The Seven Types

PSYCHOSYNTHESIS TYPOLOGY
DISCOVER YOUR FIVE DOMINANT TYPES

BY KENNETH SØRENSEN, MA PSYCHOSYNTHESIS

Dedicated to the Spirit of Psychoenergetics

The Seven Types

Copyright: Kentaur Publishing 2019
Author: Kenneth Sørensen
Translator: Anja Fløde Bjørlo
Editor: Mike Brooks
Printed at: IngramSpark
Layout: haugereitz.dk
Photo and illustrations:
Jakob Hauge, CC Vision, Imagelibrary,
Platinum, Gold, 500, 1000 and Unsplash.

Kentaur Publishing: www.kennethsorensen.dk
1. Edition
EAN 9788792252395
ISBN: 978-87-92252-39-5

Kentaur Forlag

Contents

Part One:

Introducing the Seven Types: Identifying your five dominant types

Part Two:

Working with the Seven Types: A guide for counsellors, coaches and mentors

Appendices:

Part One

Introducing the Seven Types:

Identifying your
five dominant types

Introduction to the Seven Types

Since the English translation of Roberto Assagioli's *Psychosynthesis Typology* in 1983[1] , there have been only two significant publications from within the psychosynthesis community that have dealt seriously with the theory of the Seven Types. One is Piero Ferrucci's monumental work *Inevitable Grace* (1990), which explores seven ways to self-realisation by looking at the spiritual breakthroughs of famous men and women through the lens of the Seven Types and psychosynthesis typology. The other publication is the late John Cullen's monograph *The Manager of the Future* (1988) which looks at how the Seven Types can be used for leadership training.

I hope my book will add to this legacy by offering a structured overview of the core principles of psychosynthesis typology and how it can benefit us and our clients. I will take as my starting point Assagioli's[2] writings in this area, but I will also draw upon the work of other pioneers of psychology and the perennial philosophy. My goal is to unpack the potential of this little-known area of psychosynthesis theory and to suggest how it might be implemented in counselling and coaching.

The value of typology

On first inspection, there appears to be little about typology in Assagioli's published works – for example, the only distinct references to typology in his two key books are a short appendix in *The Act of Will* and a few scattered mentions in Psychosynthesis. However, once Assagioli's support for typology is rightly acknowledged, it can be seen that typological theory was embedded in his thinking from the

---

[1] Psychosynthesis Typology was originally published in 1976 as I Tipi Umani by the Istituto di Psicosintesi, Florence.

[2] Read an online biography of Assagioli: https://kennethsorensen.dk/en/roberto-assagioli-his-life-and-work/

start of his career: it's a case of knowing what to look for because his terminology is not fully evolved (a matter this book hopes to resolve). I have described my research into this matter in-depth elsewhere[3], but let me summarise some of my findings here.

In this first quote, Assagioli (1934) explains why differential psychology (as he referred to the study of human types) plays such a crucial role in understanding our psychological life.

> The essential unity of all souls does not exclude differences existing in their personal appearances. Therefore, we must make a serious study of these different qualities. This study should become more and more a part of the new psychology. We should endeavour to understand the true nature, the underlying function and purpose, the specific problems, virtues and vices of each type, as it manifests in and through a human individual.

To "understand the true nature, the underlying function and purpose, the specific problems, virtues and vices of each type" is precisely the objective of this book. The inference here is that one of the aims of psychosynthesis is to seek to appreciate the uniqueness of each individual, which according to Assagioli (1965: 7) includes "the unique existential situation of each patient, of the problems which it presents and of the ways for their solution". In my experience as a psychosynthesis practitioner, it is our lack of understanding of the essential qualities of our clients that can prevent us from seeing the uniqueness in their intrinsic nature and problems. This psychological colour blindness, caused by an absence of typological theory, can lead to empathic failures in the therapeutic relationship. The corollary, according to Assagioli (Undated 12), is that we can improve the quality of our empathy by developing our understanding of typology, as he explains:

---

[3] My research paper can be found in the appendix.

In order truly to understand, we must be willing to make the necessary preparation and develop in ourselves the specific faculty, namely, empathy. The preparation consists in acquiring an adequate knowledge of psychology, both general and specific; this includes:

a. A knowledge of the psychological constitution of the human being;

b. A comprehension of the differential psychology of ages, sexes, types, etc.

c. An acquaintance with the unique combination of traits in different individuals.

According to Assagioli (1983: 11), developing an understanding of typology will "refine our psychological perception" and develop our empathy and loving understanding.

But increasing our capacity for empathy is not the only reason Assagioli gives for studying and applying typology. In my research, I identify 24 areas where Assagioli commends the use of typological theory, the most important of which are:

- For developing a profound self-knowledge.

- For knowing how best to apply the techniques of personal and transpersonal psychosynthesis, which will vary according to a person's types.

- For discerning a person's particular sensitivities and mentality.

- For understanding how people react to crises.

- For understanding a person's particular virtues and vices.

- For understanding how couples relate, particularly with regard to their fears and longings.

- For knowing how to help children evolve naturally according to their intrinsic qualities and motivations.

- For helping to resolve conflicts in groups with different typological features.

These reasons are a motivation for us all to study typology, especially if we are working in a professional therapeutic capacity. That said, while emphasising the importance of typology, Assagioli himself did not always elaborate on how to apply the theory, hence this present attempt to refine the theory.

I have wondered why the psychosynthesis community has shown little enthusiasm for adopting the area of typology. One reason might be an unconscious aversion to addressing the differences between us; the different types occupy different psychological landscapes, which seem incompatible. For example, dynamic types might consider sensitive types to be weak and passive, while creative types might experience practical types as rigid and unimaginative. These deep-rooted biases can be the cause of splits and conflicts in our relationships, something we might be keen to avoid. Furthermore, as we shall see, there is also the possibility of internal splitting and repression within an individual because we are in fact each a combination of several types – this will be explored more fully later.

At this point, let me offer a word of caution against applying typology too rigidly. It is a theory with many uses, but the psyche is so complex that no theory can ever fully explain a person. Assagioli (1974: 258) gave this warning:

> However useful typology may be for understanding and dealing with different human beings, it fails to give a full view, a comprehensive account of an individual. Every individual constitutes a unique combination of countless and differing factors... But important as this realisation is, it should not lead us to believe that it is hopeless to establish a scientific "psychology of the individual". Such a psychology is possible and is beginning to be developed.

Assagioli (1974: 252) also gave this advice:

"The tendency—rather, the temptation—to accord an excessive value to typological classifying needs to be resisted; and even more the inclination to attach labels to individuals. Those who are attracted by such "cataloguing" often become harmfully conditioned and limited by it, while others rightly rebel against it."

The danger of excessive labelling is reduced with the Seven Types, because we believe we always have access to all seven energies and have five dominant types on five levels as you will see later.

The seven psychological functions and the seven types

Assagioli's concept of the Seven Types developed throughout his life. He started by acknowledging C. G. Jung's four psychological types, with their introvert and extrovert dynamics, then expanded on this view, explaining (Assagioli, 1966):

Now, I may say something else about the psychological functions. As you know, Jung speaks of four functions: sensation, feeling, thought and intuition. I accepted this classification in the past, but I realised more and more that it is incomplete. Imagination, in my opinion, is an independent psychological function. It is often associated with feeling, but it has a distinctive quality of its own. Also, desire-drive and will are specific psychological functions.

In the first quote, Assagioli is describing how there are seven types based on seven "underlying functions", i.e. seven psychological functions that everyone has at their disposal. The important point is that each psychological function facilitates a different way of seeing the world and a specific type of behaviour. According to Assagioli (1934), each of the underlying functions is wired to a specific "purpose", and has "specific problems, virtues and vices… as it manifests in and through a human individual". (The psychological functions will be examined in detail in chapter three.) Hence, we can say that typological differences are caused by the development and interplay of the seven psychological functions in an individual. To summarise, we each have access to all of the seven psychological functions, and their respective energies and qualities, but we have not developed them all equally, due to internal and external circumstances.

Having made these observations, Assagioli (1983: 49) attempted a "qualitative classification" of the seven types in his typological system, but observed (1931b) "for this deeper and more specific study, modern psychology offers little help; its trend has been chiefly descriptive and analytical; it has not dealt with essential qualities". These essential qualities – which is Assagioli's term for the seven types and their underlying functions – show "specific psychological differences, those which are of a qualitative nature and which give the fundamental note, the peculiar essence, to each personality and individuality" (Assagioli: 1931b). (In this context, Assagioli is using the term individuality to refer to an individual's soul or Higher Self.)

From the qualitative perspective we can see that each of the seven types is embedded in and expresses different psychological qualities and energies in their overall behaviour. Accordingly, the study of these qualitative energies reveals that the model of the Seven Types is actually an energy typology, and that each of the types could rightly be called an energy type. Assagioli's writing reveals he was deeply interested in the study of energy. In his *Psychosynthesis Manual*, Assagioli (1965: 194) writes:

> What we hope to see developed over a period of years – and certainly do not claim has yet been achieved – is a science of the Self, of its energies, its manifestations, of how these energies can be released, how they can be contacted, how they can be utilised for constructive and therapeutic work.

Assagioli later gave the study of energies the name psychoenergetics and, in my article *Psychosynthesis and Psychoenergetics* (Sørensen, 2018), I present an overview of Assagioli's thoughts on this subject, which he termed the "fifth force of psychology".

Everything is made of energy!

Everything is made of energy. This concept is the fundamental starting point in psychoenergetics. Various iterations of this concept can be found in quantum physics, psychology and spiritual teachings, but we need only look at our everyday language to note that people seem to have a natural and intuitive grasp of this idea. For example, we might say a place has good or bad "vibes" – the phrase might lack a precise definition, but most of us can relate to the idea: we might go to a party and say it has a "great atmosphere", by which we mean there is a good energy, with joy, spontaneity, openness, etc. Similarly, when we describe someone we meet as radiant, charismatic or unfriendly we are talking about the psychological energies they are radiating. We also attach special qualities to our physical surroundings: a home or a workplace can have a positive or negative feel about it, for example. When we speak like this we are describing qualities that we sense in the world around us, in other words, energy. But while we have a natural sense of this energy, we can struggle to describe it – it could be said that we are energy illiterate in that we lack a specific language for describing the psychology of energy. Happily, psychoenergetics offers a key to understanding the energies that are in us and around us.

The following selection of quotes[4] from Assagioli show how he understood our world in terms of energy:

> Energies radiate outwards from the personality as if from a great source of light; luminous rays shine out and pervade the atmosphere. This irradiation occurs spontaneously – I would almost say inevitably

---

[4] For a fuller list of quotes visit https://kennethsorensen.dk/en/glossary/radiation/

– and this explains the effect the mere presence of a person who has had transpersonal experiences has on those with whom he or she comes into contact. (2007: 47-48)

Each of us necessarily and inevitably radiates what he is. (1968)

[Radiation] expresses what we really are, which, in both a higher and a lower sense, is much more than we are aware of. Emerson wrote in his essay on Social Aims: "Don't say things. What you are stands over you the while, and thunders so that I cannot hear what you say to the contrary. One may disguise the tone of the voice, but the radiation of the heart cannot be falsified. (1968)

Psychoenergetics proposes that there are seven universal energies. These energies constitute the building blocks of the cosmos. They reside in nature and in humanity; within people they manifest as different psychological qualities. Through gaining knowledge of these energies, we can begin to promote their development and their influence in our lives and in the world. Psychoenergetics looks at how energy is expressed throughout the cosmos, nature and humanity as a whole, while the Seven Types is a typological system that describes how the seven universal energies are expressed at the level of human psychology, specifically through the dynamic, sensitive, mental, creative, analytical, dedicated and practical energies.

Not surprisingly, from a psychosynthesis perspective, there are links between energy and the Higher Self and self-realisation. In the foreword to Assagioli's Psychosynthesis Typology (1983), the editor Joan Evans explains:

The Higher Self is a coherent point of focus which qualifies and differentiates universal energies as they individualise; the personality is the field through which these universal energies are objectified... The value in understanding the types is to see that they are qualifying energies rather than definitive in objective terms.

Each has a distinctive note or colour which shapes it from within; they are principles of limitation as well as expansion endowing the individual with opportunities along the path of Self Realisation.

Understanding your energies in daily life

Gaining insight into how the universal energies manifest in our lives can lead to healthier relationships. For example, we might find a particular person's behaviour difficult to understand. But very often we are assessing this person from the limited perspective of our own experiences and preferences. By contrast, the Seven Types offers a model for understanding the complexity of a whole range of psychological attitudes and behaviours. For example, imagine someone who is talkative: a sensitive type might experience this person as domineering and threatening, while a practical type might regard him as energetic and engaging. This sort of situation arises because we tend to interpret each other's behaviour and motivation through the lenses of our own values and typological make-up.

Clearly, understanding typology can help us to avoid difficulties and conflicts in relationships. As we learn to read the psychological energies, in ourselves and in our surroundings, we can develop a greater sense of empathy. So, in our example above, the sensitive type might realise that the talkative person is simply expressing his natural dynamic energy and not meaning to dominate; at the same time, an understanding of the Seven Types could give the talkative person the tools and insight to learn to express their energy in ways that are more attuned to different audiences, such as the sensitive type.

To begin to understand how the energies are at play in the world, we can start by looking at ourselves. Each of us has a unique energy DNA, which means we will each be more familiar with certain energies than with others. Using the theory of the Seven Types, we can begin to see how our different qualities are the expressions of the seven types of energy, each of which is related to one of the underlying psychological functions. Some people feel at ease with reason and science, while others are more comfortable with relationships and community. Everyone is different: we see and experience the world through different intelligences (i.e. psychological functions). When we identify our own unique way of seeing the world, we can start to celebrate and develop the qualities and abilities that make us who we truly are[5], we can also start to develop different types of energy.

As you will see in chapter one, we each have five dominant types in our overall typological make-up. In Psychosynthesis Typology, Assagioli vividly describes how the seven types are expressed in an individual at five different levels, namely the levels of body, feeling, thought, personality and soul. Accordingly, this book will help you to identify your unique energy DNA. We each have a dominant type – one of the seven – expressed at each of the five levels; these dominant types can be seen in our body language, predominant moods, thinking style, personality and our soul purpose. Discovering your unique combination of types can have the effect of bringing you home to yourself, leading to a deeper sense of self-acceptance and insight which can make life more exciting and meaningful.

One type or a combination of types?

What sets the Seven Types apart from most other typological models is the insight that people are best described, not as a single type, but as a combination of five dominant types – more specifically, we each have a dominant type (one of the seven) at each of the levels of body, feeling, thought, personality and soul.

That said, in this book, we will sometimes refer to people as if they were a single type. The reason for this is that while we are each a combination of dominant types at the five levels, one of these levels

---

[5] See Appendix 6. for a discussion of essentialism and the seven types

will tend to overshadow the others – either in a particular moment or context or generally as part of the role we are playing. Indeed, a complex interaction is constantly taking place between the dominant types – indeed, all seven types – both within and across the five levels of the psyche, as will be described in this book.

To offer an example, in a particular individual, the dynamic type/ energy might dominate at the level of body, the sensitive energy at the level of feeling, practical energy at the level of thought, dynamic energy at the level of personality, and creative energy at the level of soul. In everyday life, according to the context, a different one of these energies might tend to dominate, perhaps the sensitive energy (at the level of feeling) will dominate while the person is playing the role of parent, while the dynamic type (at the level of personality) will dominate while they are fulfilling the role of manager at work.

In the language of the Seven Types, we refer to a person's dominant energy at each of the five levels as their body type, feeling type, thinking type, personality type and soul type (hence, we can say that a person is comprised of five dominant types). If the sensitive energy is dominant at the level of feeling, we would refer to this person as being a sensitive feeling type. Everyone has a dominant body type, feeling type, thinking type, personality type and soul type. At any one time, one of this set of five dominant types will tend to dominate – which explains why a person who is actually a combination of types can nevertheless appear to be a single type.

As with any new language, it will take time and practice to become familiar with the words and terminology. The Seven Types is not a simplistic model, hence the language is subtle and at times complex – but we trust you will be a fluent speaker by the end of the book!

Developmental stages, including the transpersonal

The Seven Types takes into account a process of development. We are not born with a fixed personality that remains static throughout life, rather we a born into a natural and fluid process whereby our dominant types emerge and manifest at the different psychological levels at different stages of development. While all five levels are present from birth, it takes time for the energies to manifest at each subsequent level.

The first level at which our psyche starts to express itself is the level of body. We are born as a physical being, with a physical presence, and largely interact with and make sense of our environment through our physicality: it is at this stage that our dominant body type (our dominant energy at the level of body) begins to manifest. Later in life, when a few years old, the level of feeling becomes more active and a dominant energy begins to manifest at this level – this is our dominant feeling type. Next comes the dominant thinking type at the level of thought.

Many people remain at this stage – juggling, as it were, between the levels of body, feeling and thought. But it is possible for these three levels to integrate – and this activates the level of personality (each subsequent level incorporates all preceding levels). This process is what has been called personal psychosynthesis or self-actualisation. But there is a further stage, which involves the emergence of our dominant soul energy, or soul type. When our soul type emerges, we face the task of integrating our soul type and personality type, which is known as transpersonal psychosynthesis.

This last point is an important one. The Seven Types offers more than a description of how we are in the world today – working with this model will challenge us to become all we can be, which involves the possibility of discovering who we are from the transpersonal perspective of the soul and the Higher Self. Many people live their lives without venturing into the realm of the soul, which contains our highest motivations and life purpose, but those who work with the Seven Types will find themselves drawn inexorably towards the transpersonal realm and towards deeper meaning.

As can be seen, the Seven Types is a complex model. Ultimately, regardless of our beliefs about the transpersonal, the Seven Types is a system that encourages us to seek greater fulfilment in life, whether our own fulfilment as part of a personal development programme or the fulfilment of our clients if we are working as counsellors. Whichever stage of development or level of the psyche we are exploring, there is always a call towards growth, with tools at our disposal to help make growth a reality.

The structure of this book

The aim of this book is to introduce the reader to the Seven Types. Part one has a focus on the theory of the Seven Types and explains how we can identify and make use of them in our own lives. Part two explores how the theory can be applied in the context of counselling work, including psychotherapy, coaching and mentoring.

In the first four chapters, I review the key elements and building blocks that make up the model of psychosynthesis typology, namely the seven cosmic energies, the seven types (which are the energies objectified in action and expressed in psychological terms), the seven psychological functions, and the five psychological levels.

The next seven chapters describe how the different energies and types combine and the important nuances that arise from this.

The final four chapters look at how counsellors can make use of the Seven Types model in their work, with plenty of practical ideas and case studies, including my own story (chapter 15) in which I describe my personal journey with the Seven Types and describe my own combination of types. Some readers may find it helpful to read this personal account before proceeding with the more academic material.

The Seven Types is a huge topic which cannot be covered adequately in a single book. Accordingly, I've chosen to focus here on the personality model of the Seven Types, which is the foundation stone of typological theory, the best known aspect of psychosynthesis typology and something of immediate practical use for psychosynthesis practitioners. I have omitted much of the developmental psychology behind the theory, such as how the types can evolve from immature to mature types: this will be the focus of a different book.

The genesis of this book

I first had the idea to write this book in 2007. My good friend and colleague Søren Hauge and I were teaching psychoenergetics at a conference in the United States and, on our way back to Denmark, we decided we would like to offer this teaching to a wider audience. We had been studying and teaching the subject for years, via the esoteric formula of the Seven Rays, and we realised a new language and presentation of this knowledge would be needed if we were to reach more people, and this book is my contribution.

For the content of this book, I have drawn from many training courses, led with Søren, and from my own daily meditation practice, which dates back to 1988. Meditation offers direct access and insight into the world of energy. I have discovered we can change our personality from the inside out by using meditations that have been specifically designed to focus on the seven energies, and I describe this process in my book *Integral Meditation* (2017).

I have a Master's degree in Psychosynthesis. My work as a psycho-synthesis practitioner spans several thousand hours as a therapist and trainer. I have seen many lives transformed through their engagement with psychosynthesis and the Seven Types, and these encounters have also contributed to this book; I write about these experiences in detail in my book *The Soul of Psychosynthesis* (2016).

Most recently, I have been developing www.JivaYou.com, which is an online identity profile assessment tool based on the insights of the Seven Types, developed with my colleague Søren. Jiva means "unique identity" in Sanskrit, hence "JivaYou" means "your unique identity". JivaYou offers a wide range of psychological profiling tools, information about coaching courses and lectures, and much more.

In all of our work, we are indebted to the great pioneers of the psychologies of energy, especially Roberto Assagioli, Alice Bailey, Sri Aurobindo, Ken Wilber and Michael Robbins. You can read more about these pioneers in chapter one.

I would like to thank Søren Hauge for being a friend and inspiration throughout the many years we have worked together; Søren contributed chapter six in this book. I would also like to thank my many students and clients over the years who have helped me to inform this presentation of the Seven Types. Special thanks go to Jesper Bundgaard, my partner at JivaYou.com, who since 2012 has contributed to its development. And I would like to thank those who gave feedback on the first drafts of this book, especially Hanne Lund Birkholm and Lis Andersen. My translator Anja Bjørlo and editor Mike Brooks also deserve warm gratitude for their help and support with this book.

May you all have an exciting and educational journey into the world of types and energies.

Kenneth Sørensen, Gålå, Norway, 2019

A world of energy
– The five psychological levels

In this chapter we will explore how the seven types are connected with seven universal energies, on five psychological levels. In the Introduction, we saw how Assagioli suggested that each of the seven types has an underlying psychological function, which connects us to our "essential qualities". The psychological function of will provides access to dynamic energy, the function of feeling provides access to sensitive energy, and so on. These are the foundational principles for the Seven Types and we will expand on them in this and the coming chapters.

With the philosophy of the seven energies we enter the domain of psychoenergetics, which rests on the observation that everything is comprised of energy. In my article *Psychosynthesis and Psychoenergetics* (2018), I demonstrate how Assagioli conceptualised this through his well-known theory of the Seven Ways to the Soul (this theory, which is part of the curriculum for training in psychosynthesis, will be examined in detail in chapter six). Note: in this book I will refer to psychoenergetics when speaking about the big picture: the seven universal energies. And when I refer to the seven types I will be speaking specifically about how these energies are *manifested physically in individuals or groups.*

All is energy

The idea that everything is comprised of energy is nothing new and can be found in many ancient Eastern philosophies. And, with the emergence of quantum physics in the twentieth century, the idea that

Albert Einstein, 1879-1955

"all is energy" now has the backing of modern science. For example, when speaking of his famous equation $E=mc^2$, Einstein stated: "It followed from the special theory of relativity that mass and energy are both but different manifestations of the same thing".[1] This is surely food for thought. However, the focus of this book is not physical science, but psychoenergetics and the Seven Types. Quantum physics describes only physical energies, while psychoenergetics opens us up the entire spectrum of energies that lie beyond the physical realm. So, if we accept that everything in life is comprised of energy, we might ask what this means from a psychological perspective. This is the purpose of this book. I will investigate the nature of the different energies and explore how they manifest in the form of the seven types, creating psychological qualities at every level of human existence.

The field of psychoenergetics is still in its infancy, so I hope this book will be a helpful contribution in an ongoing area of study that I trust will lead us into a new world of energy. Psychoenergetics may sound vague and mysterious, so I hope this book will bring clarity. And while some of the ideas I'm describing have an ancient lineage, their presentation in the guise of psychoenergetics is quite new, so this book could be considered something of a starter guide.

We experience and talk about energy all the time, albeit with everyday names and labels. For example, when we describe someone using terms such as sweet, dynamic, graceful or genuine, we are making an attempt at reading that person's psychological qualities or radiance; in other words, we are all the time attempting to read each other's energy.

---

[1] https://en.wikiquote.org/wiki/Albert_Einstein

We base these readings on a number of factors: body language, tone of voice, behaviour, the emotions we pick up, our understanding of a person's motivation, and so on. For example, if we see a man carrying an elderly woman's shopping bags, you may think the man is being helpful and sweet, but when we discover the man stole the woman's wallet, we will change our mind. In other words, there are many factors that contribute to "reading" and understanding a person's energy and behaviour, and it can be unwise to make quick judgements. Furthermore, our ability to read each other's energies depends on the depth and richness of our language, our understanding of human nature, and our self-knowledge. Happily, the Seven Types provides a map – a set of language tools – to help us understand and access the great variety of human experience caused by the energies within us. However, it is important to note that we cannot see these energies directly, rather we observe the *qualities radiating* from the different forms of energy, whether these qualities are radiated consciously or unconsciously. Let's take a look at the different ways that energy can be expressed.

The five psychological levels

In psychological terms, the seven energies manifest at five psychological levels in the human psyche, namely the levels of the body, feeling, thought, personality and soul. These same five levels were described by Assagioli in his book *Psychosynthesis Typology* and elsewhere.[2]

Our psyche is like a five-storey building, operating at the levels of body, feeling, thought, personality and soul. At each level, we have a dominant energy (one of the seven) which determines the qualities we exhibit at that level, which can be seen in our physicality, temperament, mentality, personality and soul expression. By investigating and mapping our psyche in this way, we can create a psychological formula.

---

[2] See all the source notes in my article Psychosynthesis and Psychoenergetics, 2018.

For example, a person might display sensitive qualities at the level of soul, while being a dynamic personality type, with a creative mentality, a dedicated temperament, and a practical physicality. Such a formula – which lists our dominant type at each of the five levels – provides a comprehensive account of our personal typological make-up, our unique psychological DNA, which we can work with to actualise and express our full potential.

Figure 1 illustrates how these five levels form a psychological pyramid. Also

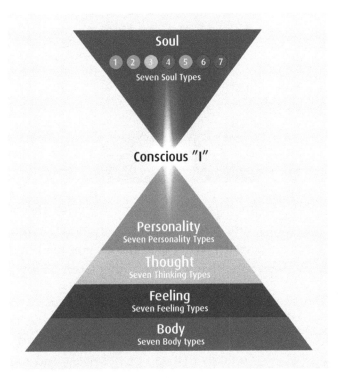

Figure 1. The five psychological levels

identified in the diagram is the white light of the conscious "I", which is seeking to reconcile or integrate all five levels. So let us begin this study by looking at each of the five levels in more detail.

The body's radiance – Our physical appearance

We experience the energy and type of the body through its shape, movement and attitude. We may interpret a bent-over, slow moving body as being weak and having little energy. We may read a smooth and quick body as graceful and full of vitality. In short, there are different body types, each with their distinctive qualities. The body's energies are most clearly recognised in the shape and contours of our face.

Mærsk
McKinney-
Møller,
1913-2012

Desmond
Tutu,
1931-

In these two pictures we have the South African bishop Desmond Tutu and the Danish shipping magnate Arnold Mærsk McKinney-Møller. What qualities do you read in their faces? One seems open and receptive, while the other seems sharp and direct. Their faces represent two different types of energy.

It is not only humans, every physical thing radiates energy: cars, animals, houses, trees, flowers and phones each have distinctive qualities that can be observed and interpreted. We can classify these qualities according to typology and, through investigation, gain a better understanding of the characteristics of each type.

Which energies we are able to observe in the world around us is affected in large part by our own typological make-up. It is like the botanist who will see and experience a forest differently from someone who knows nothing about trees and plant life – the botanist will see an oak, ash and beech, while someone else will see only 'trees'. The same is true of human types. Whether we can appreciate another person or object's energetic qualities will depend upon our own combination of types and level of self-awareness.

Our emotional radiance – Our temperament

As well as at the physical level, we also experience energy at an emotional level, such that people can be categorised according to a set of emotional types, each with its own distinctive qualities. For example, broadly speaking, we can recognise different temperamental qualities between people from different nationalities.

We read someone's emotions through the moods they radiate. People can be calm, receptive, empathic, active, restless, domineering, and so on. We all share these basic qualities, but we do not manifest them in equal measure. By learning how to read and understand these emotional energies in ourselves and others, our emotional depth and insight will deepen, and this will help us to develop harmonious relationships with others and with ourselves.

Our mind's radiance - Our mentality

Our mental life and style of thinking also has a distinctive character. Indeed, patterns of thought and communication styles differ to such an extent that it can be difficult for us to understand each another. We are not always on the same wavelength. Some people think and speak abstractly: they are curious and enjoy exploring theories and ideas. Others are more practical and concrete in their thinking and lose interest when they have to listen to theories. A third type is associative and thinks and speaks in images and stories. Another type is dynamic, focused and goal-orientated – this type prefers to speak only when they have something important and purposeful to say. These are all examples of a person's *mentality*, or unique quality of thinking. When we understand someone's mental qualities it is easier for us to adjust and harmonise our communication.

The radiance of the personality – Our persona

This aspect of the Seven Types is complex, reflecting the complexity of being human.

When we talk about the energies of the personality, we mean the overall recognisable qualities that describe a person.

Our personality emerges when as individuals we start to make our own choices and set a course for our lives. We express our personality through the quality of our will, our will-to-be-a-self. Assagioli described the formation of a strong character or personality as "personal psychosynthesis", while Abraham Maslow called it "self-actualisation". It is with the power of the will, alongside our other psychological functions, that we can create a successful life that meets our social, economic and career needs.

When we recognise the will to be ourselves and the type of ambition we want to pursue, we can then identify the qualities we need to bring forward in our personality. Our choices in life will be influenced by the qualities we feel at home with. We may not think about these qualities consciously, but unconsciously we are tuning into resources and talents that unfold in us naturally. For example, some people are distinctly dynamic, sensitive, intelligent, practical or creative in their expression. A personality test – such as the personality profile at www.jivayou.com/en/ – can help us to identify the qualities we have at this level.

Our personality contains the dominant energy that colours our external behaviour, meaning the manner in which we pursue our ambitions and individual way of life, with our mental, emotional and physical energies contributing their own shades and hues. We can observe that each of the seven types will be actualised in our life to a greater or lesser extent during the passage of normal development from childhood to mature adulthood. In this way, we move up through the pyramid (Figure 1) from the bottom up.

Our soul's radiation – Our humanity

The soul – known in many spiritual traditions and in psychosynthesis as the Higher Self – demonstrates a highly subtle expression of the energies. The soul contains the good, the true and the beautiful in each of us. It is the inner voice of conscience, it is inherent trust, and it contains the sense of community that we can share with other people and with the world itself.

Our soul's radiance emerges more visibly when we start to seek meaning and purpose in our lives. We intuit in our soul that we are connected to a greater whole and that we have a unique purpose in life. This purpose is about making a difference and contributing in our own way to making this world a better, more beautiful and more just place. The soul is therefore associated with the deepest and most valuable qualities we have to give to the world.

This unique purpose can unfold in any walk of life; we might become leaders, thinkers, artists, researchers, networkers, journalists or creators, the list goes on. We become aware of our purpose when we start to pursue a humanistic lifestyle, then the dominant qualities at the level of soul will blend with the radiance of our personality to bring about a beautiful synthesis that combines these two dominant energies.

Assagioli described the development of our soul as "transpersonal psychosynthesis" and, according to psychosynthesis theory, our soul development will be influenced by one dominant energy. This means that, although we all have access to the seven energies, our soul will naturally develop in line with one particular form of energy.

The holistic human being

We each have an incredibly rich and varied inner life, with access to a range of qualities, attributes and talents that can help us to live life to the fullest. Our psychological environment is a largely unknown land waiting to be discovered. To help us on this journey of discovery we can draw upon inherent creative powers to shape our lives, in accordance with our values and inner resources. Having a map and a language that describes these inner worlds and how they unfold is therefore very useful. We need such tools to help us to understand, recognise and master the energies in our lives. This is precisely the purpose of this book: to provide a map – or language or tool – that will help us navigate the landscape of energy.[3]

Psychoenergetics
– The fifth wave in psychology

Where does psychoenergetics sit within the larger landscape of psychology? It did not appear out of nowhere but is a natural development in the evolution of psychology.

The history of psychology shows that our understanding of humanity has been gradually expanding. Psychology emerged as an independent discipline from philosophy in the late nineteenth century – it was felt there was a need for an independent science of humanity based on observation rather than theory. Out of this came the five 'waves', or psychological schools, that have

Roberto Assagioli, 1888-1974

---

[3] Read also my books: The Soul of Psychosynthesis, 2016 and Integral Meditation, 2017 for an introduction to psychosynthesis theory and practice

shaped the discipline. Assagioli said psychoenergetics was the 'fifth wave' of psychology.[4]

The first wave

Initially, the need for a scientific understanding of human beings manifested in a materialistic and scientifically-orientated approach that studied the senses, memory and learning. People were primarily perceived as physical objects or highly evolved animals. One product of these scientific studies was behavioural psychology. Psychologists John Watson (1878-1958) and B.F. Skinner (1904-1990) were prominent exponents of this school, drawing upon material sourced from animal experiments as well as the observation of people.

The second wave

The next wave, arriving almost concurrently with behaviourism, was psychoanalysis, which emerged out of the research of the Austrian Sigmund Freud. He made popular the idea of the unconscious and its influence on our conscious life. Psychoanalysis emphasises the power and influence of our sexuality, especially the pathological effects of repressed impulses. Psychoanalysis assumes that we are largely controlled by our instincts and focuses on the exploration of the unconscious. Freud's

Sigmund Freud, 1856-1939

emphasis on pathological and deviant behaviours resulted in a fairly pessimistic view of humanity.

---

[4] Roberto Assagioli, The New Dimensions of Psychology: The Third, Fourth and Fifth Forces. (See www.kennethsorensen.dk/en/)

The third wave

The third wave of psychology began in the middle of the twentieth century. A leading proponent of this approach was the American psychologist Abraham Maslow who, in contrast to psychoanalysts, was concerned with healthy people and their needs. This approach was called humanistic psychology and its focus was on how to achieve human health and fulfil potential.

Existential psychology emerged at this point as a branch of the humanistic approach. The essential feature of existential psychology was an emphasis

Abraham Maslow, 1908-1970

on choice and its consequences in our lives. The American psychologist Rollo May (1909-1994) and the Austrian psychiatrist Viktor Frankl (1905-1997) are both key contributors in this school of thought.

The fourth wave

Psychology's fourth wave developed further the approach of humanistic psychology, with Maslow a pioneer here as well. This approach, known as transpersonal psychology, focuses on the scientific study of 'peak experiences' and expanded states of consciousness. These experiences occur when we have access to energies that lie beyond our normal every day consciousness, and include experiences of unity with nature, humanity and the cosmos. Such experiences can inspire profound insights into the meaning of life. Accordingly, transpersonal

Assagioli and Bailey were close friends and collaborators. So, in his conception of the seven types and seven ways, Assagioli was no doubt inspired by Bailey's writings. This becomes clear when we compare the names that Assagioli and Bailey used for the seven types and seven ways/rays, as shown in Table 1 (Bailey, 1962: 23, 329; Assagioli, 1983, Undated 2).

We also find in Assagioli's work, in his article *Discrimination in Service*, reference to the five psychological levels, *when he writes*: "The Rays which qualify his soul, his personality, and his mental, emotional and physical bodies." This is precisely the same terminology as in Bailey's philosophy.

Alice Bailey and Roberto Assagioli's names for Rays, Ways and Types

A.A. Baley "Rays"	Ray One Power and Will	Ray Two Love Wisdom	Ray Three Active Intelligence	Ray Four Harmony and Beauty	Ray Five Concrete Knowledge and Science	Ray Six Devotion and Idealism	Ray Seven Ceremonial Order or Magic
Assagioli "Ways"	The Way of Will	The Way of Love	The Way of Action	The Way of Beauty	The Way of Science	The Devotional Way	The Ceremonial Way
A.A. Bailey "Types"	The Power type	The Love Type	The Active Type	The Creative Type	The Scientific Type	The Devotional Type	The Business Type
Assagioli "Types"	The Will-Power Type	The Love-Illuminative Type	The Active-Practical Type	The Aesthetic-CreativeType	The Scientific-Rational Type	The Devotional-Idealistic Type	The Organizer-ritualistic Type

Table 1. Alice Bailey and Roberto Assagioli's names for rays, ways and types.

It is important at this point to note that psychosynthesis typology can stand on its own. Even though there are some concepts that overlap with esoteric psychology, Assagioli was keen to keep his work separate. Indeed, my own approach in this book is similar to Assagioli's, and can be compared with what modern writers are doing with training in Buddhist mindfulness, in that we are keen to keep practice and religious or cosmological theory separate. My aim is to focus on the practical application of typology while leaving out most of the cosmological theory.

Another thinker who has contributed to our understanding of psychoenergetics is the Indian philosopher Sri Aurobindo (1872-1950), who notes that the Vedas describe how the manifestation of the universe is an "unrestricted downpour of the rain of heaven, the full flowing of the seven rivers from a superior sea of light and power and joy"[7]. These "seven rivers" are what Alice Bailey refers to as the Seven Rays, which is also a term Aurobindo used when quoting the Vedas.[8]

Sri Aurobindo, 1872-1950

The greatest living exponent of energy or esoteric psychology is the American psychologist Michael D. Robbins. His book *Tapestry of the Gods* is a profound, systematic introduction to the Seven Rays. His monumental work is in the esoteric tradition and provides a complete introduction to the esoteric universe.[9]

Michael D. Robbins, 1943-

[7] http://surasa.net/aurobindo/synthesis/part-2.html
[8] https://sriaurobindostudies.wordpress.com/2010/09/02/the-seven-rays-of-the-infinite/
[9] Tapestry of the Gods can be downloaded for free here: www.sevenray.org/ tapestry-of-the-gods.html

In this book I draw upon the work of all these proponents of psychoenergetics, but will be focusing on the psychological qualities and behaviours associated with the seven energies. Therefore, this work will be more psychological than esoteric in nature, with the focus kept firmly within the human realm.

The seven energies in four quadrants

We can see all around us collective and individual expressions of the seven energies. Figure 2 illustrates this point. The diagram is derived from Ken Wilber's work and shows how the energies can be experienced in four basic ways – referred to as quadrants. Making use of Wilber's work in combination with the seven energies and types offers us some interesting and nuanced ways of understanding our experience of life, our relationships and how we might realise our full potential.

I will spend a little time explaining what is meant by the four quadrants because the concept will recur throughout the book.

The main use of the quadrants in the context of the Seven Types is that they can help us with the identification of our dominant types. Because we each have blind spots and defences, we are often unable to see ourselves as we truly are. Hence, in trying to make sense of our own nature, it can be helpful to gather information from other sources – and the four quadrants describe these other sources. The upper left quadrant refers to the personal/subjective field (this is how we see ourselves); the upper right quadrant refers to the personal/objective field (this is how other people see us); the lower left quadrant refers to the collective/subjective field (this field contains information about the psychological environments that impact on us, such as the cultural traits we have absorbed from our family and society and currently are embedded in); the lower right quadrant refers to the collective/objective field (this field includes our physical environment and the groups of people we associate with). By gathering information about ourselves from these four quadrants, or fields, we can build up a picture of who we are from several perspectives, rather than having a picture based only on our own personal (narrow) perspective.

Let's revisit the Wilber's terminology because it is subtle and worth spending some time to help us understand what he is referring to. There are two axes: the subjective/objective axis – with the subjective energies on the left and the objective energies on the right – and the personal/collective axis – with the personal energies in the upper half and the collective energies in the lower half. We all manifest *energies that are sensed subjectively* (left half of the diagram) *and also manifest energies that are expressed objectively in terms of our action in the world* (right half of the diagram).

We experience the subjective energies phenomenologically at each of the five psychological levels and beyond (upper left quadrant).[10] We sense inside of us the different *qualities* of the energies, for example a dynamic energy or perhaps a more creative or practical energy according to the situation. As well as this experiencing of our own internal world, we can also experience the energy or atmosphere in a group of people and can intuit the energies of our ancestors (lower left quadrant). This subjective field of energy contains our felt experience of the qualities of our individual consciousness and in combination with the collective consciousness.

The objective field (right half of diagram) concerns the more visible or tangible expressions of energy; this is what we experience when subjective energy is expressed in physical behaviour, which can be observed in the way someone speaks, their temperament and their body language. It is in this field that we can observe the seven types of energy manifested in the physical world, which are the different

---

[10] In the esoteric tradition there is also a level of spirit with many transcendent levels, which we are not using in our model, because it is too advanced for our purpose.

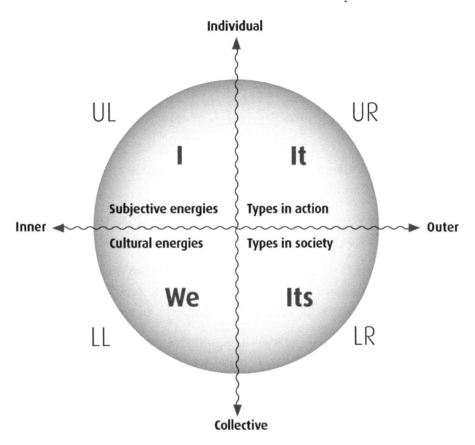

Figure 2. The four quadrants - energies and types

types of *radiation* exhibited by individuals, groups and physical spaces. This means that when we notice a person is calm, restless, energetic, focused, cold or warm, what we are actually doing is noticing qualities of energy in action. Likewise, in the objective/collective field, the energies manifest in particular ways, for example we can detect different qualities of energy in the environments of a factory, a family home and a theatre.

To summarise:

The upper half of the diagram concerns the energies and types we experience as individuals, which are either felt subjectively or expressed objectively.

The lower half shows the energies and types we experience collectively.

The left half concerns inner psychological energies, both individually and collectively.

The right half shows the manifestation of subjective energies in physical objects and in the behaviour of people.

The seven energies are expressed in all four quadrants, but our experience of them will be different in each.

In the upper left (UL) quadrant we find the "I", with all the subjective energies we experience. Here we experience the energies at the five psychological levels of the body, feeling, thought, personality and soul.

In the upper right (UR) we see the subjective psychological energies expressed in our actions and behaviour, primarily through the typological qualities of our body language, communication styles and radiance. This aspect of our energy is often more obvious to those who observe us than to ourselves.

In the lower left (LL) we find the cultural energies that we experience coming from our family, society and nation, as well as our social networks. We share this psychological atmosphere with others. This includes the norms and values of our subjective collective field, influenced by political, cultural, religious and scientific perceptions.

In the lower right-hand (LR) we find our physical surroundings and the people we interact with and who influence us. The physical landscape that surrounds us, our neighbourhood and social structures all have a distinctive radiance that affects us. The people we meet and co-operate with affect us too. Here we see the collective social behaviour in action: what we jointly create in the material world and the impact we have on each other. This quadrant is also a reflection of the invisible cultural norms from which cultural behaviour arises.

One of the implications of our exploration of the four quadrants is that psychosynthesis typology is able to describe groups and nations as well as individuals. According to Assagioli:

> Nations, as individuals, have a "body" which consists of their material means of expression; that is to say, native soil, geographical position and material assets. In addition, each nation has an emotional life consisting of feelings and the modes of reaction prevalent among its citizens, as well as its own "mentality". All this constitutes a "personality", possessing well-defined and recognisable psychological characteristics. We may even go further and say that every nation has a soul. (Undated 4)

In his book *Psychosynthesis Typology*, Assagioli designates types to civilisations, nations, buildings. An example of this can be found in a passage in which he describes the "dynamic will type":

> The Spartans and ancient Romans characterised this type in being conquerors, rulers and legislators; the English do likewise, with their will and capacity to rule, their "insularity", self-control and suppression of emotion. It is also evident both in the Germans and the Jews in some respects. (1983: 23)

Having looked at the theory, I now offer a short exercise that provides an opportunity to begin working with the four quadrants by gaining a direct experience of the energies as they arise in each quadrant.

Exercise: Experiencing energies in the four quadrants

This exercise will introduce you to the energies as defined by the four quadrants.

Upper left quadrant: Sit down and close your eyes. Take a minute to follow your breath and relax completely. Focus on your inner psychological atmosphere. Spend a few minutes observing your inner states.

What moods and qualities do you experience? Write them down.

Upper right quadrant: Stand before a mirror. Observe the energies radiating from your eyes, your body language and the psychological state reflected there.

What psychological qualities do you radiate? Write them down.

Lower left quadrant: Sit down with your eyes closed. Take a minute to follow your breath and relax completely. Imagine yourself in a social situation with your family, friends or work colleagues. Observe the atmosphere, and the expectations, values and norms that characterise it.

What cultural values and expectations characterise the atmosphere? Write them down.

Lower right quadrant: Sit down with your eyes closed. Take a minute to follow your breath and relax completely. Now imagine yourself in a social situation with your family, friends or work colleagues. Imagine you are watching yourself in this group from the outside in the company of a sociologist. Observe how you behave, what you do together and how you deal with each other.

Consider what sort of physical atmosphere is being created by your collective behaviour? Write down your reflections.

Hopefully you have now learned something about the psychological energies that you live with each day, both in yourself and in your interactions with others. All of these areas will be explored further in this book, although the main focus will remain on our individual experience. Now let's look at the seven energies in more detail as they are experienced within human psychology.

Your inner colours
– The seven energies

In the last chapter we looked at how the whole of the cosmos is a system of energy: everything is comprised of energy and energy creates everything that exists. Our own selves are comprised of energy: our bodies, thoughts, feelings and drives can all be understood as forms of energy. We can also observe that there are different types of energy, and our everyday experiences confirm this whenever we observe that we feel tired or healthy, weak or strong.

Psychoenergetics is a psychological science that shows us how everything is derived from one basic underpinning energy, and that from this basic energy seven frequencies emerge. In this chapter we will focus on how these seven frequencies of energy relate to human life.

But keep in mind that these same energies are also unfolding in all of nature and the cosmos. These seven psychological energies are sub-frequencies of the fundamental energy of the universe in the same way that white light passing through a prism

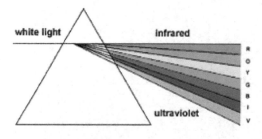

Figure 3. The seven colours of the spectrum

produces a spectrum of seven colours or seven frequencies of light (Figure 3). Just as white light separates into seven colours, so the fundamental universal energy can be divided into seven psychological and spiritual qualities. Each of these energies has a distinctive set of qualities, and taken as a whole these seven qualities constitute the sum total of the *collective energies* we embody and exchange with the world around us. See Table 2 for an overview.

To understand ourselves and our environment, we must learn how to see and feel these different qualities of energy. There are also practical benefits for our relationships because when we can understand the energies we encounter in other people we are more able to respond appropriately so that we can create good and trusting relationships; remember Assagioli's advice that understanding diffe-

The seven energies

1.	▶	The dynamic energy, expressing purpose and power
2.	▶	The sensitive energy, expressing love and wisdom
3.	▶	The mental energy, expressing activity and intelligence
4.	▶	The creative energy, expressing harmony and beauty
5.	▶	The analytical energy, expressing knowledge and facts
6.	▶	The dedicated energy, expressing devotion and idealism
7.	▶	The practical energy, expressing organisation and action

Table 2. The seven energies

rential psychology can help us to develop empathy. By contrast, without this understanding we often react negatively to those qualities we do not understand. If a relationship is particularly sensitive or tense, it is important to understand the energies at play. This will give us the option to meet other people on their terms.

The different psychological energies are not evenly distributed among people: we each have a particular combination of dominant energies. For example, people can be predominantly sensitive, dynamic, creative or practical, with each type of person having particular needs that must be understood if they are to feel accepted. In fact, the situation is quite complex. According to the theory of the Seven Types that I am putting forward, a person can be described in terms of having a dominant type of energy at each of the five psychological levels (see chapter one). Each

person is a unique combination of types and energies on five levels, so a particular rainbow of qualities must be understood in its totality if we are to appreciate the whole spectrum of a person. Indeed, developing our understanding of the Seven Types would be an important step towards increasing tolerance and healthy coexistence in our world.

How we influence each other

Look at this picture of a mountaineer perched on a rock wall 1,000 metres above ground. The next ledge is 100 metres above him, beneath him is an abys. His life depends on the safety of his rope and equipment and his own skills as climber. How do you react to this picture? Examine your inner reactions. Which energies are being activated?

You may think the mountaineer is calm, brave, fit, robust. These are all qualities of the dynamic type. This exercise in observing the mountaineer putting his life at risk provides an opportunity for you to experience the dynamic energies in action.

Now look at the image of the scientist looking through a microscope. Imagine she is analysing the result of a chemical reaction. She is focused and keeps detailed and precise accounts of her observations. How do you react to this picture? Observe your inner reactions. Which energies are activated? You may assume she is concentrated, focused and knows what she is looking for. This is an example of the analytical energy in action. You see here a scientist searching for new knowledge through her research and you have certain reactions to this image.

We always have a reaction to the behaviour of the people we meet. We identify with certain energies, while others seem unfamiliar and strange to us; we react to some energies with antipathy and to others with sympathy.

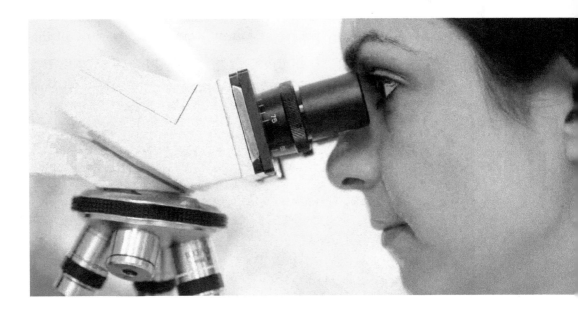

A journey into the world of energy

A basic assumption in psychoenergetics is that the seven energies are available at all five levels, i.e. at the levels of the body, feelings, thoughts, personality and soul. Our genetic make-up and personal history will provide easier access to particular energies rather than others. Our identity is shaped by specific energies and we must learn how to master these energies if we want to become all we can be.

Let's take a journey into the world of energy. Observe your reactions to the descriptions of the seven energies. Notice the ones you most recognise and which ones feel most familiar. In the following list of descriptions I do not make any distinctions according to the different psychological levels so, as you read, be open to receiving a strong sense of recognition of a particular energy on any of the five levels. The names in brackets are Assagioli's preferred names.

The dynamic energy (which Assagioli termed Will-Power) is usually the most difficult to master. This power can be too potent for some, so they fear it. Our experience of the dynamic energy is connected to our *will to power*. Many people shy away from power because of the

responsibility it brings. Yet power is part of reality and if we don't claim it for ourselves someone else will. Those who feel most comfortable with this energy are the dynamic types who tend to reach the top in their chosen discipline. We can use this dynamic power for selfish or altruistic purposes depending on our values.

This is how Assagioli (1931b) described the qualities of the dynamic energies: "Will, in the ordinary and more concrete meaning of the term; firmness, decision, concentration; the determination to attain a certain goal regardless of other considerations; energy, zeal and a fighting and aggressive spirit; a sense of justice and the urge to administer it."

Dynamic energy provides focus, courage and the power to break through resistance. With it you pursue your goals and sacrifice everything to achieve them. There's an element of destruction involved in this power. Its energy lets you cut away and remove whatever is in your path. The dynamic energy pushes us beyond the familiar, beyond our comfort zones. We become pioneers, prominent personalities in our field. This energy supplies a sense of greatness and the will to realise it. When this power is active we do not play second fiddle. We want responsibility, take action and are naturally attracted to cultures and social areas (lower quadrants) where power and strength are present. Dynamic types pursue leadership in politics, the military or anywhere where initiative and action are essential. The dynamic energy is active in areas that focus on individual achievement, such as professional sports. If you are influenced by this energy, you love to lead and fight for a cause. *Is the dynamic energy one of your primary driving forces? What do people who know you say?*

The sensitive energy (which Assagioli termed Love-Illumination) radiates softness, warmth and empathy. It takes us into the world of relationships. Like water, it purifies, heals and gives life to all it touches. If this energy is dominant in you, you will be sensitive and emotional.

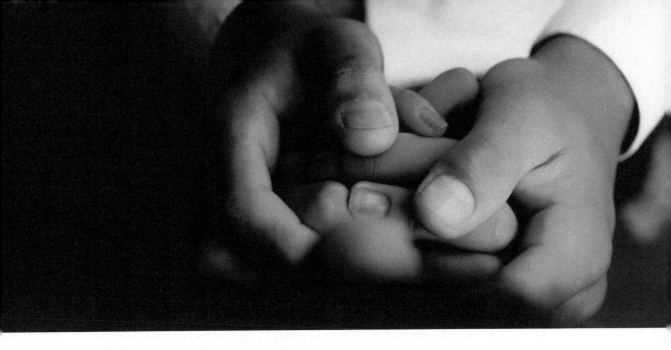

Your vulnerability and empathy can be your greatest strengths, but only when you master this energy. Empathy and understanding motivate you, not just in human relationships but in everything that deeply interests you. You want to understand something from *within* and to build bridges between whatever seems separate.

With this energy you show loving care for nature, people and all things. Sensitive types are receptive, calm and co-operative because relationships are important to them. While dynamic energy breaks things down in order to create something new, sensitive energy builds bridges. If you are influenced by this energy, you will stay in touch with and look after the people you care about.

According to Assagioli (1983: 33), people with this type of energy will be "kind and receptive; when they are not too sensitive, they are also sociable... In order to express themselves they need the stimulus of interaction with others; *they realise themselves by means of relationships.*"

In society (lower quadrants) we meet this energy in education, health and social care. It is the cohesive energy that brings people together and enables a society or relationship to work. It is an expression of love. When this energy is dominant you may work in the helping or healing professions where understanding, empathy and care are essential. This energy helps us to see the good in the world and in people, even when their actions are destructive. Love, informed with wisdom, is for you the greatest motivation. You *know* that everything is connected and you want to focus on whatever connects rather than separates. *Do you connect with this energy? Ask people close to you what they see in you.*

The mental energy (which Assagioli termed Active-Practical) sharpens our perspectives. When you are influenced by this energy you love to talk and exchange ideas and theories about the world. You are motivated by a desire for knowledge, which helps you to act intelligently and efficiently in the world.

This energy makes you light, flexible, curious and skilled at navigating the social field. Instantly you know everything going on around you and can use this knowledge to your advantage. You are aware of possibilities and opportunities available through your interactions with others. Making connections is important because this will help with your practical goals. Mental energy lacks the depth of the sensitive and analytical energies, but with it you can gather much information and form it into a whole. As a mental type you enjoy thinking and intellectual challenges; you have good general knowledge and are always happy to discover more. Also, people with this energy will have a good understanding of finances which will help them to keep on top of concerns about money.

According to Assagioli (1931b), people with this energy "are those in whom the note of activity is prevalent; those who ever try to realise, to incarnate ideas; feelings and purposes. They are vitally interested in all kinds of social activities, in progress, in culture and education."

We meet this energy in the media, journalism, finance and trade. The institutions responsible for the dissemination of a nation's culture, history and values are also influenced by this energy. Knowledge provides opportunities because those who are best informed can gain access to new knowledge first. If you are the mental type you are always keen to learn more; you are an eternal student, never tired of learning something new. You thrive in fields where new knowledge has to be created and communicated. Here you appear as the thinker or networker that finds smart solutions to problems. *Are you smart and quick witted? Ask your network.*

The creative energy (which Assagioli termed Aesthetic-Creative) encourages spontaneity, playfulness and imagination. You have a great

need for harmony and beauty. "Why should life be boring when it can be fun?" is your motto. With this energy, life becomes more manageable when it is undertaken with a sense of humour.

For creative types to thrive, beauty, light and harmony are essential. Beauty opens us up; it connects us to others and invites us to share in its magic. Reality need not be grey and boring if we use our imagination and creativity. If you are a creative type, reconciling opposites is important to you. You tend to be drawn to conflict and drama so that you might bring harmony. You can handle conflict, are skilled at mediation, and are pleased when chaos is transformed into order.

According to Assagioli (1931b), these types "evolve chiefly through the outer and inner realisation of beauty and harmony".

When trying something new, you are not afraid of losing control. You know that new opportunities arise when the old patterns break downs, and that chaos is part of the creative process. The creative energy provides you with a deep understanding of the competing forces within us, and helps you to understand that by enduring the tension of opposites we can arrive at something new.

The creative energy is expressed in the arts, entertainment, design, psychology and the media. With it, through the imagination, conflicts are resolved. With this energy predominating, your life will be lived in the here and now, filled with opportunities to enrich yourself and the world with music, play, socialising and positive relationships. *Do you often bring a smile to someone's lips? What do your friends think?*

The analytical energy (which Assagioli termed Scientific-Rational) makes you a serious, precise person who is attentive to detail and aware of causal relationships. You want to know why things are the way they are. You ask: what causes illness, why did the car break down, how can we invent renewable energy? You are curious and motivated to develop new and practical knowledge.

Analytical energy has had a major influence on the development of our modern society. The technological revolution and discoveries made in medicine, psychology, sociology, biology and other sciences have created a new world of knowledge.

If you're technically gifted, then you will know how to analyse the parts that make up the whole. If your interest is psychology, you may be interested in behaviourism and its verifiable results. Certainty based on observations and experience is important here, analysis and logic are key.

According to Assagioli (1931b), this type of individuals "are urged by the desire to know the universe, the not-self, to discover its laws, to dominate and to utilise it. They are the scientists, the inventors, all those whose occupation is that of using intelligently the forces and the materials existing in the cosmos; not only those of the physical plane but all that are to be found on the various planes of manifestation."

You are interested in knowledge that is derived from fact, especially practical knowledge that can be used to make the world a better place. You are inventive and curious, but also the highly specialised. Whatever your chosen area of research, your studies will be in-depth and detailed.

Education, research, technology and craftwork require the use of this energy. You are attracted to areas where analytical skills and certainty are needed. You might become an excellent lawyer, researcher or technician who creates a solid knowledge base which helps society to make better decisions and products. *Are you the one who fixes things, whether in a practical, social or psychological sense? Ask the people around you.*

The dedicated energy (which Assagioli termed Devotional-Idealistic) makes you excitable, goal-orientated and idealistic. The sky is the limit and you aim for the best. You are passionate and throw yourself wholeheartedly into whatever attracts your enthusiasm. You know how to motivate and bring out the best in people.

Your primary motivations are idealistic. Your dedication is expressed as warmth and loyalty in love. This energy provides you with a focus and resilience that can break down barriers. Under the influence of this energy, you do not need to be the leader, you can follow others, but only if you believe in the cause.

This energy is emotional and intense, and when it is dominant your reactions are rarely neutral or lukewarm. You glow with passion and enthusiasm, inspire others and see life in terms of causes. In society, this energy flourishes in the worlds of religion, sports, fashion and entertainment. It is present in the fields of marketing and promotion, as well as in politics, religion and activism, where people are fighting for a cause.

People influenced by this energy are, according to Assagioli (1931b), "those idealists who have consecrated themselves to a specific cause, practical or social, which they firmly believe to be a panacea for human ills. Among them we find socialists, philanthropists, and reformers of all kinds."

When you are influenced by this energy, you are inspired to make improvements. You are passionate for a good cause and are a natural advocate and activist. *Are you passionate about your beliefs? What do your friends think?*

The practical energy (which Assagioli termed Organiser-Ritualistic) makes you systematic, directive and practically-orientated. It motivates you to engage in projects requiring co-operation among many people in order to reach a successful conclusion. It also motivates you to achieve concrete results.

This energy gives you the drive to orchestrate a process from an initial idea to the final outcome. This could mean preparing a four-course meal or promoting a political campaign. You experiment with new methods

and systems in order to optimise results. You love to create order based on principles that you know work in practice.

If anything needs to be sorted, managed, organised or rebuilt, you take the lead and control the process. You can create something significant from scratch and love to watch ideas turn into real projects. You want to leave your mark on the world and want to have something concrete to show for your work. This could be a bridge, a new cultural centre, a new form of administration or a business venture.

The practical energy informs the organisations that shape, structure and regulate society. We see it in business and in large organisations that require complex management structures. Without this energy, life would be more chaotic and wasteful.

According to Assagioli (1931b), practical types are individuals "whose paramount interest is in organisation, scientific management, discipline, ritual, ceremony and magic... (They are) positive, masculine and extravert."

If you are influenced by practical energy you are good at co-ordinating and facilitating group activities. You recognise people's skills and can easily facilitate co-operation among specialists. Great things can be achieved when people with the right skills co-operate. You enjoy working with people who thrive in groups working towards a common goal. *Do you initiate and organise group activities? What do your work colleagues think?*

The spectrum of energies in all four quadrants

In this chapter we are laying the foundation for our exploration into the world of energies. Now we will work with the four quadrants to observe, evaluate and interpret our inner states and their qualities (left quadrants), while gaining greater insight into how the outer world works (right quadrants). This exercise will help us to further develop our skills at identifying how the different energies are at work in our lives.

When we look around, whatever you see – a tree, a dog, a car, a house, a landscape, a person or a group of people – you will notice that it radiates a certain type of energy, a certain quality. You can be attracted to this, feel repelled by it or feel neutral towards it. This is how we react when we encounter the seven energies as they are manifested in all four quadrants. Let me explain (Figure 4).

In the upper left quadrant (UL) we experience seven different states of awareness: dynamic, sensitive, mental, creative, analytical, dedicated

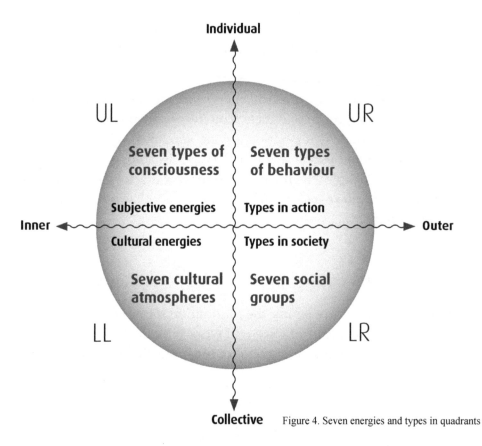

Figure 4. Seven energies and types in quadrants

or practical. These states will be experienced in different ways: imagine white light being expressed as a rainbow with one particular colour emerging as the most dominant. Once we learn the language of psychoenergetics, we can recognise which specific energy or condition is most prominent in our consciousness at any given time. We can experience these seven energies at each of the five psychological levels: physical, emotional, mental, personality and soul and beyond. Each level is coloured by the seven energies and can therefore be experienced in seven different ways.

In the upper right quadrant (UR) we find seven fundamental types of behaviours motivated by the qualities of the seven energies. Generally, our behaviour is a combination of many energies, but some will dominate. Our behaviour means our 'radiance' as perceived by others; this includes our choice of clothes, personal style, body language and facial expressions. (Later, I will explain how different types of behaviour relate to the five levels.)

In the lower left quadrant (LL) we find the seven cultural or psychological 'atmospheres' that attract and influence us. These are expressed through politics and power (dynamic), care and education (sensitive), culture and communication (mental), arts and entertainment (creative), research and technology (analytical), religion, activism (dedicated), business and organisation (practical).

In the lower right quadrant (LR) we meet the same energies as in LL, but embodied in specific social groups. At home, at work or in the wider community, we are affected by certain types of energy. If we want to develop our dynamic energy we may participate in political debates, start a course in martial arts, take up competitive sports, or register for a seminar in leadership. Our physical world also emanates the seven energies. For example, the ocean can inspire sensitive energy. Theatres and art galleries can provide access to creative energy; here the creative energies radiate from the architecture and interior design as well as the actors and artists who work there.

Exercise: Four questions to reflect on

This exercise will provide an experience of the energies as we encounter them in the four quadrants.

Upper left quadrant: Sit down and close your eyes. Focus on your breath and relax completely. Pay attention to your psychological atmosphere. Observe your inner states and then let go. Imagine yourself in a situation where you feel completely at ease and comfortable. What type of qualities characterises this situation? Feel it and relate it to the seven energies. Which of the seven energies can you access with ease? Write them down.

Upper right quadrant: Ask two of your closest friends to observe you and describe your most obvious qualities. Don't talk to them about the seven energies, just let them speak directly from the heart. What energies are clearly seen from your friends' perspective? Write them down.

Lower left quadrant: Sit in a comfortable position with your eyes closed. Follow your breath and relax completely. Now imagine a specific social situation. Notice the atmosphere and observe whatever it is that you need to do and think others should do. For example, should you be happy, strong, rational, practical, funny, or some other way? Which of the seven energies best describes your expectations? Why?

Lower right quadrant: Sit in a comfortable position with your eyes closed. Be present and relaxed. Now look at yourself in the same social situation as before. Observe how you relate to others. How do you express friendship, respect and status? What norms and what psychological qualities do you express? Are you hard, soft, ironic, humorous, polite, correct or unconventional? Which of the seven energies most influences the group's behaviour? Write down your answers.

By now you have hopefully started to gain a deeper insight into the seven energies. These energies are complex and difficult to understand, but they can be experienced. We all possess these energies and they contain untapped potential that is waiting to be discovered and used. Becoming aware of the seven energies helps in this journey of discovery.

As mentioned, the seven energies are always available but each of us experiences them differently, through the five levels of our psychology. But what determines how your unique psychology is expressed at the five levels? This is the topic for the next chapter where we will discuss the seven psychological functions.

Tools for self-awareness and self-expression – The seven psychological functions

In this chapter I will describe how the seven psychological functions relate to each other and to the seven energies and types. It is perhaps the most important chapter from a philosophical point of view because it explains how the "underlying functions", according to Assagioli, create the seven types.

From a psychological, not cosmological, perspective, the seven energies and types emerge from seven psychological functions that are inherent in every person. The Swiss psychiatrist Carl Gustav Jung proposed a model of four psychological functions that is still

Carl G. Jung (1875-1961)

widely used today, especially in the field of differential psychology. These four functions are thought, feeling, intuition and sensation, and Jung suggested we process how we understand ourselves and the world through these four functions. Accordingly, the functions can be seen as intelligences or tools of awareness.

In contrast to Jung, the model I use for the Seven Types is based on the work of Assagioli and, more specifically, his Star Diagram (Figure 5).

Assagioli suggested there are seven psychological functions that provide the intelligence and processing skills that the conscious self needs to navigate life. (By "self" I am referring to the conscious "I", which is the self-aware consciousness in all humans.)

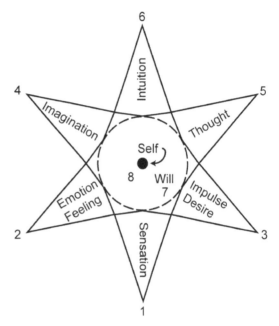

Figure 5. Assagioli's original Star Diagram with psychological functions

Assagioli writes the following about the functions as they relate to the self or "I": "In reality, all functions are functions of a living, self-conscious being and thus of an 'I'. It is the 'I' that feels and thinks, that imagines, desires and wills above all that wills." (1967b)

One could write an entire book about the seven functions, because they have such a complex nature and interplay, so I will only cover the most important aspects of the functions as they relate to the seven types.[1]

Assagioli (1967b) seems not to have described the exact nature of the psychological functions, but he quoted Jung in the following way:

> We admit that we do not know what these functions really are. We should like very much to know into what primitive elements feeling, for instance, could be resolved. But despite our ignorance of ultimate principles, we deal with these functions as if they were clearly definable organs of the mind.

The functions are, according to Jung, "organs of mind", and we might

---

[1] For more on this topic, see my MA dissertation *Integral Psychosynthesis* (Sørensen, 2008) and Assagioli's *The Act of Will*, particularly his descriptions of the Star Diagram and the ten psychological laws.

also call them seven types of intelligence. Indeed, neuropsychology, which has evolved tremendously since Assagioli, offers further insight, suggesting that the functions could be best described as *seven brain centres* or *neural networks*. Indeed, fresh insights are emerging all the time, with a great deal of ongoing scientific research into the nature of the imagination and the will.[2] A quick online search on the nature of imagination and the brain, or on any of the other psychological functions, will generate a wealth of information. In particular, the award-winning UCLA professor Dario Nardi, in his book *Neuroscience of Personality* (2011), offers some very interesting material on how the Jungian types and functions are related to the different centres of the brain.

The key idea to grasp is that the psychological functions are *receivers* and *transmitters* of the seven energies (Table 3). Will transmits dynamic energy, feeling transmits sensitive energy, and so on. So we can state that the seven energies are received by the seven psychological functions, which then distribute the energies and their qualities in various ways to create an individual's unique personality. This is the basic theoretical foundation of the Seven Types from a psychological point of view. Put more simply, rather

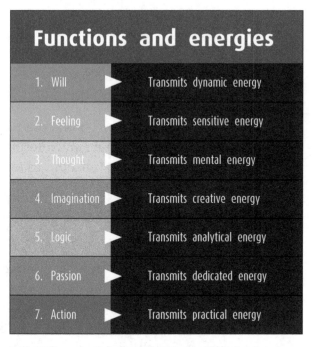

Functions and energies	
1. Will ▶	Transmits dynamic energy
2. Feeling ▶	Transmits sensitive energy
3. Thought ▶	Transmits mental energy
4. Imagination ▶	Transmits creative energy
5. Logic ▶	Transmits analytical energy
6. Passion ▶	Transmits dedicated energy
7. Action ▶	Transmits practical energy

Table 3. The seven psychological functions and their corresponding energies.

---

[2] Imagination: https://www.livescience.com/49244-imagination-reality-brain-flow-direction.html and Will power https://www.livescience.com/3553-brain-willpower-spot.html

than offering metaphysical explanations, we can take as our starting point the self-evident fact that we all possess will, feelings, thoughts, imagination, logic, passion and the ability to act.

You will have noticed that the names I am using for the functions are not exactly the same as those used by Assagioli in his Star Diagram (Table 4).

Different names for the psychological functions

Assagioli ▶	Will	Emotion Feeling	Thought	Imagination	Intuition	Impulse Desire	Sensation
Sørensen ▶	Will	Feeling	Thought	Imagination	Logic	Passion	Action
Assagioli ▶	The Will-Power Type	The Love-Illuminativ Type	The Active-Practical Type	The Aesthetic-Creative Type	The Rational-Scientific Type	The Devotional-Idealistic Type	The Organiser-Ritualistic Type

Table 4. Different names for the seven psychological functions

I have good reasons for proposing these alternative names, all of which is in keeping with Assagioli's original concepts. Let me clarify this point.

Higher and normal functions

One point at which I differ from Assagioli is that I use the term "logic" in place of "intuition". This might seem strange, so let me start by acknowledging that intuition can be described validly as a psychological function, however it can also be noted that intuition is a transpersonal function that exists beyond the range of the normal personality. Also, in his book *Psychosynthesis Typology*, it can be seen that Assagioli doesn't include an intuitive type in his list of seven types (Table 4), which might seem strange because he surely acknowledges that there is an intuitive type. I suggest there are several reasons for this apparent discrepancy, and let me offer my take on it.

Assagioli was clear in discriminating between the normal psychological functions and the higher spiritual functions, which is a distinction he discusses many times. For example, he states:

> This personal self is the human core at the ordinary level, the level of personality. It is the centre of our ordinary psychological functions: mind, emotions, sensation, imagination, etc. Likewise, at our higher human level there is an entity that is at the centre of the higher functions – artistic inspiration, ethical insight, scientific intuition. This is our real core: it is there in all of us, but the personality is generally not aware of it at the ordinary level. (Miller, 1973)

According to Assagioli (1965: 17-18), artistic inspiration, ethical insight and scientific intuition are higher superconscious functions – something he defined in his first book *Psychosynthesis*:

> From this (superconscious) region we receive our higher intuitions and inspirations – artistic, philosophical or scientific, ethical "imperatives" and urges to humanitarian and heroic action. It is the source of the higher feelings, such as altruistic love; of genius and of the states of contemplation, illumination, and ecstasy. In this realm are latent the higher psychic functions and spiritual energies.

These higher functions are higher aspects of the normal functions, so they are not something completely different, they are just natural developments, or higher potentials, which emerge when we awaken to the level of the soul. In Assagioli's words (Rosenthal, 1973):

> …each function has a lower and a higher aspect. The mind has a lower aspect—purely analytical, critical, while its higher aspect is reason and the higher mental activities. The same with emotion:

there are primitive, coarse emotions and there are refined feelings. And the will: there is a strong imperative, selfish will and the good will, the Will-to-good. Thus each function should be developed to the highest level of possible expression.

When I discuss the lower, or normal, psychological functions below, I will suggest for each of them what I consider the associated higher function to be.

Now back to intuition. Assagioli clearly discriminates between "day-by-day intuition and real spiritual intuition" (1965: 217, 220; 1983: 41)[3], and he places real intuition in the transpersonal arena as a higher function.

Furthermore, in a highly illuminating dialogue with the Canadian psychosynthesist Martha Crampton (Crampton, 1966), Assagioli states that intuition is a stage of consciousness rather than a particular type, and this makes sense because, when writing about the types, Assagioli (1983) explains that there is an intuitive expression of each of the types:

> There is mathematical intuition scientific intuition; the intuition of the inventor or the technician; the aesthetic intuition; the philosophical intuition; the mystical intuition. Intuition as a function is beyond or above — any typological difference, but it operates differently according to the psychological types.

Having explained why I have not included intuition in my list of psychological functions, why is it that I have included logic? In my view, logic can be considered a different function to thought, which is in keeping with Assagioli's idea that there are two types of mind: abstract mind, which I term thought, and concrete mind, which I refer to as logic. Logic creates the analytical or rational-scientific type, as we shall see.

---

[3] For a full discussion of this see my compilation of quotes by Assagioli: https://kennethsorensen.dk/en/glossary/intuition/

I have also replaced Assagioli's term "impulse-desire" with "passion" for the semantic reason that the word "desire" often has negative connotations. And I have replaced Assagioli's term "sensation" with the word "action", which I feel better captures the role of the body in everyday life. I will return to and expand on these points as we now look in detail at each of the psychological functions.

The seven psychological functions

Figure 6. The circle diagram showing how the psychological functions are related

We are now ready to explore each of the seven psychological functions. In doing so, I will be referring to the circle diagram (Figure 6), which numbers the functions and shows how they relate to each other. The first three functions in the list are will, feeling and thought. These three basic, or primary, functions – of which will is foundational – combine in different ways to create the other four functions, as we will see.

But before we proceed, here is a quote from Assagioli (undated 17) that will remind us of the important purpose behind this work: "Men still do not know – or do not want to – understand and appreciate individuals and groups different from them by nature, quality and function, and this prevents collaboration and mutual integration necessary for the good of all. A great help in implementing that understanding and appreciation is given by the knowledge of the various psychological types and their respective functions."

Will

The first function is will. The will channels the dynamic energy and its qualities, which manifest as the dynamic type (Figure 7). The will has received little attention in psychological literature. William James, who wrote *The Will to Believe*, is one exception. Another exception is existential psychology, which emphasises the importance of responsibility and choice – choice being an aspect of will.

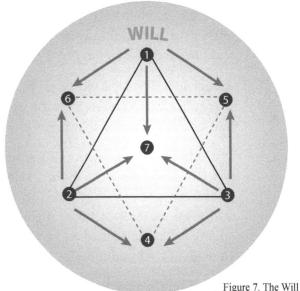

Figure 7. The Will

However, the great psychological pioneer of will is Assagioli, whose book *The Act of Will* is a recognised classic. Accordingly, I have placed will at the top of the circle diagram to emphasise its prominence in the psyche as the directing agent of all the other functions. Assagioli confirms that the will is foundational. He writes (Miller, 1972): "*The will serves, quite simply, as the directing energy for all other psychological functions.* We find that the discovery of the self is frequently connected with the discovery that the self has a will – *is* even, in a certain sense, a will."

The will is often the last function to fully develop, representing as it does the completion of our personality: the will-to-be-yourself. It is through the will that we become independent and able to freely choose how to live our lives. The will is the function that enables us to recognise and choose what is authentic for us.

Will directs our energies through purpose, choice and decision. To give an example, when we choose to study a particular subject we are using our will to help us decide how we want to invest our mental, emotional and financial energies in order to achieve a goal.

As our will develops we begin to radiate the qualities of the dynamic energy, such as courage, strength, freedom, focus and discipline. Will is the *dominant* function that underpins the dynamic or will-power type.

The superconscious aspect of the will is the transpersonal will, which is what Assagioli termed the "Will-to-good", which is a heroic call to action motivated by altruistic values. When connecting with the transpersonal will of the soul, we develop courage as our primary quality and can be said to be following the Heroic Way to the Soul (Assagioli, Undated: 19-20).

Do you find it easy to make choices, to stand up for yourself and face conflict? Looking back on your life, did you chose and implement your wishes quickly or did you deliberate at length before acting? Your answers to these questions indicate the extent to which your will function has developed. You can, of course, develop the will further. We will explore how we can develop the functions in a later chapter.

Feeling

Our feelings are manifestations of our sensitivity to psychological atmospheres. Our feelings register whether we find something pleasant or otherwise, and they help us to discern changes in the psychological atmosphere. We are each able to register and discern some feelings more easily than others. Indeed, we each experience and express feelings and emotions in different ways in line with whichever of the seven energies is most dominant in us – in this way we could each be said to be a different 'feeling type', i.e. a dynamic feeling type, a sensitive feeling type, and so on. Consider your own emotional atmosphere: are you mostly calm, intense, hypersensitive, moody, joyful or controlled? Your answer will

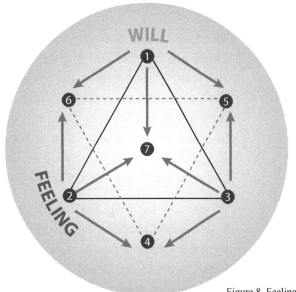

Figure 8. Feeling

suggest which of the seven energies you are most attuned to through the feeling function.

Feeling (Figure 8) is where we find the depth and grounding required to be at peace with ourselves so we can enjoy our own company and the company of others. Feeling connects us to our emotional needs, helping us to be open and receptive, connecting us to the outside world so we can empathise with what is happening around us.

Through feeling we access the inner worlds of others, and even with nature itself. The feeling function enables us to understand others' needs and to empathise. Feeling provides a kind of instinctive ability to know what's happening with those we are close to.

Feeling/emotion is the *dominant* function underpinning what I have termed the sensitive type and what Assagioli terms the "love type". According to Assagioli (1983: 30): "The emotions, as we might expect, become the centre of attention and of vital energy for the majority of those who belong to the love type."

The feeling function provides access to the sensitive energies of love. There are normal and higher aspects to this function. In this regard, Assagioli differentiated between normal love and a higher altruistic love, or ethical insight, which is the superconscious aspect of the feeling function. It is also important to note that all seven functions manifest love in their own way; this is because – as can be seen in the circle diagram – all of the functions are linked to the feeling function, which is the function most directly linked to the *energy* of love

When you develop the feeling function, you radiate empathy, care, warmth and social understanding, all of which are qualities associated with the sensitive energy. Can you detect others' feelings and empathise with them? Are you easily able to discern which atmospheres and social settings you prefer to be in? Your responses to these questions will indicate the extent to which you have developed the feeling function.

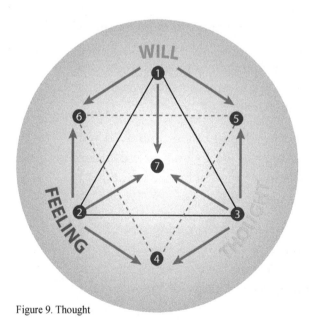

Figure 9. Thought

Thought

Through the function of thought we register information about ourselves and the world (Figure 9). Thought organises knowledge into concepts and categories and helps us to orientate ourselves to reality. (Sadly, the education system is often only focused on developing the functions of thought and logic, while neglecting the other functions.) With thought we can reflect on our experiences, weigh up pros and cons, and develop opinions about the world. Thought helps us to assess the information we receive from our other primary functions so we can gain perspective. Thinking enables us to interpret reality based on the knowledge we acquire through learning.

Thought provides an overview and an inner map so we can act intelligently in the world. Thought makes it possible to communicate and share our experiences through language. Using thought, we are able to hear other people's ideas and experiences, reflect on them and compare them to our own.

According to Assagioli (Undated 21), thought is an energy: "Creative thinking is a definite stage in objectifying ideas and higher concepts; and because thought is an energy we can use its power to develop the qualities, the attitudes, and the conditions that we think should prevail. If we use thought consciously and creatively, we can bring about changes in ourselves and our lives, as well as in our environment and in the world."

The thought function differs from the logic function: thought works with broad categorisations and networks of ideas, whereas logic has a single focus on detail.

Thought is the *dominant* function that underpins the mental (active-practical) type. According to Assagioli (1983: 39) "the fundamental quality characterising this type is intelligent *activity*", which means the function of thought operates by receiving and expressing the mental energy.

The superconscious aspect of the thought function is genius or philosophical inspiration.

We each think in unique ways and it is possible to discern our own particular thinking style, for example our style might be quick, detailed, direct, associative or methodical. When we develop this function, our mind will emanate intelligence, clarity, insight and flexibility, all of which are qualities of the mental energy.

Does new knowledge come easily to you? Do you enjoy studying? Are you a skilled communicator? Your responses to these questions will indicate the extent to which you have developed the thinking function.

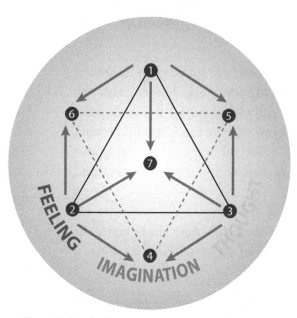

Figure 10. Imagination

Imagination

The three primary functions – will, feeling and thought – combine in different ways to create the four secondary functions (imagination, logic, passion, action). In the case of imagination, this function arises from a combination of the feeling and thought functions (Figure 10). Assagioli (1965: 144) maintained that: "Imagination is a function which in itself is to some extent synthetic, since imagination can operate at several levels concurrently: those of sensation, feeling, thinking and intuition. In one sense it is a cross-section of these four functions, or rather a combination in various proportions of them." However, while Assagioli refers to four functions combining to create imagination, I believe imagination arises primarily out of thought and feeling, a conclusion also reached by the prominent psychosynthesist Jim Vargiu (1977: 24), who stated: "The imagination is the bridge between our mind and our feelings. Images are formed in the mind and are energised by feelings."

Jung didn't consider imagination to be a distinct function, which was strange to Assagioli because Jung's work had such a focus on imaginative symbols. Assagioli (Keen, 1974) stated: "We hold that imagination or fantasy is a distinct function."

Imagination enables us to create meaningful images and stories that have emotional atmospheres. Through imagination we can visualise and picture the world as it could be. The most important images we create are our self-images. Our memory stores images from the past that influence our present self-image, and through our imagination we can explore and gain insight into these images. We can also create new self-images that express who we are today more accurately. Psychology refers to this as mental training.

Imagination opens us up to the world of magic. We can imagine alternative realities and use our other functions to make them real. We can imagine our future into being. All that we imagine will have a powerful effect on our feelings and thoughts and, in this way, all images are real in that they have consequences. According to Assagioli (1974: 52), the central function of the will can "mobilise the energies of imagination and of thought, and utilise these energies within the individual to carry out its plan".

When we develop our imagination we will increasingly emanate the qualities of the creative energy: harmony, poetry, playfulness, beauty and flexibility. Indeed, imagination is the dominant function underpinning the creative type, who is noteworthy for having a particularly vivid imagination (Assagioli, 1983: 53). Assagioli (1983: 79) adds: "The creative type is generally a channel or voice for his superconscious, a receiver of inspiration from the realms of the intuition or the imagination."

Assagioli (2007: 64) seems to be implying that the superconscious aspect of the function of imagination is intuition when he writes:

"Imagination is closely linked with intuition because when intuition enters the conscious mind it is often not in an abstract, simple, 'pure' form; rather it manifests as images."

The creative type who draws upon their aesthetic sense can be said to be following the Aesthetic Way to the Soul (Assagioli, Undated 20, 22).

Is it easy for you to use your imagination and let go and be spontaneous? Do you prefer to be in the here and now and go with the flow? Your responses to these questions will indicate the extent to which you have developed the function of imagination.

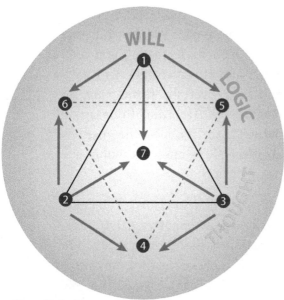

Figure 11. Logic

Logic

The logic function arises from the combination of the will and thought functions (Figure 11). Logic is a purposeful style of thinking that moves methodically from one point to the next, always adhering to the laws of reason. While the thinking function generalises, logic focuses on detail, so we can say that logic is an analytical way of thinking. Logic works with facts to reach objective conclusions.

Logic allows for accurate thinking and communication. Logic discriminates fact from wishful thinking so that reliable assessments can be made concerning what is real.

Logic enables us to manage the details of our lives and practical tasks, such as financial management. When we develop the logic function we emanate and radiate the analytical qualities: precision, reliability, order, objectivity and clear communication.

The analytical mind, or logic, is the underlying function for the analytical or scientific type. Assagioli (1983: 61-62) explained:

> The mental realm is obviously the natural environment of the scientific type. His tireless mind is always on the alert, investigating, posing questions, solving problems, searching, probing, experimenting, proving and discovering. He has a great capacity for prolonged attention and mental concentration, tireless perseverance in his research, meticulous accuracy, and an admirable ability to sift data, discover laws and conceive theories for classifying facts into coherent systems.

We can deduce from Assagioli's observations that the superconscious aspect of the logic function is scientific intuition, which occurs when intuitive inspiration is clothed in scientific facts that can be validated.

The person who uses their analytical skills to reveal the hidden mysteries of nature for the good of all can be said to be following the Scientific Way to the Soul (Assagioli, 1968c; Undated 20).

Are you someone who is adept at dealing with practical tasks? Do you love to study science and do you have a tendency to think logically? Your responses to these questions will indicate the extent to which you have developed the function of logic.

Passion

The function of passion arises from a combination of the will and feeling functions (Figure 12). Passion is feeling with a goal. The passion

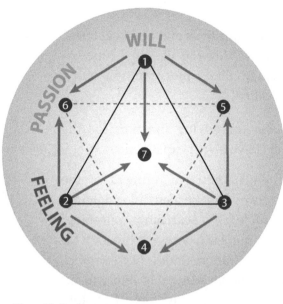

Figure 12. Passion

function is active and provides information whenever we find something attractive or repellent.

As stated above, with my model, I decided to change Assagioli's term "impulse-desire" to passion. This is because, according to Assagioli (Keen, 1974), there is a "group of functions that impels us toward action in the outside world. This group includes instincts, tendencies, impulses, desires and aspirations."

Passion is linked to our basic survival instincts as well as our devotion to the highest good. Through the passion function we can devote ourselves wholeheartedly to a goal or an ideal, such as our children, a lover, or a hero who symbolises our values and beliefs. Passion nurtures loyalty and makes us faithful to what we love.

Passion is exclusive: it selects one goal and rejects all others. This focus can offer an extraordinary strength, enabling us to enter into the world of ideals. In this way we can inspire ourselves and others simply through our enthusiasm.

When we access our passion, we emanate the energy of dedication: excitement, joy, focus, intensity, conviction and faith. Through passion we connect with the dedicated energy, which is full of will and emotion, as Assagioli (1967b) states: "Desire is or has a dynamic energy that impels to action."

Passion is the function that underpins the dedicated or devotional-idealistic type because, according to Assagioli (1983: 70): "The devotional type is intensely emotional. His feelings are often passionate and extravagant."

The superconscious aspect of the function of passion-desire could be termed spiritual aspiration, or mystical vision, because when passion has a spiritual focus it inspires a mystical approach, which many mystics have pursued on their journey to union with the divine (Assagioli, Undated 24).

Are you passionate about values and ideals? Are you dedicated to them? Your responses to these questions will indicate the extent to which you have developed the function of passion.

Action

The functions of will, feeling and thought in combination with the sensations of the body produce the function of action (Figure 13). It can be seen that any action involves choice (will), reflection (thought) and an emotional response (feeling), and this action is then carried out by the body, which utilises the five senses and its ability to act. In every action, one of the primary functions will usually dominate in its execution, in accordance with the purpose that lies behind that action. (I should make it

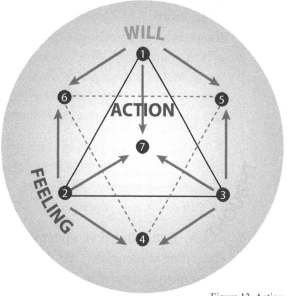

Figure 13. Action

clear that with the action function we are referring to concrete physical action. To a certain extent, our thoughts and feelings are also actions, but we don't necessarily act on them in a physical sense.)

Jung and Assagioli both termed this function "sensation", but I think action is a better word because it better describes the transmission of practical energy; the action function is essentially *the will in physical action*. According to Assagioli (1930c), the presence of sensation "indicates the sensation function or the physical consciousness and action on the physical plane". In another article, Assagioli (1934b) clearly discriminates between sensation and the action of the body, explaining: "The Orientals distinguish the organs of sensation, jnanendriyas, of which we have just spoken, and the organs of action, Karmendriyas. They are: Mouth – speaking, Hands – grasping, Legs – walking, Anus – excretion, Genitals – procreation".

If you are a practical person you will enjoy attaining concrete results for your efforts. The outcome is important to you, but you will also enjoy the process of planning, organising and executing your ideas. Efficient action requires holding awareness of all aspects of an operation. A good host, for example, must consider the requirements of her dinner guests, select the right ingredients, prepare the food and serve the meal in a pleasant way; a developed acting function enables you to do this.

A person of action moves with grace and economy towards a chosen goal. When this function is developed you will emanate the qualities of practical energy: earthiness, groundedness, co-cooperativeness, effectiveness and practicality.

Action is the function underpinning the practical organisational type. According to Assagioli (1983, 78): "The organisational type expresses himself above all in action and he is a thoroughly objective type." The superconscious aspect of the action function is the spiritual will to manifest, which will be executed using organisational skills for the betterment of society.

Do you often take charge and organise events and situations? Do you enjoy seeing the fruits of your efforts? Your responses to these questions will indicate the extent to which you have developed the function of action.

In summary, Tables 5 and 6 bring together some of the key aspects of

The Superconscious or higher psychological functions

Normal functions	▶	Will	Feeling	Thought	Imagination	Logic	Passion	Action
Super-conscious Functions	▶	Will-to-Good	Altruistic Love	Genius	Intuition	Scientific Intuition	Spiritual aspiration	Spiritual will to manifest
		Heroic action	Ethical insight	Philosophical inspiration	Artistic inspiration		Mystic vision	

Table 5. The superconscious or higher psychological functions

our discussion regarding the functions. Table 5 lists the superconscious aspects of the seven normal functions, according to my hypothesis. Table 6 lists how the primary energies and their respective psychological functions combine to create all seven energies and functions.

The combination of the energies with functions

Three primary functions	Seven functions	Three primary energies	Seven energies
Will	Will	Dynamic energy	Dynamiske energy
Feeling	Feeling	Sensitive energy	Sensitive energy
Thought	Thought	Mental energy	Mental energy
Feeling + thought =	Fantasy	Sensitive + mental =	Creative energy
Will + thought =	Logic	Dynamic + mental =	Analytical energy
Will + feeling =	Passion	Dynamic + sensitive =	Dedicated energy
Will + feeling + thought =	Action	Dynamic + sensitive + mental =	Pracital energy

Table 6. The combination of the energies with functions

The four quadrants and the psychological functions

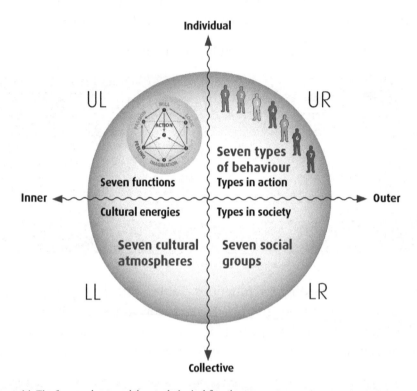

Figure 14. The four quadrants and the psychological functions

Let us now consider where the psychological functions sit within the four quadrants (Figure 14). The functions, which present themselves as inner psychological tools or intelligences, could be thought of as "organs of the mind", which would locate them in the subjective realm of the energies (UL). But we could equally think of the functions as physical brain centres, or neural networks, which would place them in the objective realm (UR).

Perhaps the functions bridge both aspects of the world – the subjective and the objective? For my model, I have preferred Jung's suggestion that the functions are best understood as organs of the mind, which therefore locates them in the upper-left quadrant. It is from this location that the functions can be expressed through concrete action and behaviour by individuals (UR: this theme will be explored in the next chapter), or collectively as cultural atmospheres (LL), or through social groupings and the physical environment (LR).

Developing the psychological functions

In reading about the seven psychological functions, you may have recognised that some are more dominant in you than others. This shows that not all of the functions are equally developed in us. For example, the thought and logic functions will be well-developed in an academic, while the feeling and passion functions will be well-developed in someone engaged in social and humanitarian causes.

We can say that all of the functions are available to each of us, but they are not all equally developed, which means we will each exhibit different qualities, talents and abilities; we emanate different energies and behave differently. Why are some of our functions more developed than others? Perhaps because our biological and psychological DNA predisposes us to develop some more than others. Also, we are all affected by the environment and the social energies that surrounded us while we were growing up (lower quadrants). For example, someone growing up in an academic household will be exposed to different energies compared with someone growing up on a farm, and they develop different functions accordingly.

Whatever accounts for our predispositions, it is important to develop our "inferior" functions, if we wish. We can train our will and imagination and develop our thinking. We must identify with the function in question and act on it (upper quadrants). For example, if we want to strengthen our imagination we must involve ourselves in situations where using the imagination is important; the easiest way to learn something is to spend time with those who already know about it and embody it (lower quadrants).

The functions have a powerful impact on how we see the world. When we see through the lens of a particular function the world will be coloured by the operation of that function. For example, if we are identified with the will function, the world will appear to be a place of competition and challenges where performance and power are all that matters. When we are identified with the feeling function, relationships will be central in our lives. When we are using the logic function, we will take more interest in how things work. In fact, we shift between the functions throughout the day. We may be ambitious at work, displaying will, passion and dedication, but when we get at home our attention may shift to our family and a desire to relax because we are more identified with the feeling function; then, later in the evening, we might settle down with a book to read about a subject of particular interest to us, thus engaging the analytical logic function.

The point to remember is that every function facilitates a different type of behaviour, with different corresponding needs and different ways of seeing the world. This next exercise provides an opportunity to reflect on which might be your most dominant functions.

Exercise: What functions do you use the most?

This exercise is designed to explore our life as individuals, rather than our role in groups or society, so we are looking at how the functions impact on our lives in the upper left and right quadrants.

How would you describe your mood and behaviour throughout the day? Which of these patterns of behaviour do you most identify with? You may find that one or two will be more prominent.

1. Focused on results, co-ordinating, habitual, organised.

2. Active, restless, communicative, mental.

3. Dynamic, goal-oriented, focused, performance-oriented.

4. Joyful, emotional, spontaneous, focused on dialogue.

5. Calm, receptive, peaceful, open, relational.

6. Practical, focused, explorative, rational.

7. Intense, passionate, one-pointed, emotional.

When you have completed this exercise, ask someone close to you to say how they would describe you – and compare your insights with theirs. In the footnote[4] you will see how the functions correspond with the list.

Colour and the psychological functions

Something we haven't yet touched on is how we can use colour to help us understand and work with the different energies and functions. We have chosen colours that are close to the classic Colour Wheel.[5] These colours can be used as a coding system to help us to work with the different functions, energies or types and to show us how they are linked.

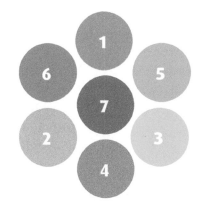

Figure 15. Colour circle showing the colours of the psychological functions

From a psychological perspective, the colours embody some of the same qualities as the different energies and their corresponding functions. According to our colour circle coding system (Figure 15), the three primary colours of red, blue and yellow are irreducible and represent the three primary functions of will (red), feeling (blue) and thought (yellow). The colours of the four other functions are derived from combinations of the three primary colours.

The Dynamic energy (Will function) resonates with the dominant energy of red.

The Sensitive energy (Feeling function) resonates with soft and calming blue.

The Mental energy (Thought function) resonates with the lightness of yellow.

The Creative energy (Imagination function) resonates with playful and harmonious green.

The Analytical energy (Logic function) resonates with energetic orange.

The Dedicated energy (Passion function) resonates with violet, which tends to lift our energies.

The Practical energy (Action function) is represented by a dark reddish brown because it contains a practical energy that comes from the will (red) and because it is the colour of the earth, which reminds us that the journey through the seven energies takes us from the inner to the outer, eventually manifesting in concrete action.

(It is interesting to note that each colour has an opposite or complementary colour: red-green, blue-orange, violet-yellow. This reflects how each energy has an opposite that contains what the other lacks. This important topic will be tackled in chapter four.)

Having looked at the seven psychological functions, in the next chapter we will look at how these functions impact on the psyche to create the seven types.

Realise your ambition
– The seven personality types

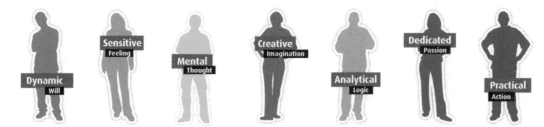

Figure 16: Seven personality types

We have seen how the seven types manifest at five psychological levels. In this chapter, we will explore how the seven types and energies are expressed at the psychological level of the personality. In doing so, we can discover our own personality type. Figure 16 shows the seven personality types with their respective psychological functions and associated colours. In fact, because psychosynthesis typology takes into account the dimension of introversion and extroversion, as with Jung's system, this means there is an introvert and extrovert aspect for each of the seven personality types, giving us 14 different expressions of the personality. But because the introvert and extrovert aspects of a type are essentially two faces of *the same basic type,* we speak about their being seven personality types.

Let us begin by exploring what is meant by introvert and extrovert. Assagioli (1967b) says the following[1]:

> We now come to the *direction of the vital interest*, and so pass from the descriptive to the dynamic aspect. One of Jung's most valuable

---

[1] For a comprehensive discussion of Assagioli's understanding of introversion and extroversion, see Assagioli (1931) and Assagioli (1967b).

contributions was the discovery and description of two fundamental psychological types based on whether the vital interest is directed outwards or inwards, and thus *"extraverted"* or *"introverted"*. I should mention at once that it is less a matter of "types" in a precise and static sense, and more of the prevailing direction of the vital interest, and thus of the consequent evaluations, choices, decisions and actions.

When we speak about introversion and extroversion we are speaking about the "dynamic aspect" of typology because we are dealing with the direction of our energy – also known as our vital interest – which determines how we *prefer to* direct our attention. Introverts are more inclined to live in the subjective world (left quadrants) and extroverts in the objective world (right quadrants). Interestingly, Assagioli (1967b) makes the observation that we can be either introvert or extrovert on each of the five psychological levels. For example, one can be introverted emotionally and extroverted mentally. Note also that we are only speaking about preferences; the ideal is that we move beyond personal preference and strive to become ambivert, i.e. able to direct our focus in either an introvert or extrovert direction at will, according to our purpose.

Note: In this book I have decided to describe the introvert and extrovert modalities of the personality types only. Space does not allow me to explore the introvert/extrovert modalities of the other types, as expressed at the other four psychological levels, i.e. the introvert/extrovert modalities of the soul types, thinking types, feeling types and body types. However, the same principles apply at all five psychological levels.

To help us differentiate between the introvert and extrovert expressions of the personality type, I have suggested a different archetype for each (Figure 17); archetypes are psychological patterns and images in the

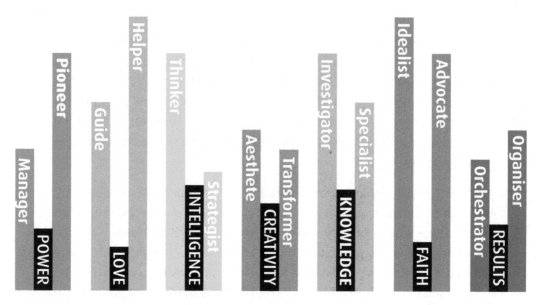

Figure 17. Introverted and extroverted archetypes

collective unconscious that express different psychological qualities and with which we can connect through identification.

Table 7 shows how the energies, psychological functions, personality types and personality archetypes are linked. For example, dynamic energy is expressed in the dynamic personality type via the introvert archetype of the Manager and the extrovert archetype of the Pioneer; both archetypes express dynamic energy but in an introverted or extroverted direction.

The personality types have both mature and immature qualities, and how these qualities are expressed depends on the overall maturity of the person and how much they have worked on personal growth. The different personality types can learn a lot from each other, and with this realisation we have found an important key to personal growth, which we discuss below.

From energies to personality types

Energies ▶	Dynamic energy	Sensitive energy	Mental energy	Creative energy	Analytical energy	Dedicated energy	Practical energy
Functions ▶	Will	Feeling	Thought	Imagination	Logic	Passion	Action
Personality Types ▶	Dynamic type	Sensitive type	Mental type	Creative type	Analytical type	Dedicated type	Practical type
Personality archetypes (i) ▶	Manager	Guide	Thinker	Aesthete	Investigator	Idealist	Orchestrator
Personality archetypes (e) ▶	Pioneer	Helper	Strategist	Transformer	Specialist	Advocate	Organiser

Table 7. From energies to personality types

The development of your personality type

Your personality type emerges during the course of your psychological development. I have based the following explanation of how this happens in Assagioli's developmental theory[2], which he aligns with Maslow's Hierarchy of Needs. The ages of development below are only suggestive because in practice there is a great deal of individual variation between people. You might like to refer to Figure 1 in chapter one which depicts this process of development in terms of the five psychological levels.

In the first seven years of life, the soul, acting through the evolving "I" and, one of the seven energies takes hold of the physical body and a particular body type unfolds. The child is also developing at the mental and emotional levels at this time, but the primary focus is on physical development and on learning about the body and what it can do: movement, speech, physical coordination through play.

---

[2] For a full discussion, see Sørensen, 2008, 2018b, 2018c, and Assagioli: 1973, 2007, chapter 9., Undated 1, 4, 1965b.

From 7 to 14, feelings take centre stage. The child integrates more fully into the family and wider social system and a particular feeling type emerges (one of seven possible).

From 14 to 21, the focus shifts to the development of thought and, assuming the person has had a rounded education, a particular thinking type emerges.

From 21 to 35, the personality type will emerge as a dominant energy if we are successful in developing our will to become an individual with our own sense of decision-making and volition. It takes courage and maturity to become an individual and not everybody succeeds in this. Many people prefer the security of conforming to society's standards and rules. The emerging personality type is shaped by the individual's *quality of will*, and it involves the integration of the three psychological levels of body, feeling and thought. *Quality of will* refers to the quality of our *ambition*; the manner in which we pursue our life path is determined by the type of energy that colours our quality of will. For example, a leader is very often a dynamic personality type whose quality of will is flavoured by the dynamic energy, while teachers are often sensitive personality types whose quality of will and ambition has been influenced by the sensitive energy. In exercising our will and establishing our personality type, we become one-pointed, and influential within our field, bringing our actions, emotions and thoughts in line with a self-initiated set of goals. The outcome, or flowering, of this developmental process has been described variously as self-actualisation (Maslow), personal psychosynthesis (Assagioli), and the Centaur Stage (Wilber).

From the age of 35 onwards, if an individual chooses to embrace the humanistic and spiritual values that are inherent in the soul, then her soul type will emerge as a dominant energy. It is important to state that, even if it has not yet emerged as a dominant energy, the energy of the soul will always be present in the background because it is a fundamental energy.

The seven personality types: their purpose, problems, virtues and vices

Let us now examine the seven personality types in both their introvert and extrovert modalities. In doing so, we will be following Assagioli's recommendation, set out in the Introduction, that we endeavour to "understand the true nature, the underlying function and purpose, the specific problems, virtues and vices of each type". By "specific problems", Assagioli is referring to the *psychosynthetic task* of each type, meaning the particular challenges that must be faced by each type in order to mature and become whole. Assagioli (1930c) explained:

> Once we have recognised to which psychological type we belong, we are confronted by the problem, which is both practical and spiritual, as to how to deal with it, how to utilise it or change it, according to our higher purposes. The inner tasks concerning each type may be synthetically indicated in the following terms:
>
> 1. *Expression.*
>
> 2. *Control.*
>
> 3. *Harmonisation.*

There is a lot here, and space does not allow for a full exploration of Assagioli's meaning, so the reader is urged to investigate Assagioli's full discussion of the topic elsewhere (see Assagioli, 1983: 13). For our purposes, I offer the following brief elaboration of the key terms: expression, control and harmonisation.

Expression concerns the process of first accepting and owning the types we belong to, then, according to Assagioli (1930c), "our chief task must be the expression and perfection of our type in the purest and most developed way possible". However, according to psychosynthesis theory, the challenge that each of us faces is that there are virtues and vices associated with each type. How the energies are expressed can vary greatly: we can do so beneficially or destructively, altruistically or egotistically; how we do so is largely dependent on our levels of consciousness and maturity. For example, an immature sensitive type can exhibit a jealous, controlling and manipulative love, while a mature sensitive type will be kind, caring and empathetic. In psychosynthesis practice we always strife for the higher expression. We will look more closely at the virtues and vices associated with each of the types below.

By *control*, Assagioli is speaking about managing the limitations of each of the types, even in their mature aspects. Assagioli (1930c) explained: "The second vital task which confronts us is that of controlling and correcting the excesses of the psychological type to which we belong. We all have the tendency to follow the line of least resistance, i.e. to go on expressing and developing the faculties which are already active in us." In practice, this means the mental type can get stuck in their head, the dynamic type can become brutal and destructive, and too much spontaneity can cause the creative type to become unstable. The challenge is to discipline ourselves to limit and harmonise our natural excesses so we can become rounded in our development.

Assagioli (1930c) said *harmonisation* is about "developing the faculties [functions] as yet undeveloped in us and which are not part of our present psychological type". Each of the types needs to integrate qualities from other types, especially the type which is its opposite (see circle diagram, Figure 6). The aim is to harmonise our typological qualities without diminishing our natural strengths. For example, a dynamic type will be more effective as a leader if they are able to integrate the qualities of the creative type, such as humour, playfulness and the ability to balance and cooperate; such a leader will further benefit if they can also manifest the sensitive qualities of love and compassion.

A full discussion of how each type can develop is included as part of our identity profile at www.jivayou.com/en/. One of the quickest ways to integrate your undeveloped qualities is to form close relationships with other types; unfortunately, this can be a disagreeable task because those who hold the qualities we lack are often the sort of people we find most irritating, precisely because they express the qualities we habitually avoid and even denigrate.

Let us now examine the seven personality types, in their introvert and extrovert expressions, mentioning also their vices and virtues and identifying the opportunities for personal growth.

1. The dynamic personality type

The red arrow pointing downwards symbolises the dynamic type. The arrow indicates the will striking like a lightning bolt, while the colour red denotes dynamic activity.

The dynamic personality type is robust, strong and determined. They are goal-orientated and resilient, and greatly value freedom and independence. This type likes to look at the big picture, and gets frustrated by detail. Their preference is to have a set of governing principles with which to guide them in their lives. When immature, such types can be selfish, domineering, impatient, difficult, and aggressive if they don't get their way. Achieving power and influence, while maintaining freedom and independence, is paramount for this type and part of their essential *purpose*.

When introverted the dynamic type is represented by the archetype of the **Manager**, who directs, protects, and focuses on the purpose and task at hand. They excel as CEOs because they relish being a figurehead who strengthens and supports the group. When extroverted we have the **Pioneer**. With their bravery, boldness and an appetite for new ideas, the Pioneer can break new ground and become a role model for courage. When immature both archetypes can be stubborn, destructive, bullying, and isolated.

The dynamic personality type must *accept* their need for power and influence, and learn to wield this power wisely. They must *control* their tendency to fight and dominate their opponents, and learn that it is easier to destroy relationships than to build them.

Assagioli *(1983: 21)* says of this type: "The most important personal characteristic of the will type is the *will to power*. This manifests itself as ambition, self-affirmation, the desire to dominate others and to be the central figure on stage. It degenerates easily into egotism, stubbornness and obstinacy. In order to achieve his goals, the person of this type can easily become arrogant and unscrupulous. Another basic characteristic, because of the suppression of the emotions, is *isolation*."

The essential psychosynthetic task for the dynamic type is to become more inclusive and adaptable without losing drive and direction. To this end, the dynamic type can develop by integrating the qualities of the other types: the creative type teaches the dynamic type to be playful and adaptive; the sensitive type offers empathy and patience; the mental type offers flexibility and strategic thinking. It is also important to integrate love which, as Assagioli (1931b) explains, will produce "a wonderful synthesis of will and love: a will which loves and a love which wills".

Professions for this type: We find the dynamic type in politics, in business as managers, and wherever leadership and responsibility are required. They are at home in the police, army, fire brigade and emergency services, and enjoy any other activity associated with risk – this is due to the dynamic energy and pioneering spirit that is required for these types of work. Similarly, this type enjoys extreme sports, martial arts, and tasks that are physically demanding or that require initiative and an ability to lead. This type is basically a warrior at heart.

Reflecting on the jobs you've had, has it been the challenge to succeed that has motivated you the most?

2. The sensitive personality type

The blue counter-clockwise arrow symbolises the sensitive type: the arrow depicts how feeling can connect and contain, while the colour blue represents the calm that can inspire people to be present with their emotions.

The sensitive type is able to tune into their surroundings and empathise, without rejecting any of the emotions. This type's emotional and mental antennae are well-developed and when mature they tend to be holistic and inclusive in attitude. Approachable, friendly and warm, this type is easy to get along with. They are insightful and welcome authentic relationships. *The purpose of the sensitive type is to sustain and develop relationships.*

The introverted expression of the sensitive type is represented by the archetype of the **Guide**, the personification of which is the counsellor who has a deep insight into human nature. The extroverted expression is the **Helper**, who supports others with their warmth, compassion and understanding. When immature this type can be sentimental, clinging to harmful attachments, over-sensitive, fearful, addicted and indiscriminate, with a victim mentality. When discernment is not developed, this type will be overly focused on subjective feelings and desires.

The sensitive type must accept their sensitivity and need for connection without succumbing to neediness. They must learn to control their tendency to be overly identified with others' needs so they can step into their authority. They also need to tackle their fear of rejection and isolation which leads to a need to be popular.

Assagioli (1983: 34) says of this type (using his own terminology): "The love type is often innocuous, good-natured and charming; his limitations are agreeable and useful to others who can easily take advantage of them; thus, he not only provokes no opposition but is often encouraged and approved of by others."

Sensitive types have a lot of good will but need to develop the strong will. The essential psychosynthetic task of this type is to learn the noble art of loving-detachment, which means being able to love wisely without becoming ensnared by the attachment and deception of "idiot compassion", as the Buddhists call it. To this end, sensitive types can learn discrimination and logic from analytical types, self-confidence from dynamic types, and objectivity from the mental type.

Professions for this type: The distinctive qualities of the sensitive type are humanistic values and a capacity for insightful communication; the goal is to build and improve character and relationships. Accordingly, the sensitive type likes to help people, which could mean teaching, coaching, therapy, counselling or social work. This type is inclined to work in the fields of psychology, social sciences or cultural studies, and they often become involved with religion, social care, sociology and human resources, indeed anything that entails healing and health. This type will also enjoy metaphysical studies and holistic topics that require deep reflection and understanding.

Has your choice of career been motivated primarily by an interest in people's well-being?

3. The mental personality type

Three counter-clockwise yellow arrows symbolise the mental type: the arrows depict the mind reaching out in many directions, while the colour yellow depicts the stimulation of the intellect.

The mental type is characterised by an active mind, shown by an appetite for planning and strategy or perhaps vigorous physical activity. This type is flexible and fluid. They are mentally creative and a rich source of ideas that they enjoy sharing. Their lack of emotional attachment to their ideas allows them to see situations from different perspectives. The purpose of this type is to be an *intelligent agent for change* through the use of their inventiveness and skill. According to Assagioli (1983: 44), the goal of this type is "to *manifest, incarnate, produce, adapt* and *invent*".

An introverted mental type is represented by the archetype of the **Thinker** or the Philosopher. When introverted, the mental type is reflective and fond of abstractions, creating smart and innovative solutions to human problems. The extroverted type is the **Strategist**, who is typically an active and busy person who is perceptive, shrewd, patient and adaptable. When immature, this type can be cold, distracted, restless, calculating, indecisive, arrogant, critical and boastful. This type has a deep fear of being seen as stupid and might compensate by being overly intellectual. The immature introverted type, in particular, can be impractical and absent-minded.

The challenge facing the mental type is that they must accept their need for change and innovation without becoming stressed or defaulting to hyperactivity. They must learn to control their tendency to being too smart for their own good, which can lead to a tendency to manipulate those who are less intelligent.

Assagioli (1983: 42) says of this type: "Their gifts: skill in action, efficiency, quickness, the capacity to manipulate, and inventiveness. This type uses and gains mastery over the 'law of economy' and can obtain the maximum results with the minimum effort and expense in time and materials."

The essential psychosynthetic task of this type is, according to Assagioli (1983: 45), "to control and eliminate the excesses of 'busyness'. He must learn the value and art – however difficult and unpleasant for him – of rest, calm, relaxation and *silence." To this end,* the mental type can learn earnestness and honesty from the dedicated type, focus from the dynamic type, and an ability to love and empathise from the sensitive type.

Professions for this type: The mental type excels in academia, research, the media, maths and the sciences. They are often journalists or writers or found in public relations. We find the mental type in think tanks and in astrology, finance, IT, commercial trading, transport, shipping and logistics. They are often farmers, craftsmen and salespersons.

Has your choice of work primarily involved uncovering and developing new knowledge?

4. The creative personality type

Two green counter-clockwise arrows symbolise the creative type: the arrows depict how imagination integrates the opposites, while the colour green represents harmony.

The creative type is spontaneous and lives in the present. This type is able to think on their feet and look at life from different perspectives. They are intuitive and artistic and often make effective peacemakers and mediators. This type is able to understand and work with opposites, which they attempt to balance through their work. Beauty is important to this type, especially in their home settings and in their work environment. Dreams are more important than truth because they prefer the imaginary to the factual. The purpose of this type is to create harmony and beauty out of conflict, chaos and ugliness.

The creative introvert is represented by the archetype of the **Aesthete**. He or she can be a designer, writer of fiction, a mediator or therapist. Aesthetes can enjoy interpreting and realising dreams. They are skilled at reconciling opposite feelings and ideas in the mind. They are able to resolve conflicts and bring harmony. The extrovert expression of the creative type is the **Transformer**, who is a thrill-seeker in search of adventures and extreme situations. This type has a facility for drama and is able to give expression to unconscious processes and conflicts. This type will be a powerful communicator, perhaps a comedian or an actor.

When immature, the creative type can be self-absorbed, boastful, lazy, undisciplined, moody, deceitful, divisive and unpredictable. Because this type is drawn to conflict and opposites, when immature they can finding themselves getting into trouble of their own (subconscious) making, even though their natural tendency is to long for peace and harmony.

The challenge facing the creative type is to accept their need for harmony and beauty. Their calling is to take inspiration from the muses and create new beautiful forms, but with their sensitive and volatile nature they must try to avoid being drawn into drama. They must learn to control their tendency to "go-with-the-flow", face reality, take responsibility and stay focused. The essential psychosynthetic task of the creative type is to develop steadfastness and balance, and to create order out of chaos without becoming overly identified with extreme points of view. To this end, the creative type can learn discipline and focus from the dynamic type, common sense from the analytical type, and a commitment to values from the dedicated type.

According to Assagioli (1983: 51), the Creative and Aesthetic type faces "the deep and complex task of creating order out of chaos. Therefore, while the essential nature of this type when it is fully realised is harmony, peace, union and beauty, it is more commonly and obviously seen in the form of unsatisfied ambitions, internal and external conflicts, struggles with intractable material and rebellious forces, and oscillations between polarities."

Professions for this type: Creative people are typically found in the arts, psychology, fashion and entertainment. They might be mediators, writers, communicators or interpreters; they may teach yoga or work in HR or, indeed, in any situation where creativity, insight, humour and spontaneity are helpful.

Has humour and spontaneity been important in your work?

5. The analytical personality type

The orange arrow pointing right symbolises the analytical type. The arrow depicts logic moving forward in a methodical manner, while the colour orange represents focused thought.

The purpose of the analytical type is to establish reliable facts about the world and improve living conditions for us all. The analytical type is dedicated in their search for truth and the advancement of knowledge. This type is patient and methodical in collecting empirical data, which they can analyse to arrive at concrete conclusions. The analyst applies logic, taking her time to gather data, working methodically to gain knowledge. The analyst collects, dissects and concludes in her search for objective truth.

The introvert expression of this type is represented by the archetype of the **Investigator** who engages in precise and factual research, seeking to generate new ideas, methodologies or products. The extroverted type is represented by the **Specialist**, or Technician, who is focused on the application of knowledge, demonstrating new skills and an ability to master the practical world.

When immature, this type can be over-analytical, absorbed in their thinking and lacking in imagination. As a consequence, they can seem overly critical, cold, arrogant and narrow-minded. They can be dogmatic, petty, unforgiving, suspicious, and sometimes cruel in their relationships. This type has a tendency to become isolated due to following obsessively rigid routines. This type can be unskilled at processing their emotions, which means they can be socially awkward.

According to Assagioli (1983: 62), when at their best, this type has "an almost superhuman objectivity and impartiality; a noble disinterestedness, and an internal and external independence that leads him to detach himself from idols, partisanship, and external authority. He is courageous, detached and almost ascetic and knows how to sacrifice himself."

The challenge facing the analytical type is to accept their need for truth, reliability and accountability, and to learn how to control their need to understand all the details, which often blinds them to the bigger picture.

The essential psychosynthetic task for this type is to let go of their materialistic outlook and to incorporate their phenomenological experience of the subjective world – in this way they can help to share the benefits of science in all domains of life. To this end, the analytical type can learn kindness, friendliness and the value of subjectivity from the sensitive type; light-heartedness from the creative type; and the value of faith and humanistic ideals from the dedicated type.

Professions for this type: The analytical type enjoys acquiring and working with specialist knowledge. They can make excellent teachers and educators, especially in the sciences or medicine. They can be skilled researchers, for example analysing DNA or investigating archaeological evidence. They will enjoy forensic work and can make effective police officers, mechanics, carpenters, dieticians, marketing analysts, opticians, biologists or lawyers.

Do you prefer work that is useful and practical?

6. The dedicated personality type

The purple vertical arrow symbolises dedicated energy: the upward-pointing arrow depicts how passion reaches for the heights, while the colour purple is associated with idealism.

Dedicated personality types are passionately committed to their cause. Their purpose is to inspire people to pursue noble ideals with a sense of passion. The dedicated type is focused, driven, goal-oriented and highly motivated to achieve goals that are the best, highest and noblest. The dedicated type is wholeheartedly devoted and humbly faithful to his ideal, idol or belief. They use the energy of devotional love to advocate for the best results, whether they are devising a new product, putting together a team, or pursuing a political vision. When immature, this type can be fanatical, authoritarian, superstitious, abusive and naive. They can be narrow-minded, unrealistic, domineering, impulsive and fundamentalist.

The introverted expression of the dedicated type is represented by the archetype of the **Idealist**: the ideal can be anything considered worthy of their devotion. The extraverted dedicated type is the **Advocate**, an activist who devotes their energy to an ideal or holy cause, which could be spiritual, political or social in its aims. As a parent, this type will idealise their children.

The challenge facing this type is that they must accept their need to pursue their ideals for a better world without becoming a missionary who views all people as potential converts. They must learn to control their tendency to being intense or extreme, holding black and white attitudes that victimise those with different points of view. Assagioli (1983: 72) said: "The good qualities of this type are as remarkable as the limitations of its less developed representatives. Besides sincerity, we find loyalty, veneration, self-sacrifice, endurance and a lack of fear, among others."

The essential psychosynthetic task for this type is to find the *still and impersonal point in the heart* from which to direct their passion without getting lost in their vision; it's a question of moderation. To this end, the dedicated type can learn flexibility and an ability to see life from different perspectives from the mental type, the value of humour from the creative type, and common sense from the analytical type.

Professions for this type: Whether introverted or extroverted, the dedicated type tends to have an "all or nothing" attitude that shows in their work. They may be missionaries, New Age gurus, PR experts, or entrepreneurs marketing a "revolutionary"' new product. They can be intensely devoted to their family or hobbies. They might be philanthropists, activists or humanitarians. As with the sensitive type, the dedicated type is attracted to nursing and any profession that involves caring, supporting or mentoring. They can also be attracted to occupations that involve fierce competition, such as politics or sport.

How committed have you been to your work?

7. The practical personality type

Three burgundy arrows meeting at the centre symbolise the practical type. The three arrows depict will, feeling and thought combining in concrete action. The colour of reddish-brown/burgundy symbolises the earth and grounding.

The practical type is skilled at coordinating people and resources to achieve a result. They are natural leaders in a practical sense, knowing how to organise and apply their energy. This type is efficient, versatile and resourceful. They make things happen through planning, collaboration and efficiency in execution. They can often be found at the centre of an activity, directing everything to achieve the best result.

Assagioli (1983: 84) said of this type: "The personal qualities of the organisational type, besides the propensity for order, are: attention to detail, accuracy, patience, perseverance, courtesy and, at the mental level, clear thought and objectivity." Assagioli (1983: 78) added: "His dominant note can be expressed as 'the ordered activity of the group' or, 'objective manifestation through organised activity'".

When immature, this type is bound by routine, power-seeking, dominating and demanding. They can be overly-formal, stubborn, manipulative, pedantic and proud. They can value efficiency over people's feelings and demand perfection. They often play the role of the grey eminence – pulling strings behind the scenes – and can use their power to outmaneuver their opponents and climb the ladder.

The introverted expression of the practical type is drawn to law and order, which is represented by the archetypical roles of the **Orchestrator** or Legislator. The introverted practical type enjoys creating smooth, efficient systems. They enjoy co-ordinating people, whether this is in a work or social setting or in entertainment: they like to conduct the orchestra. The extrovert practical type is represented by the **Organiser**, or Manager, who is at the centre of a project, focused and co-ordinating activities for the best effect.

The challenge facing this type is that they must accept their need for order, elegance and efficiency without falling into the trap of micro-managing. They must learn to control their *need to dominate* so they don't limit the creativity and well-being of their collaborators.

The purpose of the practical type is to manifest new ideas through organisation. Their essential psychosynthetic task is to keep themselves orientated towards this *ultimate purpose* and not to get entangled in the process of managing practical detail. According to Assagioli (1983: 87), they "should always be clearly aware of the difference between a living organism and a dead organisation – that is, an organisation that has become an end in itself". To help in their development, the practical type can learn empathy and care from the sensitive type, a commitment to ideals from the dedicated type, and a playful ability to balance temperaments from the creative type.

Professions for this type: The practical type will enjoy management, legislature and judicial work. They make effective project coordinators, administrators and scientists. They could be air traffic controllers, film directors, financial advisers or football coaches – indeed, any work that requires coordinating people. In recent years, many new occupations have emerged that are suitable for the practical type because they require multi-tasking and expertise in different areas.

Do you enjoy seeing the results of your work?

Overview

Having read through these profiles, readers may be closer to understanding their own personality type. Identifying your type is not always easy, and we often need help to see ourselves, so it can be useful to ask a friend or colleague for their thoughts.

You will find a full index of the types and their different characteristics at the back of this book.

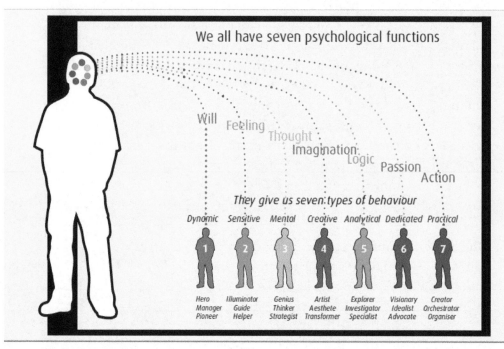

Figure 18. From psychological functions to types

Figure 18 offers an overview of the relationship between the psychological functions and the different soul and personality types. Remember, we each have access to the energies and qualities of all the types, but one of the types will generally dominate on the personality level. To find out more about your typological make-up, complete JivaYou's free personality profile or the more detailed identity profile (visit jivayou.com).

Exercise: Personality type and job history

Your job history can reveal a lot about your personality type. Begin by making a list of all the jobs you've had. If there is a large number, focus on the most significant jobs and the ones that suited you most. Now list the skills you used in each job.

Which personality type is the best match for you?

Now list your motivation for doing these jobs. Were you primarily motivated by:

Will: ambition, influence, leadership.

Feeling: care, helpfulness, good relationships.

Thought: knowledge, communication, activity.

Imagination: beauty, empathy, new experiences.

Logic: professionalism, seriousness, discovery.

Passion: excitement, competition, optimisation.

Action: cooperation, leadership, results.

Again, which personality type is the best match for your answers?

In the next chapter, we will look at the seven soul types, from which we can begin to sense our way to the soul.

The Seven Types
On a Good Day

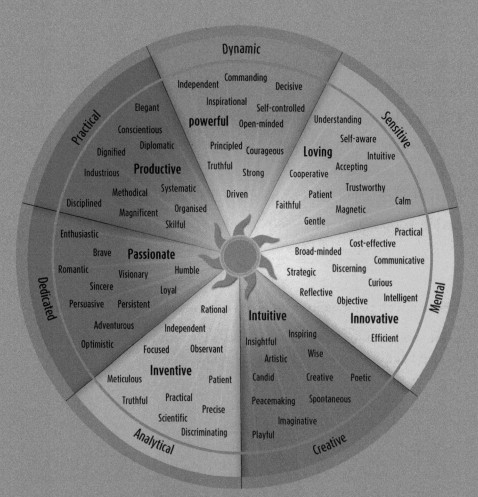

The Seven Types
On a Bad Day

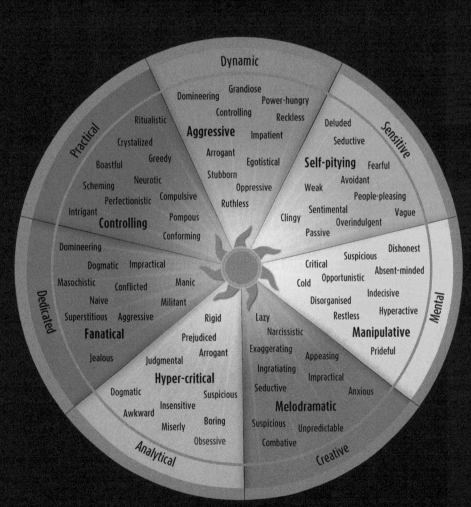

The seven ways
and seven soul types

The "Seven Ways of Self-realisation" is a familiar concept within psychosynthesis and is taught in many centres around the world. One of the prominent books on this topic is Piero Ferrucci's monumental work *Inevitable Grace* (2009), which discusses spiritual breakthroughs in the lives of great men and women. Ferrucci's extensive research offers validity for these seven ways of spiritual psychosynthesis.

Assagioli himself, prior to his death in 1974, was working on a book entitled *Height Psychology*, which he intended to include his theory of the seven ways. However, this material was later published posthumously, under the title *Transpersonal Development* (Assagioli, 1988), the book did not include the material Assagioli prepared on the ways. Happily, though, this missing material can be found in the Assagioli Archive in Florence, and I have drawn upon it for this chapter.

Let us begin with a definition of spiritual psychosynthesis and the way to the soul. For me, we are speaking about *the realisation of soul consciousness*, which means the attainment of a world-centric perspective, as opposed to an ego-centric or ethno-centric perspective. When we enter this path, we gradually let go of our identification with ourselves as a separate individual or as an isolated member of a family, nation or group. Instead, an understanding arises from the depths of our hearts that we are each an integral part of the whole. We begin to take responsibility for that whole through our service to the world; we become citizens of the world and understand that our soul purpose is to take responsibility for making our contribution to the whole. The reward for realising our soul consciousness is that we discover a deep sense of meaning; we can enjoy feeling connected to a larger purpose and will experience an inpouring and outpouring of creativity that arises from a source of endless abundance. This realisation, which is often a gradual awakening, empowers us to become all that we may be in the depths of our spiritual being.

When we set out on this spiritual path, our emerging soul consciousness will come under the influence of a particular energy, which is our soul type, of which there are seven, each with its own specific qualities. Just as there are seven energies, there are seven ways to the soul, each of which is identified with a particular archetype in the superconscious, and this archetype is what we call our soul type. The seven types and the seven ways share the same energies, functions and qualities; the seven ways refer to the manner in which we seek to realise soul consciousness.

Let us investigate how this process unfolds. In an article entitled *The Seven Ways*, this is how Assagioli (Undated 20) conceptualised the path to self-realisation:

The different spiritual approaches to reality have long been recognised in the East, particularly in India; and in the great poem *The Bhagavad Gita* this is clearly stated: "As men approach me, so do I accept them. Men on all ways follow my path." (1V, 11) The chapters in this poem admirably expound the various ways which are each suited to special types of people and their different degrees or levels of inner development.

The above passage indicates that, in Hindu philosophy, different styles of yoga are suited to different individual types. According to my own research, this is as follows: Raja yoga for mental types, Bhakti yoga for devotional types, Karma yoga for practical types, and so on. In addition, it can be noted that all the different yoga styles can be combined into a single path through the Yoga of Synthesis, as described by Sri Aurobindo.

But while there are similarities between the seven ways and the different yoga schools, they are not entirely the same. Nor so all spiritual realisations occur within a religious context. This becomes vividly clear in reading Ferrucci's book, and also in the work of Assagioli where he discusses the seven ways.

So what are these seven ways? The following list is taken from Assagioli's book *Transpersonal Development* (2007: 44-45) – it is just one of 14 references in which Assagioli describes the seven ways[1]:

> There are many different ways of expanding the consciousness as one moves upwards, and they are related to different psychological types and different individual constitutions. We can identify seven main ways. I would point out at once that these methods are not separate and that in practice they tend to overlap, so it is possible for a person to proceed along more than one path at the same time. The fact remains, however, that they are distinct and for the sake of

---

[1] Assagioli 2007: 45; 1974: 116; 1965: 25, 201-222; Undated 3, 19, 20, 22-28; 1976; 1976b.

clarity, to begin with at least, we need to describe them and get to know them separately. We can then move on to possible ways in which they can be combined. They are as follows:

1. The Way of Science

2. The Way of Enlightenment

3. The Way of Regenerative Ethics

4. The Way of Aesthetics

5. The Way of Mysticism

6. The Way of Heroism

7. The Way of Ritual

The Seven Ways and Types

	Seven Types (Assagioli)	The Will-Power Type	The Love-Illuminative Type	The Active-Practical Type	The Aesthetic-Creative Type	The Scientific-Rational Type	The Devotional-Idealistic Type	The Organiser-ritualistic Type
▶	Seven Ways (Assagioli)	The Heroic Way The Way of Will	The Way of Love The Way of Illumination	The Way of Action	The Aesthetic Way The Way of Beauty	The Scientific Way	The Devotional Way	The Ritualistic or Ceremonial Way
▶	Seven Ways (Assagioli)	The Way of Heroism	The Way of Enlightenment	The Way of Regenerative Ethics	The Way of Aesthetics	The Way of Science	The Way of Mysticism	The Way of Ritual
▶	Seven Ways (Assagioli)	Transcendence through Transpersonal Action	Transcendence through Transpersonal Love		Transcendence through Beauty		Transcendence through Self-realisation	
▶	Ferrucci	The Way of Will	The way of illumination	The Way of Action	The Way of Beauty	The Way of Science	The Way of Devotion	The Way of Dance and Ritual
▶	Sørensen	The Hero	The Illuminator	The Genius	The Artist	The Explorer	The Visionary	The Creator

Table 8. The seven ways and seven soul types

In naming these seven ways, Assagioli in different places uses slightly different terms. For ease of reference, I have compiled into Table 8 some of Assagioli's different terms, together with Ferrucci's terminology, and I have shown how they match up with the seven soul types. Each of the seven ways corresponds to a particular soul type, a specific function and a different soul energy, as shown in Table 9, p. 135. The colours depict the different qualities, for example red represents the psychological function of will, the dynamic energy and the Hero soul type.

The seven ways are different paths that lead to superconscious self-realisation, or what Assagioli calls spiritual psychosynthesis. However, it has also been noted that, as we progress and become more balanced in the final stages of self-realisation, the different ways merge to become one synthesised way. Assagioli explained (Undated 20):

> There are seven main ways of spiritual or Transpersonal realisation. The ways are not sharply divided; in fact, they frequently overlap to some extent. Some individuals may follow two or three ways concurrently; this is because there are no pure types, and also, each of us has different Ways or qualities manifesting in the different aspects or levels of our being. But all ways are directed to and lead to the same great goal, therefore, the more balanced the individual, the greater the overlapping of the ways and their blending and fusing.[2]

However, it is important at this point to mention an additional theory, hinted at in Assagioli's quote above, where he states: "Some individuals may follow two or three ways concurrently; this is because there are no pure types, and also, each of us has different Ways or qualities manifesting in the different aspects or levels of our being." In stating

---

[2] Assagioli (Undated 20) also mentions an eighth way, The Way of Transcendence, explaining: "Some of the Eastern Schools emphasise this way to Spiritual Realisation, and some of the Western Mystics, especially Meister Eckhart, have attempted to describe it." It seems to me that the Way of Transcendence is really an aspect of the Way of Will because, in Psychosynthesis Typology, Assagioli (1983: 23) identifies Vedanta Advaita and Zen Buddhism as belonging to the Way of Will, and these are both practices that are prominently used by those seeking to attain transcendence.

there are "no pure types", Assagioli is referring to the fact that we each have five dominant types in our overall combination of types (i.e. a dominant type at each of the five psychological levels), which means that no person is a single, or pure, type.

Assagioli also highlighted that the ways are not sharply divided but are more like a rainbow of energies overlapping and blending with each other as we expand our consciousness into the sublime; in other words, at the highest level, the types and ways are synthesised but without losing its primary quality. Furthermore, when the personality becomes spiritualised or synthesised – meaning the personal will becomes aligned with the transpersonal will – then the energy of the personality will merge with the soul. As a result, we will no longer be driven by the egoic needs of the personality but will be guided by the values of the soul: we try to be a good citizen of the world, while accepting our shortcomings.

It follows that our lives are greatly influenced by both our personality and our soul, therefore having knowledge of our soul type and personality type will provide vital information that we can make use of to help us in our search for self-realisation. In particular, such knowledge will help us to navigate spiritual crises – something Assagioli highlighted as crucial. In a lecture he gave at the International Centre of Spiritual Research, in Ascona, Switzerland, in 1932, Assagioli offered an invaluable discussion of the different sorts of crisis that can occur during spiritual awakening. Interestingly, Assagioli (1932: 254) indicates that these crises can arise out of a conflict between the soul and the personality:

> …difficulties may arise from the different qualities of the forces brought into play. The quality of the soul's energy, which is technically called the Ray of the Ego, may be different from that predominant in the personality. This frequently produces a period of

conflict between the two, which may cause various nervous diseases until an adjustment is effected.

For the psychosynthesis practitioner, it is crucial to understand what is going on when we witness such crises in the lives of our clients or in our own life. Our insights into the particular types and energies that are at play will make it possible to make helpful interventions.

The development from personality to soul

We have seen how a dominant energy shapes the personality, working through the quality of ambition and how we pursue it. Primarily, the personality is organised around self-serving values and motivations, such as a need for safety, close relationships, self-esteem and recognition, ambition, and a wish to be popular, powerful and creative. This is normal and understandable: it is good to look after ourselves and our close relationships.

However, some people want something deeper. At some point in life, there emerges a need for a higher meaning and purpose, for something that transcends the need for normality and success in the ordinary definition of the word. This need for meaning often arises from an existential crisis, when we find that those things that used to satisfy us no longer do. We start to feel we need to make major changes in our lives, which is a crisis of choice between the needs of the ego or personality and those of the soul. Despite

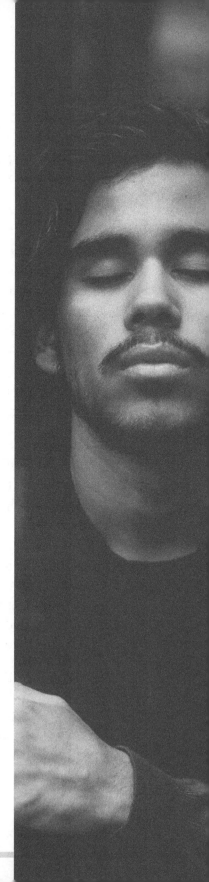

whatever success we might have had in business or society, we cannot stifle a sense of emptiness. We might start to feel empty, depressed and bored and lack a sense of vitality. We feel we *should* be happy and that something is missing. This something is the soul.

Each of us will experience this crisis differently, but in each case, if we follow through, there will be a shift in values. We will open up to the qualities of our soul type and experience new energies and motivations, with new interests demanding our attention. We will begin to experiment with different ways of being: we may change how we live and become artists or leaders.

This is how Assagioli (1932: 254) described this crisis: "All the personal affairs, which formerly absorbed so much of his attention and interest, seem to retreat into the background, to lose their importance and value. New problems arise; the individual begins to enquire into the origin and the *purpose of life*; to ask what is the reason of so many things that formerly he took as a matter of course; the meaning of his own sufferings, and of those of others; what justification there may be for so many inequalities in the destiny of men."

I recommend reading the whole of this article in which Assagioli (1932) describes the many different varieties of this crisis and how it can be navigated.

Awakening to the soul and its qualities will not remove our personal needs, but something deeper comes to the forefront. A need for personal love and status will remain, but these needs will be complemented by deeper values and a deeper ethical voice in our heart which will influence how we treat ourselves and others. It is worth noting here that some people connect with the soul before their personality has matured; such people tend to lack grounding so they become *impractical idealists* who are unable to wield influence. The theme of soul and personality integration will be discussed in detail in chapters 8 and 12.

It is from within the soul that we find inspiration to make a difference in the world. It is through our soul that we have our deepest connection to the essence of life and through which we are able to access intuitions from the superconscious. The soul is the top floor of our inner being, it is an inner penthouse that contains a wealth of talents and qualities: the good, the true and the beautiful. From this inner resource arises the inspiration to make the world a better place. The challenge we face is to balance our outer normal life (personality) with inner meaning (soul) – to do so is to discover our core identity, which triggers a new lifelong journey to harmonise the personality with the soul in such a way that the personality is the servant of the soul.

This process enables us to tune into the energy and qualities of our soul type as we find ourselves on one of the seven ways to the soul. We will start to hear our soul's calling, which will always concern a particular service that we feel motivated to pursue. Service is the most fundamental instinct of the soul, and it is accompanied by the pure joy of finding meaning.

It is important once again to emphasise that each of the seven ways contains the other six as secondary support. The ways are not separate but connected like colours in a rainbow. The ways are a spectrum of possibilities that we can all realise to a greater or lesser extent, although one of the ways will tend to have dominance – and our personality archetype will remain influential because the personality is the mask through which we will express our soul purpose in the world.

Let us now examine the seven ways to self-realisation, noting how this journey can be expressed in both secular and religious or spiritual terms. We will see how, with each of the seven ways, there is an inner calling to serve a higher purpose that acts as a compass on the path to self-realisation.

Seven Ways to self-realisation

The Way of the Hero

In his article *The Heroic Approach*, Assagioli (Undated 19) writes: "Spiritual realisation... is generally conceived in terms of religiousness, or as a purely inner experience, and therefore the fact that it can be attained through heroic action is seldom recognised. In our opinion, an unbiased observation of the facts shows that it is primarily and predominantly through selflessness and self-sacrificing *action* that a certain number or category of men rises to great heights. In their case, the reality and potency of the spirit is demonstrated through the overcoming of the major and most deep-rooted instinct existing in natural or biological man: the instinct of self-preservation. The inner quality or energy required for such an attainment is COURAGE."

What I call the Way of the Hero is *a path to self-realisation that entails leadership.* We find the archetype of the Hero in Hollywood films. He or she is the hero, the strong man/woman, the genius, even the saint. The Hero fights for noble causes, for freedom and for values that will help to create a brighter future. They are leaders showing the way. Whatever influence or power they possess are used in the service of their highest values.

Inspired by their work, the Hero in turn inspires others. Their strong will empowers them and gives them the motivation to achieve greatness.

The Way of the Hero requires courage. On this path we find pioneers with the courage to break new ground despite resistance from mainstream culture. The Hero swims against the tide, risking everything to win the prize. Their actions rise from an inner certainty which gives them the strength to stand alone. They are the great conquerors who bring new ideas to humanity.

This path is one of renewal and revolution, which also entails destruction. The hero breaks down existing rules and structures so that new life can emerge. These revolutionaries are visionaries who bring a new vision and a new reality. The Hero dismantles the old to make way for the new, risking everything to do so, drawing on their vast reserves of courage, bravery and determination.

Do you fight for a worthy cause demanding blood, sweat and tears?

The Way of the Illuminator

In his paper *The Illuminative Intuitive Approach,* Assagioli (Undated 22) writes: "Intuition comes from 'intuere' [Latin] that is to see in, and this indicates clearly the quality of this function, an inner seeing, a direct seeing. Seeing implies light, a light which allows us to see something illumined. In fact, the experience of inner light is one of the most widespread, of the most certain, described by countless witnesses of every time of every country."

What I have called The Way of the Illuminator is *a path to self-realisation through insight and compassion.* The Illuminator wants to answer life's

big questions – "Who am I?", "What is the meaning of life?" – and, drawing upon their deep insight and love of life, they find answers to these fundamental questions. Those who walk this path are wise, compassionate and empathetic.

These are the spiritual teachers who reveal life's deepest meanings. They know that everything is connected and they find many ways to teach this message. They are the ones who have fresh insights in their chosen fields or they might be healers working in new ways for the benefit of people, wildlife and nature.

The Illuminator's path is one of enlightenment. They search for the light within themselves and in others and pass on what they learn. They want to understand human suffering and how to heal the conflicted psyche. Illuminators often work as psychologists, psychotherapist, healers or in other roles that help people on the path to self-knowledge and self-realisation.

It is often through prayer, meditation and contemplation that those on this path become enlightened. They long for a connection with a spiritual being of peace and unity. The Illuminator's essential qualities are wisdom and love.

This is the path of the sensitive soul type. This type connects to life through a highly developed sensitivity. The essential qualities of the Illuminator are empathy, insight, and loving-understanding.

Is it your mission to bring light to the world?

The Way of the Genius

Assagioli (Undated 23) describes this path as *The Way of Action* or *The Way of Active Service*. He explains: "One of the ways of spiritual approach or spiritual realisation can be called the way of *dedicated activity*, or of *active service*. It is a way which is accessible to the greatest number because it does not require any special ability or inner qualities or cultural level. The simplest people can and have followed it, even better than the more sophisticated ones… It can be called Karma Yoga, or yoga in everyday life."

For this type, every physical action is dedicated to a higher and beneficial purpose or, for those of a religious inclination, to God. This is why Assagioli sometimes called this path the Way of Active Service.

The Way of the Genius is also a sophisticated path to self-realisation in which the mind makes discoveries and devises innovations for the benefit of all.

The archetypal genius recognises and comprehends life's complexities. Whatever their chosen field – culture, science, business, politics – this type can see patterns and opportunities that others are unable to see.

This is the way of abstract intelligence, that of philosophers, economists

and other thinkers. Drawing on their integral vision, they weave a network of theories that helps others to make better sense of the world. Their unconventional insights and thinking outside of the box create new fields of inquiry, and for this reason they would be at home with new technology and other areas of cutting edge innovation.

The Way of the Genius is an ethical path, which seeks to set out new guidelines for society. The Genius is not only an intellectual but also a trendsetter and a moral example of the avant-garde, bringing new elements into culture, expanding our concepts of equality, freedom and community. This type are the writers, thinkers debaters, strategists, communicators and innovators that lift culture to a higher level.

Geniuses are cultural architects. They create intelligent solutions to human problems and formulate narratives that improve culture and society. They show us the good, the true and the beautiful through concrete *intelligent activity and service.*

Do you solve problems through innovations?

The Way of the Artist

Assagioli (Undated 24) described this path as *The Aesthetic Way.* Quoting Plato, Assagioli (2007: 243-244) explained the spiritual importance of beauty for those on this path, writing: "One needs to progress from love of a beautiful form to love of all beautiful forms and of physical beauty in general, then from love of beautiful bodies to love of beautiful souls, beautiful actions and beautiful thoughts. As one ascends through moral beauty one will reach the point where a marvellous eternal beauty appears, free from any corruption, absolutely beautiful. This beauty does not consist of a beautiful face, a beautiful body, a thought or any particular science or art. It resides in no other being than

itself, neither in heaven nor on earth, it simply exists in itself in eternity and exists for itself in absolute, perfect unity."

The Way of the Artist is a path to self-realisation that finds purpose and meaning in beauty, although beauty is not the only quality that inspires this soul type.

The Artist follows the path of contrasts. The Artist archetype inspires others to appreciate harmony and beauty. However, to do this, the Artist must battle with the chaos of conflict and opposites, which must be integrated in order for harmony to emerge.

The Artist wrestles with conflict, darkness and drama, seeking to unite the opposites and black and white thinking that can divide us. This battle means the Artist's way is one of suffering. The Artist is torn between seeing the reality of how things are, while holding a vision of harmony and beauty – for how things could be. Yet their determination to manifest this vision enables the Artist to embrace the pain of life's many conflicts and contradictions.

The true artist's talent is to authentically portray the human struggle and show us the way to harmony. The Artist confronts the question: "How can we create the good life when the good we want is not what we do?" This is the question that the Artist is portraying with dance, music, theatre, film, and art forms.

But the Artist is not just a storyteller. She is the transformer who teaches us that light and meaning can emerge out of our darkness. People who walk this path are peacemakers, psychotherapists and group facilitators; they know how to dance with the opposites of love and hatred, happiness and pain. The Artist's journey is exemplified in Dante's journey into hell to find his true love Beatrice.

The Artist's path to self-realisation is the aesthetic way, with beauty serving as the guiding star. This type knows that people need humour, play, spontaneity and magic to help us to connect. The Artist believes that design, colour and aesthetic forms are as necessary for us as food. Beauty opens and motivates the Artist and, indeed, all of us, rejuvenating, renewing and bringing inspiration. The essential qualities that are being developed on the path of the Artist are grace, spontaneity, empathy and communication.

Do you need to create harmony in your life?

The Way of the Explorer

Assagioli (Undated 25) describes this path as the *Scientific Way* and offers the following insight into how scientific construction of the universe compares with ancient wisdom: "… physics has demonstrated that the so-called 'Matter' is in reality composed of minute and powerful electric charges, positive, negative and neutral, concentrated in centres and points and moving rapidly in space in conformity with laws and patterns based on mathematical formulae. The latter imply of necessity an intelligent principle or being, a Cosmic Mind which has formulated them and maintains them in operation. Thus it is that scientists have arrived – perhaps almost in spite of themselves – at the same conclusions reached millenniums ago by the most advanced philosophical thought: that the physical world we perceive is 'phenomenal', that is, apparent, and that behind and above it exits the world of reality composed of energies and intelligent powers. This is the world of causes, of which the phenomena are the effects."

The Way of the Explorer is *a path to self-realisation through research and discovery*. The Explorer archetype is curious, with a strong appetite for knowledge. We all have a need to explore and discover, but these qualities come to fore in this type. It is Explorers who develop new medicines and technological innovations and who offer fresh insights into important issues. Explorers derive great satisfaction from understanding factual truth and learning how things work from a practical and concrete perspective.

Explorers make outstanding researchers because they have extraordinary analytical skills and an appetite for detail. Their capabilities make them useful in any activity that requires analysis and research with a focus on fact-finding and evidence.

The Explorer collects information and knowledge which they use to map out new landscapes and territories. Their technical, psychological and spiritual discoveries can change the world as we know it. Those on this path will uncover the mysteries of life. This type acquires deep knowledge and employs reflective analysis and experimentation to resolve issues.

The Explorer finds joy in making discoveries that can be of real benefit to people, whether they are working within material, psychological or spiritual realms. This type is interested in anything that be of practical use, especially when that use can be tested and verified. The essential qualities of this soul type are alertness, discipline, perseverance, clarity and objectivity.

Are you moved by the promise of discovery and acquiring new knowledge?

The Way of the Visionary

In describing what he termed the *Mystical Approach*, Assagioli (Undated 26) writes: "The mystic's ardent aspiration is to achieve union with a beloved Being, who, while having divine characteristics, is conceived by him as possessing an exalted personality, and with whom he can therefore establish a personal relationship. In describing his inner experiences, he freely uses the language of human love and often that of an undisguised sex symbolism."

However, the Way of the Visionary is not confined only to religious mysticism; this path to self-realisation can take many forms of devotion.

Passion and dedication to an ideal characterise this path. The Visionary needs something to fight for, something that is good, true or beautiful. Their passion is driven by a hope for a better future. They throw themselves into idealistic enterprises in a manner that inspires enthusiasm in others to help ensure that their goal is reached.

This idealism can be expressed in many ways, depending on the person's combination of types. Where there's a religious tendency, the Visionary can inspire the devotion and worship found in church congregations and spiritual communities; these are the visionaries who have seen paradise and can show us the way. Alternatively, the Visionary's ideal might be of political nature, as expressed by the great political leaders throughout history.

Visionaries formulate and express new ideals, and can often become idols. Their ideals are often focused on beauty, excellence in performance, humanitarian goals or spiritual values, which means this type can often be found in the fashion world, competitive sports, the charity sector, in politics or in spiritual contexts. In each case, the Visionary is seeking a goal or an ideal to which they can wholeheartedly dedicate themselves.

The Way of the Visionary is also the way of sacrifice. Visionaries are willing to give up everyday pleasures and conveniences in order to achieve their goals. Their commitment is radical; when deeply committed to their ideal they will focus all of their energy on pursuing their vision and achieving their goal.

Have you dedicated your life to a cause?

The Way of the Creator

Speaking of what he calls the *Ritualistic and Ceremonial Way*, Assagioli (Undated 28) states: "This [way] was the best known and has been followed by the majority, particularly in the past. Religious ceremonies are doubly effective: their display makes a striking and lively impression on the senses and imagination of those present; while to those who understand their symbolic signification, as representing truth and spiritual principles, they carry a strong appeal."

The Creator has the ability to *organise* communal rituals, whether religious or secular in natures, such as worship ceremonies, music festivals or sporting competitions.

The Way of the Creator is a practical one. The archetype of the *Creator* motivates us to create something magnificent and useful through our ability to organise people around a central idea. This type turns great ideas into action, and subjective energies into group experiences. *Creators* know how to get things done and we rely on them to do this.

The *Creator* is inspired by a clear purpose. Their strong will helps them to make effective use of their resources. This type has organisational genius and knows how to coordinate people and manage activities. Imagine someone who is able to organise emergency aid following a natural disaster, planning everything down to the smallest detail.

The *Creator* is a perfectionist. They are often movie directors, event planners or chefs who insist on achieving excellence. This type is results-orientated and know that the result will only be as good as the people and resources they are able to work with. They are experts in selecting the right people and resources for a task. They are great planners who know how to bring projects to fruition.

The Way of the Creator is the path of greatness. They are motivated by the

chance to achieve great things, such as building impressive architectural structures or establishing innovative companies. Their dedication to expressing greatness often leads to outstanding results. This type is able to combine functionality with elegance, and balance great beauty with practicality. This type's organisational and leadership skills enable them to create new forms and new structures.

Do you feel compelled

to use your organisational skills

for a good cause?

The Seven Soul Types

Energies ▶	Dynamic energy	Sensitive energy	Mental energy	Creative energy	Analytical energy	Dedicated energy	Practical energy
Functions ▶	Will	Feeling	Thought	Imagination	Logic	Passion	Action
Seven Types ▶	Dynamic type	Sensitive type	Mental type	Creative type	Analytical type	Dedicated type	Practical type
Soul Types ▶	Hero	Illuminator	Genius	Artist	Explorer	Visionary	Creator
Personality Types ▶	Manager Pioneer	Guide Helper	Thinker Strategist	Aesthete Transformer	Investigator Specialist	Idealist Advocate	Orchestrator Organiser

Table 9. The seven soul types

The soul type and the four quadrants

In this section I will discuss the soul type and personality type in connection with the four quadrants.

The five psychological levels appear in the upper left quadrant; they are the building blocks of our inner world. The energy that passes through each of the five levels manifests as concrete action and behaviour, which we can see in the upper right quadrant.

Some of these behaviours are focused on taking care of the everyday needs of the ego, which amounts to taking care of our body, feelings, and thoughts – this is the domain of the personality. However, other behaviours are motivated by our higher needs for meaning and purpose, without excluding the needs of the personality – this is an area of activity which engages both the soul and the personality. And on rare occasions there are moments when the needs of the personality are forgotten and we find ourselves acting purely in the service of a good cause – and this is an indication that we are operating in the domain of the soul.

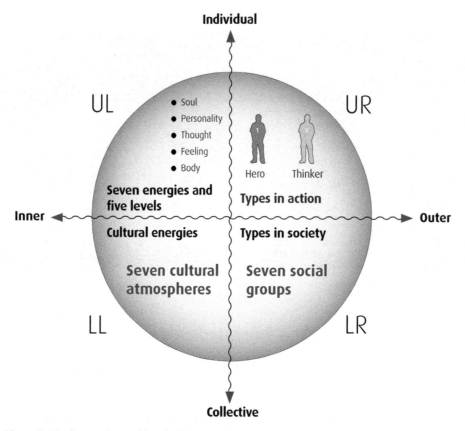

Figure 19. The four quadrants with soul and personality types

Figure 19 offers an example of what this might look like in practice. In the upper right quadrant we can see a dynamic soul type with a mental introverted personality type (The Thinker) who is following the Way of the Hero. (In chapter 8 we see in more detail of how the soul and personality come to be integrated and what this means for our personal development.)

Completing this look at the four quadrants, it is important to note that we exist in a social context, so our personal actions will also impact on the collective, as depicted in the lower quadrants. Indeed, an individual's qualities of the soul often emerge in a group context. I will return to this theme later.

Exercise: Visualise your meaningful future

You receive a letter from a lawyer in the United States who informs you that a rich uncle has left you 100 million dollars in his will. Now that you no longer have to work to earn money, you can focus entirely on living your dream.

There is one catch: 80% of the money must be used to make a positive difference in the lives of people you don't know, which rules out your family, friends, associates and local community. In short, you are required to help people who you are not directly related to or emotionally linked to.

How would you spend the $80 million?

Once you've decided, consider what lies behind the motivation.

Your answer will indicate your way to self-realisation.

You may not have inherited a huge sum of money, but now you have an indication of the direction in which your soul path lies – and you can begin this journey by taking the first small step.

In the next chapter we will take inspiration from looking at some role models who exemplify the different personality types and soul types. These examples illustrate what the seven ways of self-realisation might look like in practical terms.

Chapter 6

The seven types and notable role models

We will now look at how a few notable people each embody a different soul type. As stated in the Introduction, this chapter is written by Søren Hauge. My intention is to offer examples of men and women, past and present, who exemplify a particular soul type, or a typical combination of types, and I hope this will help us to recognise the essential qualities of the various types. In offering these examples, I have worked to the best of my knowledge, but it is not an easy task to designate types to people I have not met, so please take the following material as hypothetical. It is also important to note that in this chapter we are not looking at pure types but at soul types, which means we are looking at how an individual's expression of their soul qualities can be flavoured by the qualities of a variety of energies.

I have also included some of Assagioli's suggested examples of the types. For further examples, I highly recommend Ferrucci's book *Inevitable Grace*, which offers some deep material.

LEADERS: Dynamic soul types with Will as the dominant function

Abraham Lincoln (1809-1865), the 16th President of the United States, is an example of someone who has demonstrated strong leadership on the world stage. His role in the abolishment of slavery and his integrity as a leader made him one of the founding fathers of the United States. He demonstrated a dynamic powerful leadership that incorporated a sense of humanity and solidarity (practical type) as he sought to end slavery in the US.

Abraham Lincoln   Elizabeth Tudor   Mikhail Gorbatjov   Nelson Mandela

A few centuries earlier, Elizabeth I (1533-1603) was the Queen of England. As a progressive regent, she ruled with a firm hand (dynamic type), overseeing the birth of the British Empire while maintaining a passion for the arts and culture (creative type). She was temperamental with dramatically changing moods (creative type), but overall her determination and leadership – in both war and peace – turned Great Britain into a wealthy superpower and contributed to cultural and social growth.

A former head of state of the Soviet Union, Mikhail Gorbachev (born 1931) also demonstrated leadership on a global scale. In his own country he introduced *glasnost* (openness) and *perestroika* (restructuring). He ended the arms race with the United States and initiated the dissolution of the Soviet Union. He received the Nobel Peace Prize in 1990, and has since been involved with ecological movements such as Green Cross International and Earth Charter. Gorbachev's leadership is an expression of the strength of the dynamic type combined with the humanity of the sensitive type.

Nelson Mandela (1918-2013) is another example of the dynamic soul type. After 27 years in prison for his anti-Apartheid activities, Mandela became South Africa's first black president. His efforts to end Apartheid and tensions that existed between black and white South Africans were extraordinary. He received the Nobel Peace Prize in 1993 having supported numerous human rights organisations and initiatives. Mandela expressed dynamic leadership and power combined with the creative type's quest for harmony and balance.

According to Assagioli (1983: 22): "It is not difficult to recognise the most famous examples of this type. Various mystics and historical personalities have exemplified it. Zeus/Jupiter is a giant projection of beings of this type. His heroic antagonist, Prometheus, is another ideal model of it, and another is Hercules. The great rulers and conquerors of history demonstrate its more or less admirable traits in various proportions; we can name Alexander the Great, Julius Caesar and Napoleon."

TEACHERS: Sensitive soul types with Feeling as the dominant function

Teachers, counsellors and other sorts of helpers who want to change the world to make it a better place. The Italian physician Maria Montessori (1870-1952), a world-renowned pioneer of children's education, is one such example. Her educational philosophy, and the movement of Montessori schools that has spread across the world, have deeply influenced modern children's education. We can sense both the sensitive type and the more experimental analytical type in her work.

The Swiss psychiatrist Carl Gustav Jung (1875-1961) is another example of someone who possessed great wisdom and insight. With his analytical psychology, Jung put the soul into psychology by uniting strict empirical practice with Eastern wisdom, archetypal symbols and the collective unconscious. His practice as a psychologist is an expression of the sensitive soul type, with his work clearly coloured by his scientific interest (analytical) and an artistic aestheticism (creative).

Today, we can find many prominent examples of the sensitive soul type in the fields of spirituality, psychology, sociology and the humanities. A prominent global role model is the Indian spiritual teacher Mata Amritanandamayi (born 1953), also called Amma, the mother, who in her work unites the roles of guru, peace worker, women's activist and

Maria Montessori   Carl Gustav Jung   Amritanandamayi Devi   Tenzin Gyatso

social philanthropist. Amma is best known for her warm embraces (the Amma hug), her teachings, and her ability to mobilise relief work and social work.

The most famous global spiritual icon today is undoubtedly Tenzin Gyatso (born 1935), better known as the 14th Dalai Lama, the spiritual head of Tibet and a Nobel Peace Prize winner. Through his life and teaching, the Dalai Lama has embodied compassion, wisdom, joy, friendliness and social activism. He has written many books and travelled the world extensively to share the philosophy of Tibetan Buddhism. His message is welcome in a world that is in desperate need of peace and the values of the heart. The Dalai Lama embodies the wisdom and love of the sensitive soul type, the commitment of the dedicated type, and the Western scientific orientation of the analytical type.

Assagioli (1983: 35) says the following: "In some of the finest representatives of this type, it is the quality of 'love' that is most notable, while in others *wisdom* seems to prevail; but in reality, at the level of the Self, these two aspects cannot be separated: the one necessarily implies the other. The supreme examples of this can be seen in the life and teachings of the two greatest representatives of this type known to man: Christ and Buddha."

THINKERS: Mental soul types with Thought as the dominant function

This is the world of metaphysicians, geniuses, and other great thinkers who develop smart strategies and solutions to solve life's practical challenges. These people possess enlightened minds that generate new insights and knowledge about the world.

One of the greatest thinkers of the Western world is the German philosopher **George Wilhelm Friedrich Hegel** (1770-1831). His "absolute idealism" and historical philosophy rest on the understanding that ideas shape the world. Especially important is Hegel's dialectics, which, like other "dialectical" methods of analysis, works with contradictions and opposites to create new syntheses and dynamics that can have a huge impact on history.

Hegel's countryman, the German philosopher **Immanuel Kant** (1724-1804), is another intellectual giant, and is considered to be one of the most significant thinkers in history. Kant's theory of knowledge considers what we can know and how we can know it. His categories, dialectics, theory of perception, and moral philosophy are among the most sophisticated attempts at trying to make sense of the world. Kant, like Hegel, was a living example of the mental soul type's ability to reflect deeply on principles and ideology. Kant was also influenced by law and the rhythm of life, a distinctive feature of the practical type; his walks along the riverbank were so punctual that it is said the housewives of Konigsberg set their clocks by him.

Mental types are known for making unique contributions in the fields of science, business, communications and technology. **Stephen Hawking** (1942-2018), who had motor neurone disease, is known for his pioneering scientific research into the nature of the cosmos, black holes and quantum physics. His popular science

G. W. F. Hegel   Immanuel Kant   Stephen Hawking   Steve Jobs

books about the universe and nuclear and astrophysical theory are worldwide bestsellers.

Another icon representing the mental type is **Steve Jobs** (1955-2011). He gained cult status for his development of computer technology, for founding and managing the Apple Group, and for developing Pixar Animation Studios. The development of the Macintosh computer and all subsequent Apple innovations made Jobs the nerd's number one hero, with Jobs playing a key role in revolutionising the development of Information Technology worldwide. Jobs developed elegant graphical user interfaces and introduced the mouse, iBook, iPhone, iPad and many other innovations. Jobs was also known as a tough leader (dynamic) and a genius (mental).

Assagioli (1983: 43) cites Henry Ford as an example in this category: "Examples of the active-practical type [mental type] are well known. We will mention only one, who is very typical indeed: Henry Ford. In reading his autobiography, we cannot help but admire his genius in manipulating the 'laws of economy' in his automobile business, by finding mechanical devices and little economies that permitted not only the increase of production but the lowering of costs and the increase of profit. (It could be claimed that Ford was a good example of the combination of the active-practical and the organisational types) [practical types]."

ARTISTS: Creative soul types with Imagination as the dominant function

Examples of significant creative and artistic figures are not difficult to spot. Within the sphere of music, the German composer and pianist Ludwig van Beethoven (1770-1827) is an obvious example. A rebel with a strong pioneering spirit, we can see the dynamic type in his stern expression. We also hear the sensitive and psychological qualities of his music, which reveal the creative type in its most magnificent expression. Beethoven composed nine symphonies and numerous string quartets, piano and violin concertos, operas and choral music. The *Eroica* symphony, *Ode to Joy* and *Moonlight Sonata* evidence his enormous range and artistic genius.

In poetry and language, we can mention Johann Wolfgang von Goethe (1749-1832). Not only was he a born artist, he also showed scientific acuity (analytical) and political leadership (dynamic). Goethe wrote poetry, dramas, novels and scientific books, with his theory of colour representing a significant scientific breakthrough. His best known work is *Faust*, a deep psychological drama that describes how a successful yet dissatisfied scholar is tempted to make a pact with the devil, exchanging his soul for unlimited knowledge and worldly pleasures. Goethe was a multi-faceted, multi-talented genius and one of a kind; in many ways he exemplifies the combination of the creative and analytical types.

In today's world, we see many expressions of the Way of the Artist in show business, music and film. One example is the Canadian singer Celine Dion (born 1968), who started singing and acting as a five-year-old and went on to become a global superstar. Her singing voice and performance are at a remarkably high level, and her joy of communicating through song is well-known. Her discography is extensive, including iconic songs such as *My Heart Will Go On* from the movie *Titanic*, and *Beauty and the Beast* from the movie of the same

Ludwig van Beethoven   J.W. von Goethe   Celine Dion   John Williams

name. Her CD sales count in their millions and she is still active. As well as exemplifying the artistic type, she also embodies the intense romance and empathy of the dedicated type and the professional skills of the practical type.

Another example of this type is the composer John Williams (born 1932), who has been writing music for the movies since 1958, including blockbusters such as *Close Encounters of the Third Kind, Jaws, Star Wars, Superman, Indiana Jones, Home Alone, Jurassic Park, Schindler's List, Seven Years in Tibet, Amistad, Saving Private Ryan* and the Harry Potter films. John Williams has won five Oscars for his music, the first in 1971.

Assagioli (1983: 58) writes: "Examples of the creative-artistic type are easily brought to mind: Shakespeare, who with the magic touch of his creative genius transformed all the people and situations that he found in history or fable, permeating them with new, delightful vitality and giving them intense dramatic expression; Leonardo da Vinci, with his extraordinary ability to fuse subtle and mysterious meanings in the portraits and landscapes he painted; and many other individuals of lesser calibre found in the same fields."

EXPLORERS: Analytical soul types with Logic as the dominant function

In recent centuries we have seen a scientific revolution and, in many ways, our world is now dominated by science. Many scientific and analytical types prefer the solitude of their work to public attention, which means they don't draw as much attention to themselves as other types. Even so, there are many examples of this type. Let's start with the Italian physicist and astronomer Galileo Galilei (1564-1642) who strived to "measure everything that can be measured and make the immeasurable measurable". Galileo lived during a period of Christian orthodoxy and, with a background in medical (analytic) and mathematical (mental) studies, he faced many cultural and religious prejudices. Galileo, also called the father of the scientific method, discovered four of Jupiter's moons based on observation; he calculated the law of falling objects; and he observed that the Earth moved around the Sun, a discovery that the Catholic Church tried to hide. He developed binoculars for astronomical observations and wrote a masterpiece of mechanical physics, *The New Sciences*.

Centuries later, the Polish-born French chemist and physicist Marie Curie (1867-1934) conducted research into radioactivity, and her discovery of polonium and radium has changed how we see the world. The significance of her research is obvious considering the dangers of radioactivity. She received the Nobel Prize for her research in physics and chemistry. Her scientific efforts and achievements are outstanding: Marie Curie exemplifies the analytical and practical types in their highest expression.

The analytical type has flourished in the twentieth and twenty-first centuries. Within less traditional fields of research, we can mention Dean Radin (born 1952), an American professor of parapsychology who became known worldwide for his book *The Conscious Universe*, in which

Galileo Galilei Marie Curie Dean Radin James Lovelock

he argues that extra sensory perception (ESP) and parapsychological phenomena (PSI) are facts of human life. Radin worked as a concert violinist for five years, so he is also an expression of the creative type, but it is his experimental study into psychic phenomenon that's key. Radin continues to advocate for parapsychology to be taken seriously as a science.

Another scientific pioneer who has challenged established materialistic science is the English chemist James Lovelock (born 1919), who is known for the 'Gaia Hypothesis'. This theory argues that the Earth is essentially a living creature, with its own self-regulating balances and dynamics. Lovelock based this hypothesis on concrete, observable facts about the atmosphere, oceans and continents, which he compares with biological organisms. With his background at NASA, Lovelock's research is based on scientific methods (analytical), but it is also clear that consciousness and care (sensitive) are present in his work.

For this category, Assagioli (1983: 63) mentions the French philosopher Descartes (1595-1650), explaining: "His insistence upon clear distinctions, definitions and methodical investigation of truth demonstrates the true character of the French mind. The French culture is also an expression of the type under consideration and particularly the French language with its logical and rather rigid structure and its capacity for clear, precise, almost crystalline expression. This quality means that the language is perfectly adapted to communicating the discoveries and results of scientific research with ease and accuracy."

VISIONARIES: Dedicated soul types with Passion as the dominant function

We commonly find the dedicated soul type pursuing higher goals and values, especially in the world of religion. The French saint Joan of Arc (1412-1431) is such an example. In a short period of time, and at a very young age, she made a great impact on history. She received divine guidance at the age of 12, when she claimed to have been contacted by the Archangel Michael and two deceased female saints who encouraged her to force the English out of France and save France from unrest and war. She was prophetic and, after some of her prophecies came true, she gained access to the royal court where she impressed the king. She became the king's trusted advisor and had many triumphs at court, but in the end she was imprisoned and executed for heresy. Her fiery warring leadership was clearly inspired by an intense religious conviction that turned her into a saint and a legend.

From a few centuries earlier we can cite Giovanni di Pietro di Bernardone, from the city of Assisi in Italy, also known as Francis of Assisi (1182-1226). He was the first Christian mystic who, through his earnest religiousness, received the stigmata. Through uncompromising faith, joy and poverty, he had a deep influence on Christianity. He founded the Franciscan Order within the Roman Catholic Church, living in extreme simplicity, even in caves and forests. He established a community and was known for his humility, joy, and gratitude for God's greatness and beauty as seen in nature. As a mystic and a radical disciple of Christ, St Francis exemplifies the dedicated type, but he also shows the love and compassion of the sensitive type and the appreciation of beauty as seen in the creative type. He is spiritually related to the present

Jeanne D'Arc   Frans af Assisi   Desmond Tutu   Oprah Winfrey

reformer of the Catholic Church, Pope Francis, who cites Francis of Assisi as a role model.

Another Visionary is the South African archbishop Desmond Tutu (born 1931), who exemplifies the dedicated type, not only for his work in the church but also for his role in the anti-Apartheid movement in South Africa. Tutu is a human rights activist (dedicated), who is also known for his sense of humour and expressive nature (creative). He works tirelessly for the poor and vulnerable and for the prevention of AIDS, tuberculosis, climate change, racism and homophobia, alongside many other important causes, including health for all and women's rights. In 1984 he received the Nobel Peace Prize and, despite his advanced age, he remains active.

Another expression of the dedicated type is TV host Oprah Winfrey (born 1954). Oprah was only 27 when she became the hostess of a talk show that put spirituality, compassion, learning and solidarity into the public domain. Her shows have reached 140 countries, with 45 million viewers weekly in the United States alone. In addition to projects and idealistic initiatives, such as Oprah's Angel Network, she has proven to be a skilled actress (creative), and her shows run as a highly efficient machine, with a large number of employees, that is extremely financially successful (practical)

Assagioli (1983: 73) mentions St Paul in this category, explaining: "One is Paul of Tarsus. The complete reversal of his feelings and actions as a result of his conversion, his ardent devotion to Christ, his militant apostolic zeal, his unshakeable courage, his profound sincerity that at times amounted to intolerance, and his intense, austere style are all characteristics of the type under examination."

CREATORS: The Practical soul type with Action as the dominant function

Creators come in many guises, and we will mention just a few. The American architect, designer and author Frank Lloyd Wright (1867-1959) is a great example of someone who has the Creator's grasp of craftsmanship and an ability to invent new worlds. His visionary powers have influenced architecture throughout the first half of the twentieth century, with his ideas for reconciling nature and architecture in organic design still a great source of inspiration. We can see similarities to this organic way of thinking in Gaudi, Rudolf Steiner, Hundertwasser and Le Corbusier.

Walt Disney (1901-1966), the creator of the Disney empire, is possibly the most influential person there has ever been in the entertainment industry. He is another world-class creator; Walt Disney cartoons are legendary and the Disney theme parks have had a revolutionary impact on how we think about entertainment and movies. His work is distinctly American, appealing to those who are highly emotional (dedicated), sensitive, and adventurous (creative). One could say that Walt Disney was an imperialist (practical type) who was a pioneer in promoting fantasy (creative) that has a naïve childish aspect (dedicated).

Two very different examples of pioneers who follow the Way of the Creator are Arnold Maersk Mc-Kinney Møller and Clint Eastwood. Møller (1913-2012) is one of the world's leading ship owners, through his Maersk group. This group is active in 125 countries, involved primarily

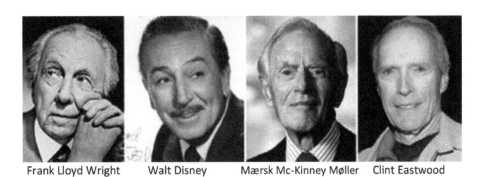

Frank Lloyd Wright   Walt Disney   Mærsk Mc-Kinney Møller   Clint Eastwood

with transportation, oil and natural gas production, and supermarkets. The Maersk shipping company runs a fleet of more than 300 large vessels, mostly container and tankers. Møller has run the company with an intense discipline (practical) and highly effective management skills (dynamic), all of which was expressed in his company's motto "Timely care".

Our other example is the artistically gifted pioneer Clint Eastwood. Eastwood (born 1930) is a movie star (creative) who demonstrates an extraordinary ability to make characters come alive, such as Rowdy Yates in *Rawhide*, the character of Dirty Harry, and Walt Kowalski in *Gran Torino*. Eastwood usually plays the tough hero (dynamic), and this type is visible in his personality. But Eastwood is also a gifted film director and producer. His film company, Malpaso Productions, was established in 1967 and created more than 50 movies, many of them starring Eastwood. He is known for his friendliness and efficiency, in the same way that his company is known for its efficiency, being able to produce films faster than most other companies (practical). At the same time, Eastwood is a composer and a pianist (creative). Eastwood was also the Mayor of Carmel, California, for two years, which is another example of his practical nature.

Assagioli (1983: 84-85) offers no historical figures for this type, but writes: "They include the highest priest at the head of a magnificent religious procession and the nurse who feels the pulse and takes the temperature of a patient at regular hours, transcribing them in order on a chart and supervising all the doctor's prescriptions for him. There is the chamberlain of the court, profoundly interested in intricate questions of precedence, and the tough football coach who imposes regular exercises on the team. There is the energetic commander of an army who, with his organising ability, makes fresh bread and hot coffee available to soldiers in the front line, and the refined philologist who patiently tries to harness the living body of a language in a structure of synthetic and grammatical rules, but having to accept a large number of exceptions. Then there is the archivist, intent on recording and precisely ordering the feverish activity of his company in innumerable multi-coloured filing cabinets; the individual who invents the rules of a new card game – and many others."

In light of the above descriptions, which prominent people have been your role models?

Make a list of your most important role models.

Which psychological qualities are most prominent in their characters?

Can you see a pattern in the qualities you are especially inspired by?

What does this tell you about how you set about seeking to have a positive influence in the world?

So far, we have looked at the seven energies and seen how they are expressed in seven different ways, from the dynamic to the practical type. We have also reviewed the five psychological levels of body, feeling, thought, personality and soul. With these foundations in place, we will now look at another factor that is essential for understanding our personality type and soul type, namely the seven motivators.

Find your drive
– The seven motivators

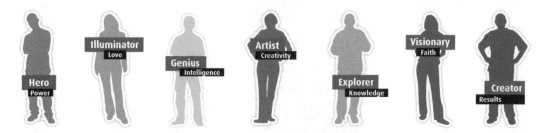

Figure 20: The seven types with motivators

To recap, the Seven Types is a model of typology based on the concept of psychoenergetics, according to which the universe and everything in it is composed of energy. Furthermore, this foundational energy can be divided into seven types – similar to how light can be divided into seven colours. So we can say that everything is comprised of energy, including our own selves. Another key concept of the Seven Types model is that the human psyche is comprised of five psychological levels – body, feeling, thought, personality and soul – with a different type of energy being dominant at each of the levels. This chapter looks at some of the difficulties involved in identifying these dominant types – and I will explain how an understanding of our underlying motivations and values can help.

Let me give an example to illustrate how an understanding of motivation can help us to distinguish between types. The dynamic type might exhibit the same behaviour as the dedicated type – both are one-pointed, forceful and dominating – however, their respective underlying motivation is quite different. The dynamic type is motivated by a wish to obtain power and influence – and this applies no matter whether power is being expressed at the levels of body, feeling, thought, personality or soul. While the dedicated type is motivated by the need to pursue an ideal. So, while the outward behaviour might look similar in some respects, the underlying motivation is different. However, we will also be able to observe clear differences between the types – in this case, we can observe that the dedicated type is highly emotional, while the dynamic type tends to suppress emotion.

To the untutored eye, making sense of the similarities and differences between types is a challenge. To give an idea of what we will be looking for, Figure 20 lists the seven types and identifies one of the prominent qualities that motivates each.

Assagioli wrote about the difficulties in identifying the types and he explained how understanding the underlying motivation can help. In the following passage, he offers the example of the mental type (what he calls the active-practical type). Having described how the mental type uses action in his quest to attain a higher purpose, Assagioli (1983: 49) continues:

> While this way of living is within reach of all, as we have said, there will still be a fundamental difference in this respect between the various types, for their motives for action are always different. In others, the stimulus to be active, to work, and to find expression in the external world is not *primary* and spontaneous; this stimulus is possessed by or, even better, *it possesses* the active-practical type. So, for the will type [i.e. dynamic], the impelling stimulus to act is ambition; for the love [i.e. sensitive] type, it is love for his family, property or country; for the idealistic [i.e. dedicated] type, it is devotion to some ideal, etc. This fact should be well understood to know others truly and to avoid the error of seeing all those who work actively and ceaselessly as belonging only to the active type. What constitutes the fundamental basis of this qualitative classification

is *the power of deep motivations* that indicate the essential nature or "keynote" of the individual and not the external manifestations of these motives, which can be determined and conditioned by very diverse factors. The same type of activity can be induced by many motives, while the same motive can create completely different channels for its expression.

The essential point is that identifying an individual's type cannot be deduced from that person's actions or outward behaviour, but requires an understanding of his underlying *"deep motivations"*. In other words, we need to understand what motivates someone if we are to come to the right conclusion about their type – and this is particularly important when discriminating between types which are very alike. Assagioli (1983: 61) offers the following example, in which he compares the mental and analytical types: "The analytical scientific type is as fully alert to and acutely interested in the external world as the active-practical type [i.e. mental] but the motivations that arouse each one's interest are completely different. The motivation of the active type is to make good use of *things*, while the scientific type is interested in phenomena *per se*, in knowing the structure and function of the cosmic mechanism both in its broad sweep and in its tiny details."

Motivation gives direction and power

What is motivation? You know how it feels. Motivation is an inner power that energises us to do whatever we need to do; when we feel motivated, undertaking difficult tasks can be enjoyable.

By contrast, when we don't feel motivated, the same tasks become a chore and we have to draw upon all of our will

power and discipline to complete them, which is exhausting, our inner engine can stall, and we feel we have no energy for anything.

Another key point about motivation is that it is associated with *value*. Each of the types holds different values. For example, the dynamic type values influence and power, while the dedicated type values the pursuit of an ideal. Indeed, the dedicated type is so convinced of the importance of his values that he will pursue his ideal even when it has caused him to become isolated and to lose all his influence.

When we focus on those things that naturally motivate us, we will feel energised and alive. So it is important for us to understand our motivations, then we will be able to maximise our energy and achieve our goals.

Seven Types and motivation

Energies		Dynamic energy	Sensitive energy	Mental energy	Creative energy	Analytical energy	Dedicated energy	Practical energy
Functions	▶	Will	Feeling	Thought	Imagination	Logic	Passion	Action
Seven Types	▶	Dynamic Type	Sensitive Type	Mental Type	Creative Type	Analytical Type	Dedicated Type	Practical Type
		Power Influence Freedom Greatness	Love Insight Relations Empathy	Intelligence Overview Inspiration Network	Creativity Peace Transformation Beauty	Knowledge Truth Discovery Precision	Faith Ideals Future Loyalty	Results Efficiency Order Elegance
Soul Types	▶	Hero	Illuminator	Genius	Artist	Explorer	Visionary	Creator
Personality Types	▶	Manager Pioneer	Guide Helper	Thinker Strategist	Aesthete Transformer	Investigator Specialist	Idealist Advocate	Orchestrator Organiser

Table 10. The seven types and motivation

Table 10 shows the qualities that motivate each of the seven types, both in a general sense and at the particular psychological levels of soul and personality. To take an example, the dynamic type is motivated by power – and this power can motivate in different ways. At the level of personality (ego), the motivation will be a self-centred desire for personal power; at the level of soul, the motivation will be a wish to use power for the welfare of humanity. The difference in how power is expressed is determined by the underlying value. In the case of personality, the underlying value is personal ambition, whereas at the level of soul the underlying value is the good of humanity. (Assagioli suggests that the value underlying the dynamic type is ambition, but I think this term is too general in that all the types have a sense of ambition, so in my model I am using the term "greatness" instead.)

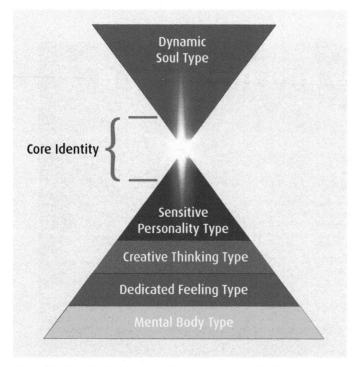

The more we understand about our motivations and values, the more effective we will be in pursuing our goals and fulfilling our purpose, whether at the level of personality or soul. Through understanding our motivations, we can learn how to keep ourselves energised, meaning that when life feels difficult, we can keep going because we will know where to focus our attention and how to direct our energy.

Figure 21. Example showing a dominant type at each of the five psychological levels

The topic of motivation becomes complex when we take into account that a person has a dominant type at each of the five psychological levels – which means each psychological level is influenced by a different quality of motivation. As a consequence, our emotions and thoughts might be motivated by different qualities and values, which can leave us experiencing all sorts of inner ambivalences and conflicts, all of which need to be sorted if we are to understand ourselves through our combination of types (see Figure 21).

Let us consider the psychological level of the body. Our bodies differ according to our specific constitution, which in turn determines how we use and generate energy. Our dominant type at the level of body will determine the diet and sort of exercise that is best for us. For example, certain body types thrive on a rich diet and regular demanding exercise, while others value a lighter diet and gentler movement. It is similar at the level of emotion: some value calm atmospheres, while others are motivated by lively surroundings. And, at the level of mind, some might be motivated by working with detail, while others prefer to see the big picture. (We will look in detail at how the dominant types manifest at the levels of body, feeling and thought in chapters 9, 10 and 11.) At the levels of personality and soul, our underlying motivations and values reveal themselves in the form of our choice of profession, the way we live, and the manner in which we pursue personal and spiritual development. (This aspect of our typological make-up will be examined in detail in the next chapter.)

As mentioned, identifying your dominant type at each of the five levels is not easy, but observing our values and motivations at each of the five psychological levels will help. I suggest you take some time to consider your qualities at each level. You might like to seek help from a skilled typologist. The hard work is worthwhile because when we can identify our dominant types we can start to fully understand our personal typological DNA, and we can mature and grow as a result.

The following sections will help us to disentangle some of the complications we encounter in trying to observe our motivations and values.

Masculine and feminine energies

Motivation can have a masculine or a feminine quality according to the nature of the type. Of the seven types, the dynamic, mental, analytical and practical types are more masculine. Masculine types are mostly motivated by action and tangible results; they tend to be focused on the mind and are generally more interested in things than people. By contrast, the sensitive, creative and dedicated types are more feminine, being motivated by subjective values, such as relationships and psychological development, and they are more interested in people than things. However, it is important that we don't confuse matters

by falling into gender stereotypes: there are feminine and masculine energies *in all genders*.

The presence of competing feminine and masculine qualities is an example of one of the conflicts that can arise when trying to identify types – something commented on by Assagioli (1931b), who wrote:

> The study of the qualities and methods of the different Rays is interesting and illuminating, but that of their vital relationships, of their harmonious or inharmonious interactions, of their difficulties of adjustment, is even more interesting, as it shows the source of many misunderstandings, antipathies and conflicts arising among men and points the way to their elimination.

> In examining these relationships, we find that the Rays of alternate numbers are congenial to each other, while those directly following each other are apt to clash. We have an interesting analogy in the musical notes: For instance, C (do) E (mi) G (sol) make a perfect chord while C (do) and D (re) or F (fa) and G (sol) create a dissonance.
> Thus the First, Third, Fifth and Seventh Rays are harmonious to each other and represent a definite line of expression and development which may be broadly described as positive, masculine and mental, and the Second, Fourth and Sixth Rays have a corresponding affinity to each other and represent the negative, feminine, feeling and intuitive line.

To illustrate his point, Assagioli (1983: 53-54) offers the following example:

> The artistic types are often sensitive to subtle psychic impressions; they are subject to telepathic phenomena, precognition etc. This sensitivity belongs not only to the creative-artistic type. The love type, with its marked receptivity, often possesses it and the same holds for the more mystical people of the devotional type. But those who belong to the will, practical, scientific and organisational types, who are more positive and objective, generally lack this sensitivity.

Differences in purpose, qualities and motivation

Those who work as psychosynthesis practitioners will often be called on to resolve conflicts that arise between the types – whether in the intra-personal or inter-personal field. These conflicts emerge because each type has a different purpose and is motivated by different values.

In this section, I will focus on some of the more common conflicts that arise between the types. Assagioli (1931b) highlighted some of these conflicts (my terminology in brackets):

> We often find misunderstandings and conflicts between First [dynamic] and Second [sensitive] Ray individuals, representing the qualities of power and love and between Fourth [creative] and Fifth [analytical] Ray individuals represented for instance, by the artist and the scientist. The clash between the Sixth [dedicated] and Seventh [practical] Rays, between the man of devotion or the idealist, and the magician and ritualist is particularly acute.

Conflicts between love and will

A conflict relevant to us all is the conflict between the sensitive and dynamic types, which is the duality of love and will. Assagioli wrote a great deal about the synthesis of love and will in his book *The Act of Will*, chapter 8. The fundamental problem, he said, is that the sensitive type has a lot of *good will* and a weak *strong will*, which means this type has good intentions without the power to manifest them. The opposite is true of the

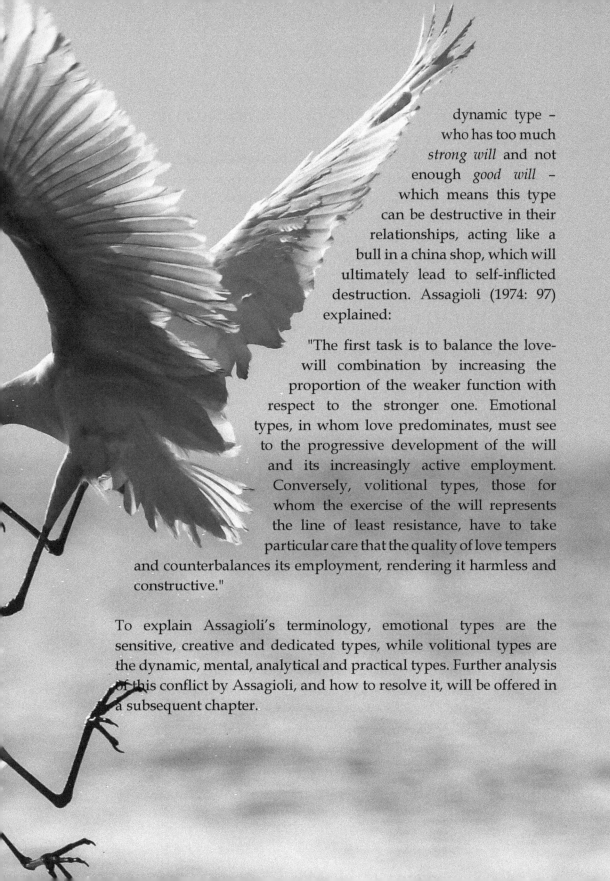

dynamic type – who has too much *strong will* and not enough *good will* – which means this type can be destructive in their relationships, acting like a bull in a china shop, which will ultimately lead to self-inflicted destruction. Assagioli (1974: 97) explained:

"The first task is to balance the love-will combination by increasing the proportion of the weaker function with respect to the stronger one. Emotional types, in whom love predominates, must see to the progressive development of the will and its increasingly active employment. Conversely, volitional types, those for whom the exercise of the will represents the line of least resistance, have to take particular care that the quality of love tempers and counterbalances its employment, rendering it harmless and constructive."

To explain Assagioli's terminology, emotional types are the sensitive, creative and dedicated types, while volitional types are the dynamic, mental, analytical and practical types. Further analysis of this conflict by Assagioli, and how to resolve it, will be offered in a subsequent chapter.

Conflicts between imagination, logic and passion

The conflict between the artist (creative type) and the scientist (analytical type) arises due to a clash between the qualities of their respective functions: imagination and logic. The conflict can be expressed in this way – *Which is most true: that which we can imagine or that which we can analyse through facts?* Imagination opens the inner eye to subjective realities, while logic establishes a solid base by analysing objective data in detail. These two types operate in different psychological domains, with plenty of opportunity for conflict.

We should also mention the dedicated type, in whom we find a similar conflict, this time between religion and science. The dedicated type seeks metaphysical realities through faith, while the analytical type rejects faith as unscientific.

Wilber (1999b) describes how we can obtain a synthesis between the two types of cognition: subjective and objective. Wilber explains that there are objective facts which are perceived through the eye of the flesh (sensation analysed by logic); there are phenomenological facts which are perceived through the eye of the mind (thought and imagination); and there are spiritual or mystical facts which are perceived through the eye of Spirit (mystical perception through transcendence and devotion). When we can acknowledge all three modalities of perception, we have taken a first step towards the integration and synthesis of these diverse functions of the mind.

A similar conflict that can be seen in our culture is due to a clash between the energy of the practical type and the devotional (religious) energy of the dedicated type. The premodern longing of the dedicated type for paradise or nirvana – a transcendental heaven in which all hardships of the physical world are resolved – has dominated our culture for at least two thousand years. However, these dedicated energies have declined rapidly with the rise of modernism, which values the analytical and practical energies with their focus on science, economic growth and materialism. This shift in energies can be seen in how spirituality increasingly has a focus on the body, health and well-being, which is a clear expression of the practical energies – this is a shift towards God as immanent rather than transcendent. Little wonder these huge cultural shifts create conflict between people and groups which have different typological and religious temperaments.

Sensitive and dedicated love

The dedicated type is a blend of the dynamic and sensitive energies, a blend of will and feeling. Consequently, we will notice a similarity between dedicated and sensitive types, both of which are full of love, and it will be difficult to discriminate between the two unless we have

a sense of the underlying values, motivations and qualities of love being expressed. Assagioli (1983: 75) notes that dedicated love tends to be domineering, insistent and conditional; he explains:

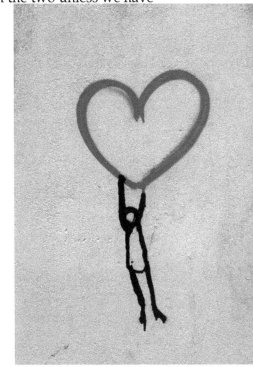

> An accurate analysis reveals that what [dedicated types] "love" is often their subjective image of the ideal, whether it is a person, an idea or some kind of philanthropic work, as these are reflected in their minds and not as they are in reality. This is proved by their internal reaction and behaviour in certain situations -for example, when the person they venerate does not satisfy their expectations or when they discover gaps and limitations in their ideal.

This is rather different from the love [i.e. sensitive] type, and it offers us a clear way to distinguish one from the other in spite of their superficial resemblance. When the love type discovers the person he loves has previously unsuspected defects, or behaves badly, he is aggrieved by the knowledge but has no reaction against the person. They tend to excuse him and defend him, and immediately proceed to love him with greater intensity than before. The devotional type reacts with resentment in a similar situation. When the idealised person fails to live up to the peak of *his* expectations – which are often unreasonable and unattainable – he feels personally offended and does not wish to forgive or help him; his instinct is to turn against the cause of his disillusionment. (It is true that we sometimes find a mixed attitude and reaction in the same individual; this is due to the existence of mixed types, and to the fact that the combination of the love and devotional [i.e. dedicated] types is, fortunately, not unusual.)

The sensitive type is motivated by good relations, based on acceptance and mutual understanding, while the dedicated type is motivated by the pursuit of an ideal in terms of what we could be or achieve. The sensitive type is calm, open and nurturing; the dedicated type is fiery, passionate and intense.

Differences in the expression of will

The masculine types are, in different ways, all influenced by will – the mental type to a lesser degree, the dynamic, analytical and practical types to a greater degree. These different influences of will manifest in different ways of being and different underpinning motivations. Assagioli (1983: 78-79) explains (using his own terminology for the types):

When it is fully expressed, the organisational [i.e. practical] type demonstrates will and purpose, a clear mind, constructive activity and practical ability. These qualities make him similar to other types. He could be confused with them, or seem to be a mixture of them with no distinctive characteristics of his own. His will resembles that of the will [i.e. dynamic] type, his clear mind the scientific [i.e. analytical] type, his constructive activity the practical [i.e. mental] type; and yet he is different from any of them. The will type is principally interested in putting on a display of his power, or in dynamically and inflexible directing himself and others towards a precise goal. The organisational type, however, uses his will precisely, slowly and persistently in order to materialise his or another's plan gradually. In common with the scientific type, he has a clear, exact mind but, while the former uses it largely with the purpose of discovering and knowing, he uses it with the purpose of *doing* - of attaining tangible results.

Mental types tend to exhibit *skilful will*, which is the strategic and tactical use of the mind, with its ability to attain concrete results through the smart use of all the psychological functions. This type usually lacks focus because they tend to avoid being direct, preferring to operate tactically, which can impede their dynamism and effectiveness. (Assagioli writes extensively about skilful will in this book *The Act of Will*, chapters 5-6.)

Regarding the dedicated type, Assagioli (1967b) acknowledges this type as containing a great deal of dynamic energy, explaining "desire is or has a dynamic energy that impels to action". Accordingly, the dedicated type's expression of will tends to be emotional in tone and, in some respects, blind due to its instinctive basis. But despite this difference in motivation, the dedicated type in practice will look similar to the other masculine types in exhibiting a one-pointed focus, discipline, endurance.

Different forms of discipline

Another way of considering the differences between types is to look at the different ways in which each type is able to apply discipline. In the following extract, Assagioli (1983: 80-81) describes how different forms of discipline are motivated by different values: "Discipline is not only a characteristic of the organisational [i.e. practical] type; the will [i.e. dynamic] and the idealistic [i.e. dedicated] types often manifest it even more energetically. In them, however, discipline assumes a different tonality or character. The discipline of the will type is hard, implacable and even cruel both when he applies it to himself and when he imposes it on others; but his sole aim is to achieve the willed result, with the maximum speed and competence and at whatever cost. The discipline that the idealistic type imposes on himself or others can be just as rigid and austere, but it has an ascetic character and purpose. His aim is to eliminate real or imaginary faults or "sins" and to purify the person, rendering him, presumably, more acceptable to and beloved by God; in a word, to save his soul. The discipline of the organisational type is generally more moderate and respectable in comparison with the others. His goal is to eliminate loss and waste of time, energy and materials, to avoid friction and establish in the end more productive cooperation.

From what has been said it is clear that while discipline is *one* of the characteristics or qualities of the will and idealistic types, it is in fact the central and specific means by which the organisational type operates and with which he reaches his goals. All his organisation and his order seem to be the product of both external and internal discipline. When the organism or organisation has grown to maturity and functions smoothly, this discipline ceases to be exercised from the outside and no visible pressure to reinforce it can be noticed; but discipline is there, intrinsically, in the form of tradition, habit or custom. This is demonstrated in the fact that when tradition declines, or when some new factor or situation compels a change in habit, the organisation can fall to pieces unless new infusions of discipline and order save it."

We can add the observation that the analytical type expresses a mature discipline, as demonstrated by the inventor who is methodical and persistent in his search for the most suitable materials. In highlighting the value of persistence, Assagioli offers the example of Edison. Assagioli (1974: 29) writes:

Another kind of persistence is that exercised in spite of repeated failures. This is the secret of many successful inventors and scientists. It is said that Edison tried about two thousand substances before finding carbon wire for making his electric bulb. Let us think how much we owe him for this extraordinary persistence. He would have been well justified if he had given up the attempts at the thousandth or even the five hundredth trial.

Creative and practical types

All the types can be and are creators, but two of the types are especially creative due to their capacity for employing imagination and organisational skills. The creative type draws upon their openness and their desire for something totally new and joyful to happen, making full use of their attunement to the subjective world of the imagination. The practical type also wishes to see change and improvement in the world, but this type draws primarily on an efficient will in order to organise all the available resources. Assagioli (1983: 79) says of these types:

> [The practical type] "is in a certain sense, a creator because new elements are born through his activity, but his method of working is quite different from that of the creative-artistic type. The difference can be expressed in the two words: to create, and to construct. True creation is a *vital* and mysterious process, initiated outside the ordinary field of consciousness. To construct, however, consists of consciously gathering materials, generally belonging to so-called inorganic matter, and assembling them into an objective structure. The creative type is generally a channel or voice for his superconscious, a receiver of inspiration from the realms of the intuition or the imagination, while the organisational type initiates his activity himself with clear awareness and deliberation, and carries it out methodically to a conclusion.
>
> The creative type works from the inside out, while the practical type works more from the outside in, and we often find that highly creative people are a healthy combination of both these types."

Mental and practical types

The mental and practical types can also be difficult to differentiate between because they are both active, intelligent and focused on the external world of culture, finance and science. However, according to Assagioli (1983):

> The active-practical [i.e. mental] type is plastic, adaptable and even a little dishonest and meddling; the organisational [i.e. practical] type tends instead to be rigid and formalistic. The former tends to be independent and prefers to work alone; the latter prefers to work with or *through* others, assigning them tasks. The active type is exclusively interested in results and success and is quick to use whatever method seems to be effective. The organisational type tends instead to be interested above all in organisation for its own sake, which can become so important in his eyes that it can make him almost forget his object. The active type works in an active, aggressive, often disorderly manner; the organisational type works calmly at the centre, projecting future activity and registering and coordinating the results of previous activity.

Perhaps the most obvious difference between these two types is that the mental type seeks change, flexibility and new possibilities, while the practical types prefers stability, order, and a routine that upholds the structures they have worked hard to develop and sustain.

Attitudes to the law and conflict

Someone's attitudes to the law, or laws, and conflict reveals a lot about their underlying motivations and qualities, and this will help us to identify their type. Let us begin this section with a very interesting observation by Assagioli (1983: 80):

> Another way of looking at the different attitudes of various types is

by observing their reactions when confronted by a factor such as the law. The will [i.e. dynamic] type loves the law and is always ready to punish those who infringe it. The scientific [i.e. analytical] type is simply interested in discovering the existing laws of nature. The organisational [i.e. practical] type is interested in formulating laws with punctilious care, or in using them carefully for constructive ends. The active [i.e. mental] type seeks either to extract the maximum benefit from laws, or to dodge them skilfully. The creative type generally takes exception to those laws that he is aware of while unconsciously continuing his creative activity according to unknown laws that he does not fully understand.

There is a lot to ponder on here. Let me offer an example to help illustrate the motivations underlying the different types; let's consider what happens in situations of conflict (a subject that is related to the law). What happens when the different types find themselves in conflict? The dynamic type will confront the opposing force directly, with a clear intention to defeat the other. The sensitive type will reflect deeply on the conflict, using empathy to try and understand the other's perspective and using love to try and resolve the issue. The mental type will try to understand what motivates the other, then use skilful and powerful negotiation to try and resolve the conflict. The creative type will seek to bring balance by enacting the different emotional qualities in the conflict, sometimes creating a drama to bring the underlying tensions to the surface in the hope that all parties can be heard and a peaceful resolution found. The analytical type will focus on the facts and suggest a solution that is fair, objective and agreeable to all parties. The dedicated type will focus on what is right from a moral perspective, urging people to tune into their ideals to try and solve the problem, and if this doesn't work then they will fight for what they believe is right. The practical type will focus on the end result, i.e. on what needs to be done so that all parties might be *reasonably* satisfied, perhaps using his diplomatic skills to create alliances that will unite opposing factions.

Money and the sensitive and mental types

This last section will explore the different underlying motivations of the types in their approach to money. In this quote, Assagioli focused on the mental and sensitive types (1983: 40):

> We generally find, that the active [i.e. mental] type anxiously pursues activities for gain and is concerned with prosperity and material success. In this respect he can resemble the love [i.e. sensitive] type, but close observation reveals an important difference between the two; the love type wants money and other possessions for its pleasure, comfort, security or other advantages; his desire is to have these things without effort or worry, to obtain them by inheritance, gift or luck. The active type is chiefly interested in the *process* of making money, in the *game* of managing it in business, banking etc. He appreciates money as a symbol or touchstone as well, signifying his ability, his success and his "social value". The American phrase, "This man is worth so many dollars" characterises this attitude very simply.

The above example is, to some extent, a caricature of the mental personality type: we can find many examples of mental types who are not identified with money. That said, all mental types will tend to work through the use of money because this is one of the principle domains in which they operate. Practical types are also known for their

ability to create and organise economic resources, with a motivation that is more about what they can *create* using money rather than the accumulation of wealth.

The four quadrants and motivation

Where does motivation sit with respect to the four quadrants and the five psychological levels? Figure 22 will help to explain.

Upper left quadrant: personal subjective world

In the upper left quadrant, we see the five psychological levels in the context of *consciousness* (our subjective inner world). We see the five levels, from the body up to soul (the number seven reminds us that there will be a dominant type – one of the seven – at each level).

Upper right quadrant: personal action in the world

In the upper right quadrant, we find five levels of *motivated behaviour*. The qualities of behaviour at each level are a manifestation of the dominant type/energy at the corresponding levels in the upper left quadrant.

At the level of body, the motivation for our behaviour is *survival* (i.e. the need for food, sleep, and the expression of our basic instincts). Much of our lives are spent ensuring that our physical and material needs are met. The number seven indicates that there are seven ways of meeting our survival needs according to the type which dominant at the level of body.

At the level of feeling, our behaviour is motivated by a need for *security*, love and belonging. These needs are all related to our emotional life and they can trigger a range of behaviours depending on our dominant type, which will determine our preferences and values for the sort of security we want and the sort of people we want to be with.

At the level of thought, we are motivated by a need for *status*, recognition

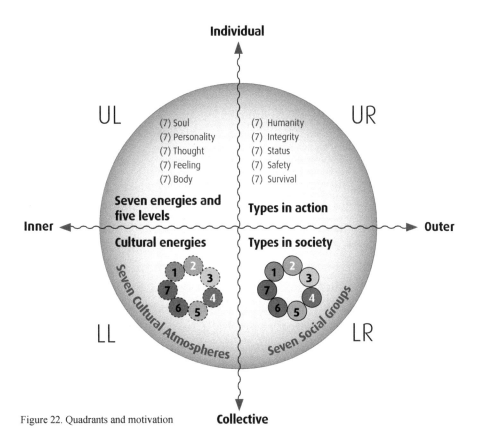

Figure 22. Quadrants and motivation

and self-worth. These needs relate to the mind, and our dominant type at this level will determine how we search for status and self-confidence through education, employment and society.

The level of integrity, or *integration*, concerns self-actualisation, or personal psychosynthesis, which is the process of becoming a unique individual. This is the level at which we begin to define ourselves, achieve independence, act responsibility and show the world our true personalities. We will begin to express our authority in a manner determined by the qualities of our personality type.

The level of *humanity* concerns our soul and our life purpose. At this level, we are motivated by our concern for the world and the positive changes we want to see. Our ethics and values extend beyond the personal as we begin to see ourselves as citizens of the world with a concern for global challenges. We express the energy of our soul in ways that are innovative and creative.

The lower quadrants: the collective fields

The lower quadrants are concerned with our place in the collective, which includes both the collective unconscious (inner subjective world) and its outward expression in society. Motivations can be shared by the collective, by families, communities, organisations, nations, even the whole world. The quality of motivation will affect which social groups are formed and which we want to belong to. Any changes in these shared motivations can lead to a reorganisation of our collective functioning, which can affect everything from our immediate social circles to the whole of culture. Interestingly, the personal and collective fields are also influenced by the past.

Assagioli (1930) offers an example of how we can each be influenced by the qualities and motivations present in the collective field:

> The psychological characteristics prevailing in different regions and even in different towns of the same nation (are important). In Italy, for instance, the psychological make-up of a Florentine, a Bolognese and a Roman show wide differences, in spite of the geographical proximity of these towns, and I think that each of you could make a similar observation about the citizens of various towns of your country.

Assagioli (1930) continues with his description of how the individual can be influenced by collective or external conditions:

> The numberless psychological influences which concur in modifying the growing personality may be grouped under the following headings:

1. *Race* – which acts not only in the form of heredity, but also as a present and continually operating factor, giving the fundamental colour or tone, so to say, to the psychic atmosphere by which the individual is surrounded.
2. *Climate* – as well as scenery and environment, which, besides their physiological effects, have also a definite psychological influence upon us.
3. *The national soul.*
4. *Family and relations.*
5. *Nurses, teachers and professors.*
6. *Schoolmates and friends.*
7. *Books, magazines and journals.*
8. *Influences directly from the inner planes*, as the great waves of emotions and impulses which sway humanity as is clearly seen in important historical crises, and also other subtler and more mysterious, but no less powerful, mental and spiritual currents, which are said to be projected by the Great Beings who are directing human evolution. These currents are caught at first by a few pioneers, particularly receptive and attuned to them, and which gradually influence all the more advanced and progressive souls, and, through them, the bulk of humanity.

All of the factors listed by Assagioli can have a direct energetic impact on each of us as individuals, with an impact that will vary accordingly whether the energetic qualities are aligned or misaligned with our own dominant types. In other words, these aspects of the collective will either stimulate our natural growth or stifle it, which means it is vital for us to know how we are aligned with the prominent energies in our nation, our family and the groups we belong to. A practical consequence is that we might realise we are out of tune with a particular environment, and so we might decide it is important for us to make a change.

Having looked at the theory, I now offer the following exercise to help you identify your own particular motivations.

Exercise: what motivates you?

What *really* motivates you? What makes you shine? What brings you joy? Is it running, drawing, dancing, architecture, playing with the kids, writing your blog? You might like to ask your friends for their impressions. Make a list.

Examine this list and identify the underlying themes: what are the tastes and preferences that run through the whole list?

You are now ready to name your motivations: what are the motivations that underpin your choices?

Considering now the five psychological levels, see where your different motivators sit with respect to the needs and aspirations of the five levels.

Having explored many general aspects of the Seven Types, it is now time to look in detail at how the soul and personality combine to create our *core identity*.

Your integrated identity
– The 49 core identities

In this chapter, we will look at the important psychosynthetic task of integrating the soul and personality.

Our personality anchors us to the everyday physical world, while our soul connects us to a wider world, of deeper meaning, within which we each have a unique role to play. Therefore, if we are to manifest our total being in the world, it is essential that we bring together personality and our soul – and this integration of our personality type with our soul type is what I term our *core identity*. It follows that this process will often involve the integration of a different combinations of types, as Assagioli (1983: 51) explains: "…mixed types can and do exist. One person can possess essentially, in the depth of his being [i.e. soul], the quality of a certain type, while his external personality can demonstrate the traits of another type."

Janus, the two-faced god of Roman mythology, illustrates this duality. According to one account, Janus was created by the sky god Uranus as a gift of love to Hecate, the goddess of the underworld. But Janus hated his new life in the underworld; he longed for the heavens, so he ignored the gods and fled from the underworld. His punishment was thereafter to occupy the space between the two worlds, being never wholly in the heavens or in the underworld. The plight of Janus is our plight: we all long for a better world (soul) but find ourselves living in an imperfect one (personality). These are the two forces we must unite.

It is not possible to flee the world. On the contrary, the challenge facing us is how to introduce into this world more of the true, the good and the beautiful, not as impractical idealists or narrow-minded materialists but rather, as the saying goes, we should aim to keep our head in the clouds and our feet on the ground. This chapter will explore how we can do this.

But before we proceed, let's remind ourselves of how Assagioli (1983: 21) described the difference between soul and personality:

> Before considering the characteristics of the personality and those of the Self [i.e. soul], I would like to explain how I distinguish between the two... I consider as characteristics of the *personality* those that can be regarded as egocentric and separative qualities which the human personality has *before* it comes into conscious contact with the Self and feels its influence. On the other hand, the characteristics of the *Self* are those that possess a true transpersonal quality and that are expressed when the Self permeates the personality with its light, shining through and working in it to some extent.

The soul awakens when we realise that life is about more than just looking after ourselves and our family. When we truly see this, our heart opens to a wider sense of meaning. Often, we discover our soul's calling during a life crisis when we start challenging our values only to find them inadequate: we are no longer satisfied with our former way of life – our soul, which has lain dormant, has woken up from its slumber! Most self-help literature is based upon a general sense of yearning for something *more*, for something *better* in life – this is a yearning for our soul to manifest. To use the terminology of the Seven Types, we might say that what millions of people need is the integration of their soul type and their personality type.

The development of our personality is largely governed by a sense of lack; we have a needs deficiency, as Maslow showed, and our personality is the driving force that compels us to meet these needs and, in the process, our personality becomes more robust, effective and grounded. But while the personality is concerned with our active engagement in the world, we cannot ignore our soul, which is a constant underlying essence, our essential being. From within our soul we can sense a deep calling to become all we can be and to fulfil our life purpose. However, as we can see, soul and personality can have quite different agendas – hence the need for synthesis.

Psychosynthesis believes that we must learn to harmonise our soul and personality. The image presented is that of the personality as a chariot that must be driven by the soul, the charioteer. When this happens, self-realisation has taken place.

Figure 23 illustrates the optimal interaction between soul and personality. This diagram was inspired by an important article by Vargiu and Firman (1977) that explores in detail the crisis of awakening. The vertical axis represents *being* and charts the new values and possibilities that are available to us in the spiritual domain. The horizontal axis represents *doing* and depicts our actions and behaviours as we progress along our life path (diagonal line). The nature of the interaction between these two axes will determine the extent to which our talents and qualities manifest in the world. Let's look at this diagram in more detail.

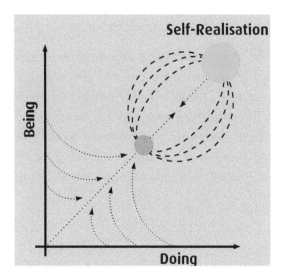

Figure 23. Being–Doing axis

When the conscious "I" (orange circle) harvests the energies and resources available from both dimensions – being and doing, soul and personality – tremendous personal power is generated. The six arrows show how the conscious "I" is supported by our qualities of body, feeling and thought (doing/personality) as well as the qualities of intuition and inspiration (being/soul). This confluence of qualities provides us with the power to realise our dreams and visions and to discover our inner selves.

The sun (large yellow circle) represents our vision: it symbolises our need to balance being and doing. When this balance between our conscious "I" and our vision is achieved, we are inspired to act creatively and selflessly in the world.

The diagram depicts an optimum balance between *being* and *doing*. Sadly, this rarely occurs. In the Western world because our lives are typically focused on our work, status and achievements in the world, which pulls us towards the doing axis, creating a materialist culture and causing stress in our personal lives. The symptoms of this imbalance can be seen in a widespread sense of emptiness and boredom which people try to escape through work, drugs and entertainment.

Happily, there is another way. When the soul awakens, we have an opportunity to integrate and balance being (soul) and doing (personality). But the personality is not easily won over: when the soul starts to exert its influence, the personality fights back. So how does this relationship between personality and soul play out in real life? In answering this question, I want to begin by presenting a case study from my clinical practice as a psychotherapist.

Michael's rebirth

From my first session with Michael, it was clear his life was in chaos. He was an attractive, fit man in his mid-30s. He was charming and energetic, with a sense of humour and a great appetite for life. People admired his self-confidence and he was often the centre of attention. But beneath this confident exterior, Michael was far from happy. His girlfriend had left him, he had no family, and his friends did not fill his inner void. He dreamed of success as an actor but his career had stalled; and even after a great performance, he did not feel happy. Alarm bells were ringing; something was missing. So what was wrong?

During our sessions, it became apparent that Michael was avoiding something. Through awareness-based psychotherapy, Michael slowly learned to observe, identify and communicate with his key motivators. While aware that he craved attention, but he also realised that no amount of attention could fill his emptiness. I suggested to Michael that we work together using the Seven Types. We discovered that Michael was a creative personality, embodying this type's finest qualities, as well as its inconsistency and restlessness. For example, he'd had many girlfriends but none had been able to satisfy him, so he was constantly moving on in search of new adventures; he was flying from flower to flower like a honeybee, never committing to anyone – and, like someone who has overeaten so that the sight of food becomes sickening, Michael's affairs began to produce a kind of nausea in him.

When I explained to Michael about the creative type, the pieces of the jigsaw started to fall into place. Michael strongly identified with this type. He loved beauty and being surrounded by happy people, but he also realised his life was superficial. Living was easy and he had endless opportunities, but he started to realise that quantity of relationships is not the same as quality. Michael realised that his inner void could only be filled by a kind of love that would provide him with a deep and consistent connection to life and other people. We worked with this realisation for some time and eventually concluded that his soul was motivated by love. So here we had a creative personality type with a sensitive soul type.

As we continued to work together, Michael's need for attention was gradually replaced by a longing to give attention. During these important months of therapy, his sensitive soul type began to emerge, manifesting the Illuminator and Teacher archetypes. Michael decided to remain in the world of acting, but he became a drama teacher, helping others to improve their craft and develop their careers. There was also a change in his attitude to love and relationships, such that he was prepared to stay in relationships for longer. Michael started to be able to contain his sense of emptiness; he could still feel pain, but he no longer felt the strong need to escape it. Indeed, he was able to make use of his pain, realising that part of his journey was to help heal the world's pain by *being love* and through offering a love that could accept the imperfect.

When our sessions together concluded, Michael was still working on certain issues, but he had undergone a transformation and his life had taken a new direction. He had found new meaning and purpose, and this would see him through life's challenges. Now it was up to him to be the captain of his ship. This was possible because he had begun to integrate his creative personality type with his sensitive soul type. Integrating the soul and personality can be a slow process – perhaps taking many years, depending on the types involved and the effort applied – but, ultimately, the reward is a kind of rebirth.

The balance between being and doing

Michael's transformation demonstrates that we can bring new qualities and motivations into our lives without losing old ones. The positive aspects of the creative type were retained, with Michael learning how

to express them differently and for a different purpose. Deciding that love would be the foundation of his life meant Michael had to abandon everything superficial. He could still enjoy himself, but he would steer the chariot in a new direction.

Doing comes naturally to creative types – they are motivated by success, love and a need to be the centre of attention – but when Michael started to listen to his soul's calling, the peaceful, sensitive and holistic qualities of the sensitive type emerged and he felt inspired to discipline his personality to serve a higher purpose. Being aware of his underlying motivations meant he could learn from his mistakes.

As mentioned, the ideal balance between being and doing is not a 50/50 split because the soul should be guiding the personality. At the centre of our being, our soul is an eternal source of energy that flows into the world through our persona, which is our mask or personality. And when personality and soul are integrated, the life energy of the personality is sublimated into the flow of energy from the soul. Over time, as the influence of the soul qualities increases, our personality evolves and matures so there is a fuller expression of who we are. In Michael's case, he became a calmer person who was able to take other people's needs into consideration, which are qualities arising from his soul – Michael now sees his role in the world as being a source of truth, beauty and goodness.

The integration of soul and personality can happen naturally, but knowledge of the seven types and guidance from a trained counsellor can support this process. We can begin by identifying our energies and types, and with this understanding we can learn to master and channel our energies. Broadly speaking, this process of integration follows two stages. The first stage is the integration of the personality, which Assagioli called "personal psychosynthesis" – this provides the foundation for a good and stable life. The second stage involves the opening of the heart to experience the soul, leading to its integration with the personality, which Assagioli termed "transpersonal psychosynthesis". Out of this two-stage process arises our core identity, with soul and personality, doing and being, in optimum balance.

Sometimes, people experience energies emerging from their soul before they are an integrated personality. Such people tend to become impractical idealists or dreamers who lack will and stamina. They may dream of a better world but they lack the power and grounding necessary to make their vision a reality – their heads are in the clouds, but their feet are not on the ground. To fulfil their soul purpose, they first need to strengthen their personality. Idealists might sometimes feel guilty about having an ego with needs – they don't understand that they need a sturdy chariot if they are to have any hope of reaching their destination. In practical terms, it is helpful to establish a sturdy personality – which can help us achieve financial security, emotional fulfilment and a sense of self-esteem – because then our soul can manifest in a manner that is grounded, which will help us to be of service to the greater good.

Hopefully, the reader will now have a clearer understanding of what is meant by the integration and harmonising of the personality and soul. You can find case studies in chapter 12 that show what this integration might look like in lived experience, while chapter 9 to 11 will look at how the personality forms via the integration of our dominant types at the levels of body, feeling and thought. In the following section we will explore some of the different combinations of soul types and personality types.

The 49 identity types

When the personality type and the soul type become integrated, we discover our *core identity*. Given that there are seven different soul types and seven different personality types, this means there are 49 possible core identities, or, as we will refer to them, identity types.

The top half of Figure 24 shows how seven types in relation to the seven psychological functions and the sorts of behaviours they manifest. The bottom half of Figure 24 lists the seven soul types and the seven personality types, with their respective primary motivators indicated in brackets, and shows the full range of combinations that are possible.

I describe identity types with two numbers. Highlighted within Figure 24 is the example of Michael (see above), who has a 2-4 core identity, i.e. an Illuminator soul type (2) combined with a creative personality type (4). (Note: the real picture is more complicated given that each personality type has an introverted and extroverted aspect, but I am not going into that level of detail at this point.) As well as giving a number-code to each of the identity types, I have also given each of them a name to describe their core qualities. In Michael's case, the 2-4 identity type is a *Sensitive Performer*.

Let's take another example. The 1-1 identity type is the *Brave Redeemer*. It is worth noting that it is rare for someone to have the same type at the levels of both soul and personality, but it is not impossible.

Assagioli brings to our attention another particular combination of types, namely when a person's soul type and personality type are both masculine (type 1-3-5-7) or both feminine (Type: 2-4-6) in nature. Assagioli (1931b) describes how this can lead to a particular sort of awakening crises:

> We find that when the Ray of the personality and the Ray of the Ego [soul] belong to the same group the life of the individual is generally harmonious; it has a definite line and homogeneity, but it is apt to be one-sided and static. Instead, when the personal and individual Rays belong to different groups, there are often inner strife and difficulty of adjustment. The man is divided within himself; his

conscious and sub-conscious tendencies clash and, in the language of psychoanalysis, he is particularly subject to repressions and complexes. Yet while these complications and struggles entail much suffering, they often produce richer and more vital experiences, and result in greater spiritual progress.

In light of this observation, we can deduce that when soul and personality are both masculine types or both feminine types then integration will be smoother compared with when one is masculine and the other feminine.

To help give us a sense of this journey of integration, I have selected seven identity types for us to examine in more detail. In each case, I will describe the personality type, then the sort of crisis that will typically arise when the soul begins to awaken, then I will describe the consequences of integration. A full description of all 49 identity types is included in the identity profile available at the JivaYou website.

Michael Robbins' article *Combinations of Soul Rays and Personality Rays* also offers a good introduction to this theme.

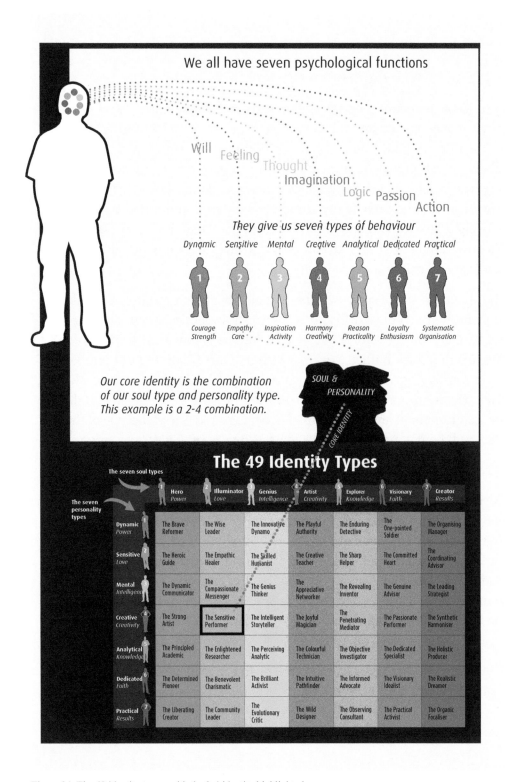

Figure 24. The 49 identity types, with the 2-4 identity highlighted

1-2: The Heroic Guide

You have excellent people skills (sensitive personality type) and crave warm, nurturing relationships characterised by mutual care and understanding. You are a good listener who values and respects others, which gives you a great capacity to help others, meaning you might typically choose a career as a teacher, counsellor or caregiver. However, despite your many competencies, you are limited by a fear of being disliked: your ego needs to feel appreciated, loved and secure. The awakening of your soul can be disturbing for someone with your gentle and considerate personality.

The dynamic soul type awakens in you an inner pressure to attain more influence in the world and accomplish something great. The Hero insists that you fight for a cause and that, as a powerful leader, you dare to enter into conflict. Your personality fears becoming unpopular, but an emerging need to show courage and leadership and to take risks becomes more important. You seek holistic solutions and fight for enlightenment and education. Once integrated, the archetype of the Hero will help you to meet your goals as the *Heroic Guide*.

2-1: The Wise Leader

Decisiveness, focus, power and resilience characterise your dynamic personality type. You are motivated by a need to take charge and exert yourself. You have got to where you are in life by aiming for the top within your chosen field. You often find yourself in a position of leadership, whether formally or informally, and you easily dominate your surroundings. You are strong and independent and enjoy being on the frontline. You seek out challenges and enjoy testing your strengths against competitors. You accept risks that prove your courage.

Your domineering character will most likely lead you into a power struggle, which will become the trigger for a crisis that will awaken the quality of love-wisdom that abides in your soul. The continuous exertion of your power may have ruined your relationships and led to a sense of frustration and emptiness. But when the soul awakens you start to sense that your power could be used for the greater good. You start to feel you no longer need to control everything, your hard shell softens, and peace and tranquility enter your life. You receive inner wisdom, feel inspired by positive role models, and recognise opportunities for spiritual growth. This love-wisdom comes from the Illuminator archetype, which invites others to work with you to achieve your goals. Once integrated, you become the *Wise Leader.*

3-4: The Intelligent Storyteller

Your sense of humour and ability to entertain have shaped your character and they help you to attain success, a characteristic common to the creative personality type. You influence your environment with a spontaneity and charm that helps to create a relaxed and positive atmosphere. You want to be the centre of attention, and it does not matter whether this means being admired or being seen as a tragic figure. For you, the world is a stage and you feel alive when you are able to draw attention to yourself and create more beauty and harmony. However, a lack of harmony disturbs you and motivates you to seek peace and balance. For this reason, emotional tension tends to attract you, often drawing you into conflicts that you want to resolve.

The intelligence of your soul type can emerge as a deep need for knowledge which pulls you away from the limelight, causing you to have a sudden crisis of identity. As

the crisis deepens you will feel the need to retreat from life's dramas to a place of detached observation from which you can gain a new sense of perspective. You discover a desire to approach life more rationally and you begin to understand that being at the centre of things is not always important. As your soul awakens, you become aware of a thirst for knowledge and understanding that helps you to discover new ways to make a difference in the world. The Genius archetype, integrated with your creative personality type, finds its greatest satisfaction in communicating these emerging ideas in an engaging way, and you become the *Intelligent Storyteller*.

4-5: The Colourful Technician

Your logical and sensible approach to life is the key to your success as an analytical personality type. You are a specialist who knows the facts and can separate real information from fake news. You are motivated by a need to hone your intellect and technique and to become the smartest in your field. You seek out knowledge that is useful and practical and that will help you arrive at concrete solutions to real problems. You pride yourself on being 100 per cent reliable.

The qualities of the Artist soul type awaken in you a great longing for beauty, love and magic and an interest in things that cannot be measured or weighed. This can lead to a crisis in how you understand the world. Your former logical approach has made your world a cold place devoid of sunlight, beauty or poetry. Now you want to create space for the intuitive levels of your being to emerge. Out of this inner well arise stories, images and symbols, and your imagination inspires you to create well-crafted work that inspire others and generates a sense of togetherness. Your skill as a craftsman enables you to realise ideas in a very practical way. Giving concrete form to your intuition allows others to share your experience of beauty and harmony. Your analytical personality has integrated the Artist archetype to make you the *Colourful Technician.*

5-6: The Informed Advocate

As a dedicated personality type, being an enthusiastic spokesman for your cause has given you success in life. You want to be a part of something special, something you can believe in with all your heart. Your inner fire inspires you to convince others to share this enthusiasm. Your wholehearted commitment attracts followers. Your innocence and naivety mean you have a tendency to see only the best in people and situations, and this desire to see the best in everything is your strongest motivator, but also a liability. You are competitive and willing to go for broke if it helps with the realisation of your vision.

A crisis arises when you realise the cause you have been championing is an illusion. You gave your all but now you see your passion was misdirected. As the cool clear light of the Explorer soul type emerges, you start to analyse and re-evaluate your life. As a consequence, you become better able to differentiate between true and false values. You begin to view life more objectively. Rather than seeking only to achieve personal goals, you start to draw meaning from reality itself, just as it is. You start to share your research with the world and see that it can make a difference. Your newfound passion for true knowledge brings out the best in you and gives you a sense of purpose. By integrating the archetype of the Explorer with your dedicated personality type you have become the *Informed Advocate*.

6-7: The Practical Activist

A highly organised life characterises your practical personality type. You live a goal-oriented life that is built upon routine and a systematic approach that makes you trustworthy and reliable. Your elegant planning makes you a natural leader. You are efficient and able to take responsibility and achieve results. You are motivated by a need for order and control. You want your efforts to have practical benefits. Your ability to organise people and projects has carried you a long way, but sometimes you resent always being the one who is responsible.

As the qualities of the Visionary soul type emerge, you start to realise you don't always need to be in control, and you grow tired of always attending to detail. For someone who has always prided themselves on being orderly and efficient, this is a crisis. You realise your compulsion to be in control has caused you to overlook your deepest values, and you start to suffer. You start to envision a new cause, one with higher and more noble goals, something you can commit yourself to wholeheartedly. Your newfound devotion to this higher cause will inspire others to join you and to share your values. You are a practical utopian seeking to bring innovation into your chosen field. Integrating the Visionary archetype with your practical personality type makes you *the Practical Activist*.

7-3: The Leading Strategist

The mental personality type means you are an active communicator who likes to share knowledge. You have a tendency to establish networks, perhaps specialising in sales or trade or in the development of innovative ideas. Your encyclopaedic knowledge makes you a valuable source of information; your curiosity and versatility have opened doors. You know something about everything, and this gives you a unique perspective on life. You have professional and financial concerns and are motivated to develop the right contacts to help you become the smartest in your field. Being able to keep your options open has presented you with many advantages and opportunities.

However, as your soul awakens, you feel anxious that you have been spreading yourself too thinly – and the realisation that quality is more important than quantity will lead to an existential crisis. You start to feel restless and search for something you can truly value. You want to use your skills to create something that is of lasting value. You start to tune into your soul purpose, which helps you to clarify and prioritise your goals, and eventually you will understand how you can combine strategy and management to realise your vision, combining the tactical skills of a chess master with incisive leadership qualities. Integrating the mental personality type with the archetype of the Creator makes you the *Leading Strategist.*

Core identities and the four quadrants

Now let's look at the four quadrants in relation to identity types. Figure 25 uses the example of Michael, a 2-4 identity type (see above), and shows some of the processes taking place during integration, highlighting both the inner-subjective and outer-objective perspectives.

The upper left quadrant shows the five inner levels of Michael's consciousness, from body to soul. The personality type combines the influences of body, feeling and thought: Michael is a creative personality type, so this grouping is given the number 4.

The soul type incorporates the personality, hence Michael's sensitive

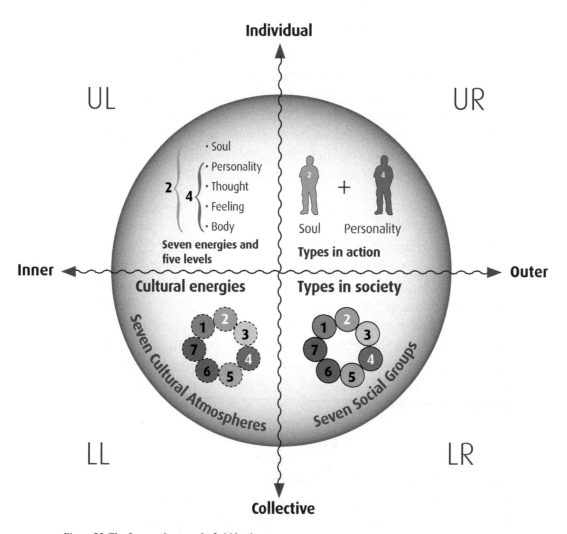

Figure 25. The four quadrants and a 2-4 identity type.

Illuminator soul type, numbered 2, shows a grouping of all five levels of consciousness. When the soul awakens, a broader, less egocentric, perspective emerges and begins to guide the personality away from itself and towards others. In Michael's case, the emergence of the soul has made love his central purpose in life, and all his resources are being called upon to fulfil this purpose.

As a consequence of this soul awakening, we can see in the upper right quadrant that Michael's behaviours begin to change. This will be seen most visibly in changes to Michael's lifestyle, career goals and relationships; his motivations have been transformed.

The lower quadrants depict Michael's social world. Before his awakening, Michael's social circle was dominated by creative types (green circle), but now he has a new interest in education and psychology (blue circle).

With the awakening of Michael's core identity, his entire psychological environment will change because now the soul is in charge instead of the ego or personality. As a consequence, Michael will become more concerned about his physical environment and the world in which he lives (lower right quadrant) and this will typically express itself as a concern to be environmentally conscious. Relationships will also be affected, with his need for self-esteem lessening and his consideration for others growing. When the soul awakens, we start to consider how our choices impact on others; we become less self-conscious and more focused on the group and the collective consciousness. In this way, the soul moves us to identify as a global citizen, but without losing our capacity to love and take care of those we are close to.

Exercise: What groups do you belong to?

Your relationship to your social groups, and the types of groups you are engaged with are a reflection of your level of consciousness because they reveal the values and interests that determine how you relate to the world.

1. Make a list of the groups and communities that are most important to you, which may include family, religious groups, work, social clubs, etc.

2. What interests or values hold these groups together? What are the concerns and interests of these groups and what are their qualities? Try to describe these groups in terms of the types they exhibit.

3. Make a list of groups you don't belong to but would like to join. What are the values, qualities and concerns of these groups?

4. Examine both lists – your current groups and the groups you would like to join – and summarise the key qualities of each.

5. Now consider that you are on a soul journey in which you are transitioning from the first set of groups (which represent your personality type) to the latter (which represent your soul type). What might this tell you about your identity type?

6. Consider any crisis that you are currently facing and consider what this challenge might mean with respect to the awakening of your soul. (Spiritual crises often arise in connection with our social world.)

We will now explore the different qualities of our types at the psychological levels of body, feeling and thought. Once we know more about our body type, feeling type and thinking type we can combine this information with our identity type to provide a more complete five-fold typological profile – which we will discuss later in this book.

Your mentality
– The seven thinking types

We know that people are different, with distinctive appearances, postures, movements, temperaments and attitudes. This chapter, and the two that follow, will look at these differences from the perspective of the Seven Types. As we have seen, we each have a typological DNA that consists of a dominant type (one of seven) at each of the five psychological levels. We have already explored typology at the levels of soul and personality – and how these two types integrate to create our core identity, or identity type – now we will be looking at the psychological levels of body, feeling and thought, with this chapter examining the level of thought and the seven thinking types, and the following two chapters looking at the levels of feeling (seven feeling types) and body (seven body types) respectively.

Of course, we are each unique and cannot be reduced to labels or formulas – no typological model could ever capture the subtleties that arise from the many layers of experience that have moulded our characters. However, a knowledge of our types and the types of others can help us to see and understand ourselves and each other, which will help us to communicate, cooperate and reconcile conflict.

Just as we encounter different types of people in the world, we also find there are different types within our own unique typological DNA. We can experience internal conflicts between our dominant types at the five levels – for example; there can be conflict between our bodily needs, feelings and thoughts. This can inhibit us – we might not do what we want to do due to an inner resistance – and these conflicts can seem insoluble. However, when we understand how the different levels of our being interact we can take steps to integrate our types and achieve synthesis and harmony.

One of my clients had a conflict between her communication style and her temperament. She expressed herself directly and categorically but felt hurt when people responded in the same way. When she realised that she was a dynamic thinking type and a vulnerable, sensitive feeling type, this gave her valuable information so that she could work to create inner harmony and manage her relationships in more helpful ways.

When we understand our dominant types at the levels of body, feeling and thought, we can begin to utilise their unique resources more consciously and harmonise conflicts between them. Of course, we will also need to accept that there are certain psychological qualities we cannot change, which is what Assagioli called accepting our typological structure.

The five levels and seven psychological functions

Few typological models speak about the five psychological levels. Most typologies are one dimensional, operating at the level of the personality only. Models based on Jungian psychology, for example, tend to focus only on personality types in terms of where they lie along the introvert/extrovert dimension; the different types appear in different combinations, but these models only speak about the level and the different developmental stages of the personality. Wilber (2000c: 53) described these typologies as having "horizontal orientations", explaining:

> Finally, a word about "horizontal" typologies, such as Jungian types, the Enneagram, Myers-Briggs, and so forth. For the most part, these are not vertical levels, stages, or waves of development, but rather different types of orientations possible at each of the various levels. Some individuals find these typologies to be very useful in understanding themselves and others. But it should be understood that these "horizontal" typologies are of a fundamentally different nature than the "vertical" levels – namely, the latter are universal stages through which individuals pass in a normal course of development, whereas the former are types of personalities that may – or may not – be found at any of the stages.

These horizontal typologies suggest that a person has a basic personality type that is constant throughout the different stages of development (including the pre-personal, personal and transpersonal stages) and in the realms of the unconscious, conscious and superconscious: the personality might evolve and change, but an individual is only ever described in terms of their personality structure.

By contrast, the Seven Types takes a holistic view of the human psyche, distinguishing between five psychological levels – in addition to the level of personality we have the levels of body, feeling, thought (which combine to create the personality) and soul (which combines with personality to create the core identity). Each level is dominated by one of the seven types, and each level undergoes its own stages of evolutionary development. This understanding of our psyche allows for a greater degree of detail, variety and complexity than a one-dimensional horizontal model. Because it is a more complete typological model – including body, thought, feeling and soul types, as well as personality types – the Seven Types is able to explain why people with the same personality type might still be very different.

We describe an individual's unique combination of types using a five-number code, as follows. Each of the seven types is numbered from one to seven: 1-dynamic, 2-sensitive, 3-mental, 4-creative, 5-analytical, 6-dedicated, 7-practical. We then list the dominant types at the five levels in this order: soul-personality, thought, feeling, body. Figure 26 gives the example of a 1-2-463 composition, where 1 is a dynamic soul type, 2 is a sensitive personality type, 4 is a creative thinking type, 6 is a dedicated feeling type, 3 is a mental body type.

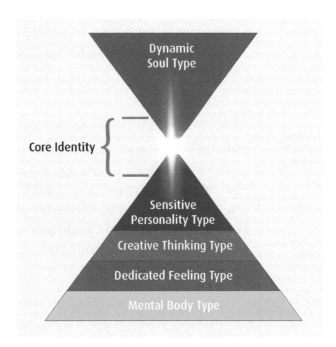

Figure 26: A 1-2-463 combination of types

When comparing psychosynthesis typology with Wilber's integral psychology[1], it is clear that when Assagioli (Undated 6) refers to "the *Rays* which qualify his soul, his personality, and his mental,

---

[1] See Integral Psychosynthesis (Sørensen, 2008), a comparison of Wilber's and Assagioli's systems.

emotional and physical bodies", he is referring to the energy bodies or sheaths that are described in Vedanta philosophy, which Wilber also incorporates into his teaching. This is an advanced theory, so I will delegate it for further reading[2].

My view is that the Seven Types gives us the only vertical typological model that focuses on all aspects of a person – not just the personality, but our psyche at all its stages and levels, including the spiritual. Indeed, the spiritual aspect of typology (the Spirit and Monad) is itself a vast topic which is not touched upon in this book.

Let's now look into the art of reading energies and, more specifically, how we can distinguish between the seven thinking types that colour our mentality.

The art of reading energies

Identifying types is difficult. Though we might have a sense that our lives are built out of energy, we are not practised at distinguishing between the different qualities and radiations of these energy fields. We are not in the habit of observing distinctions between our bodily sensations, feelings and thoughts, so it is to be expected that initially we will find this a challenging task, an endeavour that is made more complicated by the fact that these energies overlap and affect each other.

It might be assumed that our dominant type at the level of body would be the easiest to identify because we can see our bodies directly with our eyes. But, in fact, the body can be the hardest type to identify because the energies of the other types – feeling, thought, personality

---

[2] Ken Wilber writes extensively about how the energy bodies relate to the seven chakras in his book *The Religion of Tomorrow* (2017). Previously, Wilber published two well-known papers on subtle energies: *Toward a Comprehensive Theory on Subtle Energies* (2006) and *Sidebar G: States and Stages* (2007). In the former paper, Wilber wrote: "The traditional 'Great Chain of Being' is usually given as something like: matter, body, mind, soul and spirit. In the Vedanta, for example, these are, respectively, the 5 sheaths or levels of Spirit: annamayakosha (the sheath or level made of physical food), the pranamayakosha, (the level made of élan vital), the manomayakosha (the level made of mind), the vijnanamayakosha (the level made of higher mind or soul), and anandamayakosha (the level made of transcendental bliss or causal spirit."

and soul – all express themselves *through* the body or affect the body's appearance. Indeed, the body is the physical mask through which we express our entire being.

To identify the dominant types at the different layers of our being we must become experienced psychological observers. This is difficult! We might have one view of ourselves, but others will see qualities in us that we don't – and some aspects of ourselves might be outside of our own or anyone else's awareness. For example, we might appear self-confident but actually feel vulnerable and not know why – and, based on this partial self-awareness, we might develop a distorted self-image by focusing on our vulnerability rather than on our confidence.

Wilber's four quadrants can help us with the task of identifying our types because we need to practice looking at ourselves from all angles: our inner experience (upper left quadrant), how others interpret our behaviour or how we might appear to ourselves if, for example, we were to see ourselves in a video (upper right), and how others see us in group contexts (lower quadrants). Note: making use of the upper right and lower right quadrants require that we ask others for feedback about our behaviour.

The Seven Types model is being verified and finessed through ongoing research and experience. Ultimately, it is a model that not only describes the human psyche, but everything in the universe. It is informed by many schools of philosophy, thought and teaching. Roberto Assagioli and Alice Bailey are the two key theorists whose work I have drawn upon, but I am also indebted to the work of Michael Robbins, especially his book *Tapestry of the Gods* volumes I-II.

As we begin the task of identifying our thinking, feeling and body types, the following principles should be held in mind.

1. **Dominant energies at different levels can affect each other**. The dominant energies at all five levels impact on each other, colouring their manifestation and expression.

2. **All seven types of energy are present at each level**. We find all types of energy at each level, however some types of energy are more common than others at certain levels.

3. **An individual's maturity or level of development determines whether positive or negative qualities will be prominent**. The types at each of the levels can manifest in healthy or distorted ways; the further we are on our journey of self-development, the healthier the expression of our types will be.

The seven thinking types

To identify our thinking type – which incorporates our manner of thinking and our style of communication – we start by looking at our intellectual **interests**. These reveal our type's natural disposition, which is the "mental channel" that underpins our thinking. We then look at *how* we **think**, which includes our mental habits and how we collect and processes information. Finally, we look at our **communication** style.

While we will each tend to exhibit one dominant thinking type, through maturation we can learn to make use of all seven thinking types (Figure 27). However, some of the types are less compatible with the level of thought/mind than others, which can make it difficult to think clearly. However, where there is a challenge there is also an opportunity: if our dominant type at the level of thought is causing us difficulty then it follows that there is a specific lesson we need to learn as part of our soul journey. The same issue of incompatibility can arise at the levels of body and feeling, and I will address this issue in the relevant chapters.

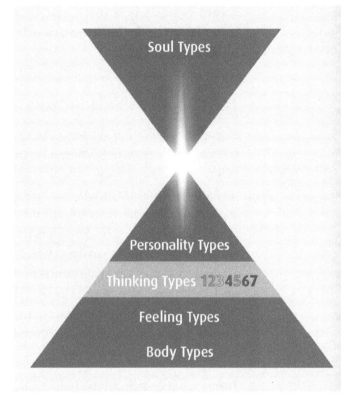

Figure 27. The Seven Thinking Types

The following section contains descriptions of the seven thinking types. As mentioned above, each type can be tempered with qualities from other energy fields – both other energies at the same level and other energies from different levels – so it is unlikely that we will observe a thinking type in its purest manifestation, so to speak. For example, a proud intellect (dynamic thinking type) can be tempered by a quality of humility from the temperament (sensitive feeling type), which is a conflict one must learn to balance.

Identifying our types is challenging work. My advice is not to be too hasty in making an assessment of your own thinking type. It might benefit you to revisit this chapter several times, perhaps gathering feedback from friends and family also, before making an evaluation.

The dynamic thinking type

Assagioli (1983: 20) writes: "At the mental level, the will [dynamic] type often has *clear vision,* uncoloured and undistorted by emotions. When mature, he has an open mind and a synthetic vision, and he considers the broad view rather than the details. He has great powers of concentration and a dynamic one-pointedness. He expresses his combativeness, on the mental plane, in the love of argument and criticism, and this is one of his chief defects."

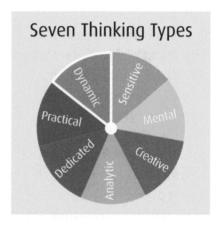

Seven Thinking Types

Interests: You are interested in the laws and principles that underpin the world. You want to understand the mechanisms that govern people, nature, technology and any other area of interest. Whatever the focus of your interest, you want to become an expert and master it. You are interested in power and your talents are well suited to management, politics, planning and anything goal-oriented. You are sharp like a knife, focused and ambitious with an ability to think in big pictures.

Thinking style: You are free and independent and draw your own conclusions. Your intellect is powerful and quick to tune into new ideas. You are probably a trendsetter whose opinions have authority and influence.

You have firm convictions and will rarely be persuaded to change your mind. That said, you can take in many points of view and

Interests	Power, whatever is essential, governing principles and laws. Management, politics, strategy, setting aims and objectives, greatness, ambition.
Thinking style	Individualistic, free, future-orientated, strategic, cutting to the chase, generating ideas, taking perspective, hierarchical, goal-orientated. *Distortion:* Isolated, one-track minded, selfish, arrogant, immovable, patronising.
Communication style	Direct, honest, confrontational, directing, setting the agenda. *Distortion:* Suppressive, crude, brutal.

assess an argument's strengths and weaknesses. You have excellent concentration and can be very focused. You don't study just for fun but want to become a master in your field; you want to be the best and to share your expertise with others.

You fear being dominated so you stand firm in your beliefs. This can lead to a tendency to think you're always right, making you proud and arrogant.

You prefer solitude when thinking through decisions and conclusions. You consider asking for advice to be a weakness, and this can further isolate you and inhibit your effectiveness.

You organise your thinking linearly and hierarchically, clarifying and prioritising by importance. And, because you are action-orientated, you don't spend too much time on philosophical contemplation unless there is a clear objective. Your challenge is to not be too closed minded.

Communication style: An excellent spokesperson, you communicate with authority and clarity. You make strong arguments and insist upon defining principles, laws and rules. Knowing that arguments will arise when people have strong opinions, you consider the weaknesses and strengths of a topic before engaging. You like intellectual debate because it sharpens your arguments. The English parliament is a good example of your style of debate. You debate well because you express your convictions strongly and to the point. You maintain a cool overview lest emotion impair your clarity. You can argue crucial points brutally and are inclined to suppress others' right to expression.

You are proud of your ideas and respect others who are independent thinkers.

You excel at issuing directives, delivering them with a sense of clarity and perspective. A person of few words, you avoid elaborate explanations; you tend to present the big picture and fill in the detail only if necessary.

You are concerned with the most efficient way to communicate and share information. As a consequence, you might look down on those who are slower than you or who talk in circles or digress. This impatience means you can be intolerant of indecision and reckless in how you achieve your goals.

You prefer clarity over beauty or relationships, which can make you appear cool and impersonal. You also have a tendency to display your power, which can make you seem self-centred and boastful.

The psychosynthetic task: The task facing the dynamic thinking type is to *develop* an ability to dominate your field of influence by understanding the core principles and facts. You must *control* your tendency to engage in mental warfare and harmonise your communication style by allowing more space for dialogue so you can balance opinions.

Are your thinking and communication styles dynamic?

The sensitive thinking type

Assagioli (1983: 34) writes: "The identification tendencies of this type are generally revealed in their inclusive mentalities or in their ability to see all sides of a question, which produces breadth of vision and equanimity but sometimes these are accompanied by lack of firmness and resolution."

Seven Thinking Types

Interests: You love knowledge and seek to understand the world holistically. You possess an open mind and are interested in people and everything connected to you. You want to strengthen social and intimate relationships through understanding.

Thinking style: You are contemplative and receptive, absorbing knowledge instantly and intuitively, but this can also mean you are easily influenced.

Clear, concrete thinking can be a challenge for you. You would benefit from practicing discrimination so you can distinguish more easily between what is relevant and irrelevant, true and false, otherwise you can fall into the trap of believing everything is of equal value. Also, because your sensitivity can make you indecisive, you might find it difficult to dismiss some options and find your voice.

You absorb a great deal of information and become so absorbed in your thoughts that it can be difficult for others to connect with you or to keep track of where you're at.

You know that everything is connected and you look for similarities and patterns. But being holistically-minded means you can be vague, seeing analogies and connections where others can't. You love knowledge but find it difficult to apply knowledge practically, preferring to remain the eternal student.

You are receptive to intuition but find it difficult to formulate your ideas clearly so that others can make use of them. Indeed, at heart you are a poet who is focused on subjective truth and who employs emotional language. You see the best in others, and this is both your greatest strength and greatest weakness.

Interests	Connections, holism, relationships, nature. Healing of broken relationships.
Thinking style	Quiet, receptive, broad-minded, open, considerate, holistic, social, humanistic. *Distortion:* Naïve, inaccurate, indecisive, diffuse, impractical, vague.
Communication style	Friendly, understanding, careful, bridging, inclusive. *Distortion:* Conflict-avoidant, unclear, unsure, self-annihilation.

Communication style: You are gentle, inclusive, empathetic and considerate, wanting to avoid offending anyone. To avoid conflict, you would rather agree with others than assert your opinion. In fact, you do not always know what you think and often need to talk something through to help you know your own mind.

In general, you are a loving person who is focused on relationships, a good listener with a sensitive communication style who wants to help others.

The psychosynthetic task: The task facing the sensitive thinking type is to *develop* your capacity for inclusive thinking and fine differentiation between nuances. You need to *control* your tendency to be over-inclusive and vague. You can *harmonise* your thinking and communication by increasing your capacity to think analytically and to discriminate between subjective and objective facts.

Do you make sense of the world through a sensitive mindset? What do your friends think?

The mental thinking type

Assagioli (1983: 41) says of this type: "He is often intelligent, mentally active, enterprising and quick to find the right methods"

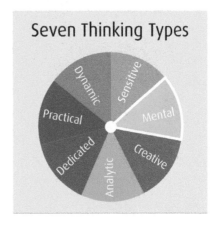

Interests: You are interested in the big picture, in making connections, and in devising theories about how the world works. You keep well informed and want to know about everything in your field of interest. You like to gather information and share it with others, having a particular interest in economics, business, the services industry, communications and philosophy.

Thinking style: You like to take an overview and look for patterns, and from this you are able to develop theories about the world. You don't cut to the chase as the dynamic type does, but rather want to gather as much knowledge as possible. You can think across systems and see new connections among different fields of knowledge and so generate new possibilities. Discovering new ideas motivates you, so you keep an eye out for new trends.

Your quick, active and curious mind absorbs much knowledge and you enjoy combining this in new ways. You like to develop well-defined theories. You love to plan and devise smart strategies, that produce concrete results. You are well informed, having a large network that helps you to gather the information you need. You have sound critical judgement and can see quickly whether something makes sense. However, while you never run out of ideas, you can sometimes be too smart, calculating and manipulative, which means your communication can distort other people's reality like a spin doctor.

You have a good critical sense and can quickly see when something doesn't add up. You tend be arrogant – like a dynamic type – and can become muddled or over-complicate things. Also, because you know so much, you have a tendency to see others as stupid. And because you are able to remain objective, this can make you seem impersonal, cool and calculating. In extreme cases you can become obsessive and inclined to paranoia.

Interests	Theories, planning, strategies, philosophy, information sharing, networking, trade, communication.
Thinking style	Active, fast, curious, sharp, smart, taking a broad perspective, inventive, connecting, diverse. *Distortion:* Arrogant, overthinking, conspiracy-minded, manipulative, cold, distracted.
Communication style	Clear, intelligent, structured, light, quick, large vocabulary. *Distortion:* Secretive, calculating, manipulative, indesicive.

You enjoy challenging your intellect and seeking out difficult mathematical, philosophical or technological problems. You enjoy mysteries and solving puzzles. You understand complex relationships better than other types, but you can get lost in your thoughts, which easily distract you.

Communication style. You speak a lot, with a concern to express yourself clearly. You question everything and are constantly searching for new knowledge. You rarely get straight to the point, but you're an excellent and easy conversationalist because you are so knowledgeable and can always think of something to say.

Your quick and easy going nature is attractive and you know how to generate a positive atmosphere. However, you tend to play your cards close to your chest, revealing little of your true feelings – although avoiding public declarations means you are able to keep your options open.

You are quick to understand what is being said and can move a conversation in whatever direction you want. You communicate well, conveying your message in the most strategic way. However, with this skill comes a temptation to manipulate and deceive others and, because you unconsciously expect others to do the same, this can result in you becoming suspicious of others.

Because you are able to see all sides of an issue, you can find it difficult to reach a conclusion, and even when you do it will be with reservations. To you, the truth is often relative.

The psychosynthetic task: The task facing the mental thinking type is to *develop* your mental flexibility and acuteness by holding many perspectives. You need to *control* your tendency to be too smart for your own good, communicating only what suits your agenda. You can *harmonise* your thinking style by identifying your core values and objectives more clearly so they become your guiding stars.

Have you an active and curious mind that loves to work things out?

The creative thinking type

Assagioli (1983: 54) said of the creative thinking type: "The chief mental tendency is to harmonise, include, unify and perfect, but the contrast between the beauty of the ideal and the prevailing conditions that prevent its realisation in the world easily rouses their instinct to combat the stupidity and blindness of those responsible for this inadequacy."

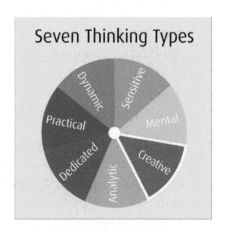

Interests: You explore alternate realities using your imagination. You draw inspiration from interacting with others and making connections.

You like to be in harmony with other people and enjoy psychology, humour, and relating to others spontaneously.

Your mind is visual, aesthetic and active and you express yourself best through storytelling. You are a natural talent, telling real life stories based on your experience with other people and life in general.

Thinking style: Your thinking style draws upon your aesthetic sense and imagination. You are more interested in beauty and real-life experience than facts.

You love to dramatise your understanding, telling anecdotes and stories. You take your time getting to the point, weaving stories that are full of imagery. It is through telling these stories, or by tuning into the immediate situation and atmosphere, that you are able to process and gain insight into your life.

Interests	Aesthetic expression, development of language, storytelling, making connections, peace-making, humour, play, imagination.
Thinking style	Aesthetic, imaginative, focused on direct experience, dramatising, positive, creative, inventive. *Distortion:* Indecisive, torn, fearful, avoidant, moody.
Communication style	Large vocabulary, well spoken, funny, storyteller, engaging, resolving conflict. *Distortion:* Exaggerates, misrepresenting reality, selfcentred, conflict-avoidant, instigating conflict.

You like to build bridges, make connections, find common ground and create harmony. You prefer thinking with others to solitary work. You can see both sides of an argument, which can make you indecisive, and you can become frustrated when new perspectives and opportunities arise.

You struggle when dealing with data, for example in the fields of economics or technology. Similarly, too much structure will restrict your fluid, creative thinking. You tend to be influenced and inspired by your emotions, which can make you seem vague, so you can be misunderstood. However, your spontaneity and creativity mean you can always think of a way to express yourself.

Your strong imagination can exaggerate your fears. You are often

happy and outgoing, but your moods can fluctuate. Humour can help to remedy your darker moods and can balance your tendency to worry. You love to play with words and their meanings – this lightens your mood and presents you with alternative perspectives.

Communication style: You are talkative and wordy. You try to express yourself beautifully and evocatively. You are concerned to have an impact, so having the right effect is more important to you than being factual – and, as a result, your performance may overshadow the content of what you are trying to say.

You have a wide vocabulary and are a lively and engaging speaker. However, your imagination and fluency can sometimes work against you and cause you to lose your thread. You also have a tendency to see life through rose-tinted spectacles, and avoid unpleasant topics, which can make you seem lightweight.

You are humorous, charming and spontaneous. You connect easily with people. Being able to see all points of view means you are most likely a good mediator and peacemaker. You weigh the pros and cons of an argument and tend to oppose extreme viewpoint in principle, regardless of your own beliefs, in order to establish balance. Ironically, to help establish harmony you might sometimes generate conflict in order to bring issues out into the open so they can be fully discussed. Overall, your highest quality is an ability to turn a bad situation into something good.

The psychosynthetic task: The task facing the creative thinking type is to *develop* your talent for expressive and colourful language, which captures the moment in a beautiful way. *Control* your tendency to let your imagination run wild and distort your sense of reality. Your creativity and spontaneity will become *harmonised* as you develop an ability to stay focused by keeping a clear awareness on your goals.

Do you love to play with words and tell stories instead of facts?

The analytical thinking type

Assagioli (1983: 61) said of this type: "His tireless mind is always on the alert, investigating, posing questions, solving problems, searching, probing, experimenting, proving and discovering. He has a great capacity for prolonged attention and mental concentration, tireless perseverance in his research, meticulous accuracy, and an admirable ability to sift data, discover laws and conceive theories for classifying facts into coherent systems."

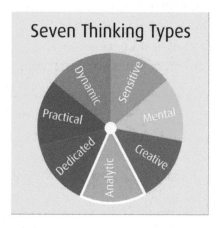

Interests: You are interested in objective truth and have a professional attitude and a serious concern to distinguish fact from fiction. You are curious, with an interest in understanding how things work. You immerse yourself in specialist research, especially in science and practical know-how. You are committed to objective truth. If interested in psychology, you will aim at developing proven methods to help the human condition. Your in-depth investigations lead to discoveries which have a practical expression.

Interests	Practical knowledge and know-how, research, science, academia, discovery.
Thinking style	Sharp, precise, penetrating, attention to detail, analytical, logical, critical, examining, specialising. *Distortion:* Stubborn, dogmatic, narrow-minded, arrogant.
Communication style	Precise, careful, logical, thorough. *Distortion:* Overly detailed, boring, dry, cold, rejecting.

Thinking style: Your sharp and logical intellect is good with detail. You have immense powers of concentration and an analytical approach to gathering facts and seeking practical solutions. Your ability to work with detailed information means you are knowledgeable about many subjects, but this can come with a tendency to be arrogant and narrow-minded.

Your mind is sceptical and critical. You test ideas to see if they are credible and fit with what you already know. You analyse and verify. Your manner can seem cool, serious and reserved, so you can come across as curt, somewhat dry and even something of a nerd. You are a no-nonsense, cut-to-the-chase sort of person who is in a hurry to discover the facts. Indeed, you can be so concerned to discover the facts that you can miss the wood for the trees. For you, truth and efficiency count for more than beauty. You narrow-mindedly ignore the intuitive dimensions of reality, especially anything that cannot be proven physically. You have an unhelpful tendency to take a dogmatic view on topics in the subjective domain about which you have little knowledge. Still, you have much to offer and your type commonly excels in education and academia.

Your search for clarity means you have a tendency to focus on differences rather than similarities: you separate before synthesising. If presented with something about which you know little, you tend to be sceptical. You are cautious and look for errors and omissions. You have a detective's eye for detail and see patterns others miss.

You want to use your knowledge and are satisfied if it can help you to improve things. Your perseverance and thoroughness can make you an expert in your field. You are curious and inventive but your approach to life is basically literal; you have little time for symbols.

Communication style: You are a person of few words unless you need to make a detailed point where making clear and precise statements is

necessary. You think before you speak and communicate what you have to say accurately, thoroughly and methodically. However, this need to present the facts in a painstaking way can make you a poor speaker because your listeners lose interest.

You lack spontaneity. When encountering something new you need time to study and evaluate it, so very often you prefer to say no to things you don't know about before you say yes. You ask questions and research a subject extensively. Sometimes, you will struggle to say what you think because you want to go away and study something so you can work out what you think. When something strikes you as illogical you can become highly critical, even brutal in rejecting it. Your attention to detail can leave you with a narrow perspective, so you can seem stubborn, but you are reliable, which is a great strength.

The psychosynthetic task: The task facing the analytical thinking type is to *develop* your ability to analyse and draw out solid conclusions while *controlling* your tendency to lose perspective by focusing on the detail only. Your thinking style will become *harmonised* if you can allow space for subjective values and goals and for dialogue with different perspectives.

Do you love to communicate facts with a serious agenda?

The dedicated thinking type

Assagioli (1983: 71) says of the dedicated thinking type: "In the mental field, this type tends to exhibit more limitations than good qualities because his intelligence is very often dominated and activated by his strong passions; he therefore easily becomes narrow-minded, intolerant and critical. His views are uncompromising and rigid, and whenever he adopts an opinion or theory, it is very difficult to change his mind."

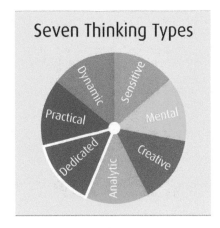

Seven Thinking Types

Interests: Your focus is on ideals, idols and utopian dreams. This passion will often be expressed through a religious devotion, but you could be drawn to any vision or cause that arouses your enthusiasm and commitment, from poetry to politics. Your thinking will be influenced by your emotions, which can be problematic.

Interests	Visions, ideals, idols, religion, poetry, politics, emotion.
Thinking style	Goal-orientated, intense, sacrificial, passionate, strong convictions. *Distortion:* Fixated, narrow minded, dogmatic, closed, fanatical, possessed.
Communication style	Passionate, agitating, dominant, inflaming, powerful. *Distortion:* Propaganda, bombastic, warring, creating conflict.

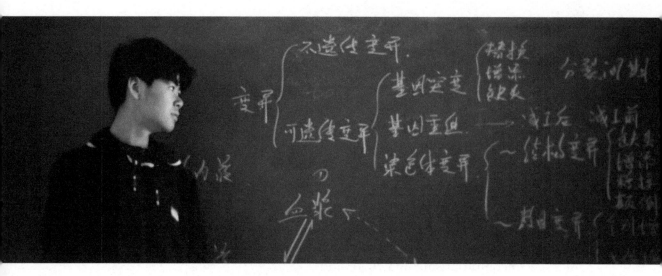

Thinking style: Highly idealistic people can become so focused on their vision that they ignore everything else. This type is goal-orientated, focused and intense, which means they are well placed to overcome challenges.

This is a mentality largely guided by desire and passion, and these emotions can cloud thinking and make you dogmatic.

Your thinking is directed by your passion, which motivates you to dig deeply into the meaning behind your mission. It is therefore important for you to refine your passions and make them more inclusive, because this will make your thinking more complete. Religious, political or philosophical views that dismiss other beliefs as false are typical for your type of thinking. When passion takes over, your thinking will become irrational and closed to criticism. When your feelings and emotions are not open to debate, you can become a fanatic and a zealot; there is a danger that you could become a crank, unable to view your beliefs objectively. You tend to have a closed mind and can focus only on what *you* know to be true. You have a tendency to think in black and white concepts, further arousing the passion that can distort your thinking.

Communication style: You are a fiery and intense advocate for your cause. You find dialogue difficult because you already have all the answers to everything worth knowing so you ignore other perspectives and beliefs. You channel your passions, whether loving or hating, into your communication.

You are a campaigner who uses slogans and rhetoric to make your point, but ignoring what other people think will create conflict and generate opposition, and you might find yourself in a kind of mental warfare.

Being so single-minded will not make you a good communicator, even though your convictions mean you are powerful in your manner of communication. Given that your passion is to encourage others to share your vision, this style of communicating will be counter-productive.

The psychosynthetic task: The task for the dedicated thinking type is to *develop* your ability to discern your truest values and formulate them into attractive ideals. You must *control* your tendency to be dogmatic and dominating in how you communicate your perspectives. *Harmonise* your single-mindedness by debating your points and through being open to dialogue and to different values and points of view.

Are you the true believer pursuing a utopian dream?

The practical thinking type

Assagioli (1983: 78) said of the practical thinking type: "His mental activity is exercised in *projecting*, accurately and in detail, and in thinking out and outlining precise, elaborate models of what he intends to manifest."

Seven Thinking Types

Interests: You are focused on order, systems, hierarchies and rituals. You enjoy creating well-functioning systems using a variety of elements, whether it might be an IT system or a social event. You govern, direct and bring things together in a beautiful and elegant manner.

Thinking: You are skilled at organising your knowledge into well-defined systems where everything has its place. You know how to make practical use of knowledge and process detail in a systematic manner. You are not a specialist, like the analytical type, but a generalist who is interested in knowledge that is practical and used to achieve results. You can be conservative in your mindset because you tend to settle for what you know works. When you know something works you stick with it, which can make you rigid and over-regulated. But you are sensible and quickly understand what makes something tick. You look for the laws and rules that govern the world, and seek the optimal balance between conservation and renewal. Generally, you are constructive and pragmatic.

Your thinking is purposeful. You don't waste time playing games, unless they are power games through which you can bolster your need for control. You have a need to understand the whole system, which could be a society or a language, and you carefully analyse all the detail

Interests	Order, systems, organisations, hierarchies, rituals, processing, efficiency, flow, elegance.
Thinking style	Systemic, organising, practical, generalist, constructive, pragmatic, cooperative. *Distortion:* Rigid, controlling, compulsive, stiff, obsessive.
Communication style	Diplomatic, well-spoken, elegant, mastermind, group orientated, facilitator. *Distortion:* Superficial, formal, snobbish, elitist, proud, easily insulted.

and the context. You are keen to master and control, leaving nothing to chance, but you can become obsessed with micro-management. Knowing the best way of doing something is the ultimate purpose of this kind of intellect.

You formulate your thoughts with a certain elegance, carefully selecting the appropriate words, as a chef might the ingredients of a meal. You are good at following processes, cataloguing information, and applying new knowledge, but you can become obsessed with words and rules and reject anything that doesn't fit your system. Your efficiency can help you, but your tendency to force an issue won't.

Communication: You speak with elegance, carefully weighing your words because you know words have consequences. You can be diplomatic if this will help you achieve the best results in the most efficient manner. However, always trying to say the right thing can make you overly formal and polite, while what you are saying will lack substance. You like routine, which means you tend to talk about favourite topics. You don't like idle chatter and prefer to talk only when there is an issue that needs addressing, which can make you appear rigid and snobbish.

You communicate with politeness and grace, and people enjoy working with you. Indeed, as the practical type, you excel at getting people to cooperate, even being able to mastermind large operations. You tend to give people attention and offer them praise and constructive criticism. Ultimately, your greatest talent is an ability to express yourself in a manner that provides a framework and direction and that promotes cooperation. However, you will feel demoralised if your efforts are overlooked or not appreciated. You are easily offended if you feel your status has been overlooked.

The psychosynthetic task: The task facing the practical thinking type is to *develop* and fine-tune your ability to gather detail and organise, while *controlling* a tendency to be overly structured and rigid. You can *harmonise* your systematic approach to life by allowing the subjective realms of feeling and imagination to influence your way of reaching conclusions.

Are you an efficient communicator and planner who is always working on a to-do-list?

Exercise: How do you communicate?

Ask someone who knows you well to help you identify your thinking type. Consider the following statements and, with their support, identify the ones that sound most like you.

These statements have been carefully worded to include reference to the motivators that underlie the different thinking types, so please take care that you are able to agree with all aspects of a statement before selecting it.

1. I often seek to convince others about my ideals, and can push my views onto others.
2. I often use humour to create a good atmosphere.
3. I am elegant and diplomatic when speaking because I want to facilitate cooperation.
4. I'm good at mediating because I can understand people's feelings.
5. I listen more than I speak because I want to make sure others feel heard.
6. I enjoy a good argument because it allows me to test my intellectual strength.
7. I am considerate in my communication because I don't want to hurt or insult anyone.
8. I care about how people talk to each other – courtesy, respect and formalities are important.
9. I speak a lot because I am knowledgeable – and people benefit from my knowledge.
10. I love to discuss details and explore different possibilities.
11. I am serious and professional in my communication, always making use of the facts.
12. I know I'm right in what I believe and people listen to me.
13. I always cut to the chase when speaking to people.
14. I tend to be critical of others, especially when I think people haven't checked their facts[3].

Before looking at the footnote, connect the statements to the thinking types. In the footnote the first number is the question and the second is the type.

---

[3] Statements (the number in brackets is the feeling type, where 1-dynamic, 2-sensitive, 3-mental, 4-creative, 5-analytical, 6-dedicated, 7-practical): 1.(6), 2.(4), 3.(7), 4.(4), 5.(2), 6.(1), 7.(2), 8.(7), 9.(3), 10.(3), 11.(5), 12.(6), 13.(1), 14.(5).

Your temperament
– The seven feeling types

In this chapter, we look at the seven feeling types and how they create different temperaments. According to our type, we may be quiet, warm, open, reserved, impersonal, observant – some of us have strong emotional reactions while others can remain calm and seem not to react at all. These differences in temperament reflect the energy of the emotional field in all its variety.

From the perspective of psychoenergetics, the ultimate purpose of our emotional life is to express love in all its aspects: parental, romantic, spiritual, friendship, self-care, love for all people, animals and the world we live in. The purpose of our emotional life is to make love possible.

Love is an energy that unites. Through love we experience belonging and connectedness. However, the way we love, and the way we want to be loved, is different for each of us. All seven feeling types are motivated by love, but they will express love differently according to their motivation, as discussed in chapter 7. We can say that the seven feeling types demonstrate the seven ways of expressing love that come naturally to humankind (Figure 28).

There are many unhelpful misconceptions about love so, for clarity, I will sometimes refer to love as "sensitivity" because it is the sensitive energy that enables us to become attuned to other people's feelings, to empathise and to form relationships.

We should also note that love is expressed at all five psychological levels – and this totality of expression is what colours our experience of love. At the level of body, we like to touch and be touched; at the level of feeling we need to give and receive love; at the level of thought we each value and conceive of love in different ways; at the level of personality we are focused on achieving our ambitions so love is experienced in terms of our engagement with the world; at the level of soul, love is altruistic and concerned less with our own needs and more with the well-being of all.

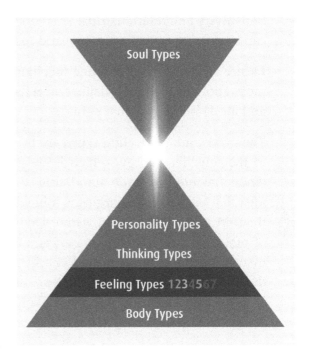

Figure 28. The Seven Feeling Types

It is through our feelings that we can express love, and we will each do this in one of seven ways according to our dominant energy at the level of feeling – and this is what we call our feeling type. In the descriptions of the seven feeling types below, we will focus on three key criteria:

Basic temperament and love language: This concerns how a type prefers to give and receive love, how they feel safe, and the sorts of relationship they are drawn to.

Sensitivity and relationships: This concerns the degree to which a type can be open, sensitive, receptive and responsive within relationships.

Desire strategies and defence mechanisms: This concerns the type's motivation, its likes and dislikes, and its strategies for seeking out love and for defending against pain.

The most common feeling types are those that are most closely linked to the sensitive energy, which is the energy most connected to our emotional life. To understand this, we need to consider again the idea that each of the energies is a blend of the other energies, two of them in particular – in the same way that some colours are a blend of other colours. The creative energy is a blend of the sensitive and mental energies; the dedicated energy is a blend of the sensitive and dynamic energies. Hence, at the level of feeling, the creative, sensitive and dedicated energies will most likely dominate – these three types are the most effective mediators of love.

The other energy types – dynamic, mental, analytical and practical – are also present at the level of feeling but, because they are the energies with the least connection to the sensitive energy, rather than facilitate the flow of love, they are most likely to impede love and present emotional challenges. This will become apparent below when we examine the seven feeling types in more detail.

Another general point is that our emotional life will be more or less mature, with an immature feeling type having a less harmonious experience of the world. We each face the psychosynthetic task of balancing our emotional life – with each of the seven feeling types facing a different task, so identifying our feeling type is essential.

It should also be noted that qualities from the other psychological levels can influence and colour the experience of our feeling type. Hence, when seeking to identify our feeling type it is important to consider which qualities seem fundamental to who we are, and which qualities are secondary and therefore perhaps caused by the influence of our dominant types at the other levels.

With these basic principles in place, let's take a close look at the seven feeling types. Consider which of the types you resonate with most strongly – and which seem to describe the people in your life. I will begin each description with a quote from Assagioli to set the scene.

The dynamic feeling type

Using the term "will type", Assagioli (1983: 19) says of the dynamic feeling type: "In his emotional sphere, the will type is decidedly introverted. He inhibits all displays of emotion and feeling, since he regards them as obstacles and dangers to the efficiency of his actions and the one-pointedness of his aims."

Basic temperament and love language: Your dominant dynamic temperament gives you an aura of strength and authority, as well as firm and clear boundaries. Because you keep people at a distance, you can appear reserved and secretive, even intimidating. You tend to repress vulnerable feelings because you see them as a sign of weakness and prefer to have your emotions under control.

In your relationships you need to feel strong and free. You are attracted to other independent people. You prefer relationships where there is an element of competition and where you don't feel the need to wear kid gloves. You want to develop your strengths, so a good partner for

Temperament and love language	Dominant temperament, reserved, wilful, controlled, free, short and sharp, respectful, focused on status, courageous.
Sensitivity and relationships	Not very sensitive, loyal, supportive, help to self-help. *Distortion:* Clumsy, oppressive, controlling, shy, closed-off.
Desire strategies and defence mechanisms	Strong drive, goal-orientated, eliminating fear, nerves of steel, aiming for greatness. *Distortion:* Explosive, ruthless, warring, proud, isolated.

you would be someone who can point out your weaknesses and help you to fix them.

You want power and respect, and you set about getting this in a courageous manner, being thick-skinned and willing to stand up for yourself – all qualities of the dynamic feeling type. You are a warrior at heart and see the world as a battlefield in which the strongest take hold of the best opportunities.

Sensitivity and relationships:
Your sensitivity is under-developed, which means you are often unaware of other people's feelings. Because of your emotional illiteracy, when it comes to romance you can be like a bull in a china shop. But you are loyal and trustworthy and will fight for those you love. You show your love through being respectful, loyal and reliable in a crisis.

Your strong emotional life can be domineering, giving you a tendency to control your partner. You have a strong sense of others' weaknesses and tend to use this against them. You can easily end a relationship once it has served its purpose and can cut ties without a second thought, like a gardener disposing of weeds.

You tend to express love by giving gifts and other outward displays of affection. Because of your shyness you tend to isolate yourself so that even those who are closest to you may not know who you really are. You are out of your comfort zone when loved ones need some TLC. But what they can count on is your strength and your ability to help people help themselves.

Desire strategies and defence mechanisms: You have a strong emotional drive and can be ruthless to get what you want. You are so strong you could even end an addiction through sheer will power.

You have nerves of steel and are willing to engage in risky behaviour. You can use reason to suppress your feelings, but your emotions will eventually erupt like a volcano. You are sensitive to any challenge to your self-esteem or status and you can retaliate disproportionately when defending yourself.

Your basic defence is to isolate yourself. You pride yourself on being self-sufficient, but this go-it-alone toughness can be counter-productive. You desire recognition and authority but find it difficult to engage with people. You are a warrior, with great power, but this power must be used carefully because it could make or break you.

Psychosynthetic task: *Develop* your courage and stoic emotional presence. *Control* your tendency to suppress your feelings because you need them to give you valuable information and support. *Harmonise* your emotional life by learning to share your feelings in a mature way, which others will see as a sign of strength.

Can you turn your feelings off and on at will?

The sensitive feeling type

Using the term "love type", Assagioli (1983: 30) says of the sensitive feeling type: "The emotions, as we might expect, become the centre of attention and of vital energy for the majority of those who belong to the love type. Passionate and romantic love, often mixed in varying proportions, tends to be their principle interest in life."

Seven Feeling Types

Basic temperament and love language: Your temperament is calm and sensitive, which makes you open and receptive. You are very at home with feelings and have a knack for distinguishing their many shades and nuances. You enjoy having a warm, kind and loving connection to the world, and you tend to create such an atmosphere through your accepting and inclusive nature, with your mere presence often being enough to achieve this.

Temperament and love language	Calm and sensitive temperament, open, receptive, accepting, intimate, seeking union, loving, caring, warm.
Sensitivity and relationships	Hypersensitive, considerate, delicate, receptive, positive, healing. *Distortion:* Poor boundaries, easily exploited, suffering, fearful, dependent.
Desire strategies and defence mechanisms	Calm, empathetic, friendly, innocent, patient, resilient, peaceful. *Distortion:* Manipulative, martyr, hopeless, isolation.

You have a strong desire to express and receive love; you cannot live without human contact, which opens your emotional life like a flower. You have a tendency to surrender to love which, through identification, can cause you to become merged with those you are closest to. Therefore, this capacity for love and empathy are both your greatest gift and greatest liability.

Mutual care and physical presence are important in your relationships, and you attain this through empathy and warmth. You build bridges, bring people together, lower their defences and heal their wounds.

Sensitivity and relationships: Because of your porous boundaries and strong desire to feel connected, you can often feel invaded. You have a delicate sensitivity – even hypersensitivity – and a suggestibility which means you are often in need of protection: people can take advantage of you, so having a sharp mind is necessary so you can set boundaries.

You gain a sense of security from the people, places and things you are attached to, but clinging onto them could hold you back and prevent you from growing. You should also be wary of your strong desire to be loved and to be popular, which can lead to you making unhealthy compromises.

You relate to others easily, picking up on their feelings and identifying with their pain, which can be a source of great suffering. This ability to accept and enter into emotions makes you an adept carer and healer: you are able to absorb negative emotions and transform them with love to create a positive atmosphere.

Desire strategies and defence mechanisms: You move towards your goals with calmness and a sense of responsibility. When you are set on a goal, you have a patience and endurance that surpasses the other types. You also have an instinct for opportunities.

You are kind and inoffensive and averse to conflict. You attract what you need because you are friendly, sympathetic and attentive. More than anything else, it is your need for love and understanding that motivates you. You help and protect the vulnerable, creating peaceful atmospheres so that people can find shelter. You avoid extremes, preferring to maintain a peaceful atmosphere.

Your sweet nature can be gently manipulative: you can use your innocence and vulnerability in ways that make others feel obliged to give you what you want.

Your vulnerability makes you sensitive to emotional outbursts and you can be thin-skinned when faced with hostility. Your hypersensitivity might cause you to avoid others, even to isolate yourself, and this will cause you great suffering. The solution is for you to work hard on setting boundaries, which is difficult for you but necessary if you are to protect yourself from other people's feelings and behaviour. You rarely react in ways that lead to a breakdown in the relationship, preferring to express your disappointment with others inwardly in the form of sadness and depression. By not asking outright for what you want, you can tend to become a victim.

Psychosynthetic task: *Develop* your capacity for empathy and calmness.

Control your tendency to become absorbed and overly-identified with other people's emotions. *Harmonise* your emotional life by setting clear boundaries where necessary.

Are you a calm, soft and warm-hearted person who creates good relations?

The mental feeling type

Using the term "practical" type, Assagioli (1983: 41) says of the mental feeling type: "In the subjective field, in the complexity of the life of feeling, in matters that require psychic sensitivity and in flights of aesthetic imagination, the practical type tends to be obtuse, perplexed or simply uninterested. These functions are generally dull or undeveloped in him. The 'feminine' aspect of the psyche, changeable and plastic, is an impenetrable mystery to him"

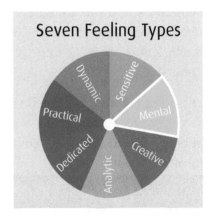

Basic temperament and love language: This is a complex feeling type because reason and feeling are often in conflict, which makes for restless, turbulent emotions. Your temperament is active, even nervous. Consequently, you tend to feel safe when you are on the move or when circumstances are changing rapidly. Indeed, being open to external influences means you will often be subject to sudden changes in direction.

When at your best, your emotional life is guided by reason and you can articulate your feelings concisely. You could even formulate a philosophy of emotion, differentiating precisely between different nuances of feeling. This is possible because your thoughts can control your emotions and you can intellectualise your feelings. As a result, you can find it difficult to really *feel* your feelings.

In a romantic relationship, it is important for you to talk about your emotions because this is how you become aware of what you feel. You enjoy this experience because you are a master at speaking words of love. For you, friendship is a vital quality in a romantic relationship, so it is essential that your partner shares your interests and values.

Sensitivity and relationships: Guided by reason, you can be unaware of other people's emotions. You want to know how to react but you rarely sense other people's feelings. Some people may see you as unreliable.

You can't commit to a relationship unless you are completely sure of it. You prefer relationships where there is enough freedom for you to pursue outside interests. Your relationships are informed by agreed rules and values.

You might desire many intimate relationships and aim for quantity, not quality. As long as a relationship serves a purpose, you will put energy into it. You rarely just "hang out" – you prefer relationships where you are engaged in an activity or have an objective of some kind. You focus on the present moment – for you, being out of sight means being out of mind. You may shower your significant other with showy gifts that say as much about your status as your degree of affection.

You are good at forming relationships as long as they are based on explicit rules and common interests. This is your relational style.

Temperament and love language	Restless and active temperament, changeable, communicative, friendship.
Sensitivity and relationships	Unaware, insensitive, quantity, non-committal, materialistic. *Distortion:* Superficial, calculating, unreliable.
Desire strategies and defence mechanisms	Strategic, flexible, intelligent. *Distortion:* Making excuses, lying, twisting the truth, calculating, irrational, splitting.

Desire strategies and defence mechanisms: You approach what you want strategically, exploring opportunities without giving too much away. You calculate your thoughts and feelings, weighing pros and cons, like a lawyer in court. This tendency for calculation can lead to the belief that money can buy you love.

Because of your shifting desires, you like to leave room for manoeuvre, so you tend to avoid emotional involvement and long-term commitment. You want one thing one moment and something else the next, with your restless desires and flighty emotions pulling in different directions.

To defend against feelings that are difficult for you, you use excuses and white lies which sow confusion so that no-one knows the truth, not even you. You also defend against feelings by rationalising them, which can cause a split in your psyche, giving rise to irrational outbursts and incomprehensible reactions. Because of the unpredictable nature of your feelings, and your difficulty in handling them, you tend to avoid intimacy. Your challenge is to develop a more positive and mature relationship with your feelings.

Psychosynthetic task: *Develop* your capacity for emotional flexibility and your understanding of complex emotions. *Control* your tendency for being superficial and non-committal. *Harmonise* your emotional nature by becoming aware of your long-term needs and values.

Are you the sensible type, always on the run?

The creative feeling type

Using the term "aesthetic" type, Assagioli (1983: 53) says of the creative feeling type: "The emotional life of this type is very active and often leads to a lack of equilibrium. These individuals are very changeable; they often swing between extremes of optimism and pessimism, times of vitality and uncontrolled happiness alternating with others of discouragement and despair."

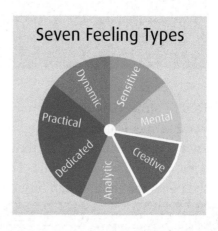

Basic temperament and love language: Because your temperament is influenced by your aesthetic sensibilities, you are the most colourful feeling type. You crave beauty, harmony and a rich variety of experiences. You express spontaneous joy and are playful, but you are also sensitive to pain and suffering. Your temper responds so quickly to nuances of harmony and disharmony that you are often pulled in different directions.

You are generally comfortable with your emotions, but they do tend to conflict because your emotional life is very polarised. You can move easily from one extreme to another, from love to hatred, joy to sorrow. Your lively, changeable emotional life demands a rich variety of experiences. Your curiosity and thirst for experience gives rise to a considerable emotional repertoire.

Temperament and love language	Colourful, craving beauty, receptive, polarised, rich emotional life, expressive, harmony through conflict, humour, lightness, honesty, erotic.
Sensitivity and relationships	Empathy, sensitive, creating harmony, experimentation. *Distortion:* Dramatic, self-obsessed, creating conflict, changeable mood, seductive.
Desire strategies and defence mechanisms	Charming, attraction. *Distortion:* Manipulative, chaotic, avoidant.

You demand honesty in your relationships and cannot abide excuses or rationalisation. You want authentic connections with people who tell it like it is. Beauty and harmony are essential and you will go to great lengths to experience them, even putting up with conflict. Erotic love is important and you can be something of a flirt. If you are met with humour and spontaneous play, you can be very cooperative.

Sensitivity and relationships: Your sensitivity gives you access to emotional energy. If emotionally mature, your understanding of other people's feelings will allow you to accept even aggressive and destructive elements. Being able to sense the source of a conflict means you are well placed to be able to help restore balance, providing what is needed to create harmony. On the other hand, if you don't get your way you can be a drama queen. You like to be the centre of attention, even if it means starting an argument to achieve this. Creating conflict is sometimes the best remedy for you, as a means to achieve harmony. Hence, conflict is not necessarily a distortion. Those who work with conflict resolution know you must bring the opposing energies into the light before peace can become an option. This is why the creative energy is said to deal with "harmony through conflict".

Relationships with you are something of a rollercoaster ride. Your moods go up and down, which can be a strain on others, but at least it isn't boring. Accepting your mood swings will make it easier for you to manage them. You are in your element in emotionally-charged atmospheres because of the sudden shifts in mood. When you are emotionally mature, one of your beautiful qualities in a relationship is your willingness to keep going through thick and thin. But you find beauty to be a temptation, so you can be flirtatious and unstable, imagining that the grass is greener on the other side of the fence.

Desire strategies and defence mechanisms: You use your charm and beauty to get what you want, creating the impression that will benefit you the most. You know what people want to hear and this makes you very attractive; through flattery you appeal to their vanity.

You feel inner conflict around your true desires. You want peace and security but also crave the excitement of taking risks. This friction can cause you great suffering that could take years to resolve.

When there is friction you can become defensive, with a tendency to overreact, which can make you unpredictable. But you can often ignore

friction and enjoy yourself in spite of it – even when life gets messy, you can throw your hands up in the air and walk away. Your biggest challenge is to grow up and take responsibility for yourself without losing touch with your inner child. But you really shouldn't worry: having a varied emotional life means you are usually able to make the most of a situation and you will invariably land on your feet.

Psychosynthetic task: *Develop* your capacity for emotional insight and for expressing a wide range of subtle feelings. *Control* your tendency to let your emotions run away with you due to your vivid imagination. *Harmonise* your emotional life by disciplining your volatile temperament: you do not need to express everything you feel in public.

Are you a changeable feeling type person, full of smiles and spontaneous joy?

The analytical feeling type

Using the term "scientific" type, Assagioli (1983: 61) says of the analytical feeling type: "In his emotions, the scientific type seems to be cold, insensitive and even inhuman and cruel. Often he shows a curious inability to feel and express human sentiment or tenderness, and in having such a lack of elementary sensitivity he exhibits the indifference and coldness of the vivisector.

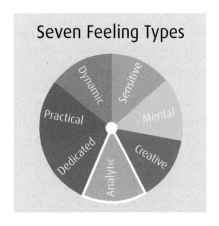

However, if we study him more carefully, we find that in many cases this is due to the fact that all his capacity for feeling and devotion, all his love – and it can be great – are directed towards *impersonal* objects."

Temperament and love language	Bland emotional life, controlled, cold, dry, neutral, ascetic, simple, predictable.
Sensitivity and relationships	Reduced sensitivity, emotional control, analysing, fair. *Distortion:* Anxious, fearful, compulsive, isolated, frozen, split.
Desire strategies and defence mechanisms	Careful, indirect, punish or reward. *Distortion:* Restricted, clumsy, conflicted, rigid, frozen

Basic temperament and love language: This is a complex feeling type because your need to be in control serves to obscure your temperament, meaning it's difficult for people to get a sense of what you're really like.

You live a simple, almost ascetic, life that is focused on your interests, and this creates the stability and security you need. You are cool, dry and objective and a creature of habit. You like order and routine. Personal relationships, especially romantic ones, are not your strong point.

A solitary life may suit you best, but a simple life shared with a significant other could also be agreeable. Sharing practical tasks – any creative work with visible results – would serve as a bond. In this way, love for you would involve helping each other in a practical sense to meet life's challenges.

Sensitivity and relationships: For you, feelings are so fleeting they can't be used as a

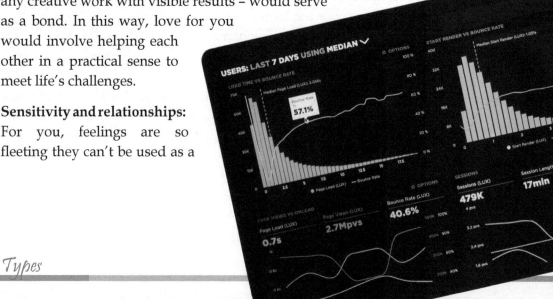

foundation from which to build your life. Consequently, because you do not trust your feelings, you are not at your best where sensitivity is required. In fact, your need to inhibit your sensitivity and control your emotions can cause you to become anxious or compulsive – when this happens, your strong sense of rationality means your neurotic behaviour will strike you as inexplicable.

You find it difficult to relate to people emotionally, and romantic relations are a complete mystery. You fear the loss of control that true intimacy entails. To avoid this, you tend to analyse your feelings until there is nothing left of them. This is the key danger for the analytical type – when your natural inclination to analyse gets out of control it turns your emotional life into a desert.

Your relationship style is based on a model of reward and punishment. This helps to give you a sense of control which helps to prevent you from being overwhelmed by your emotions, which is linked to a fear of abandonment. But because you value logic, you try to be fair and objective in your relationships.

Desire strategies and defence mechanisms: When it comes to romance, you approach the person you desire carefully, having analysed the risks thoroughly in advance – you would rarely make a direct approach. This is partly because you are unsure of your feelings, but also because you want to avoid the risk of embarrassment.

When trying to express your emotional needs you become inhibited and clumsy. You prefer to make your feelings known indirectly, trying to get what you want without having to ask for it. This approach rarely works and often leaves you feeling worse. You are drawn to the more emotional types, especially the sensitive type – this is because, while you may repress your own sensitivity, you know this is exactly what you need.

A rigid emotional life is bound to produce conflict and resistance within. On the surface you may seem frozen and stiff, with no apparent emotion, but outbursts of irrational fears and wild desires show what's bubbling beneath the surface. These eruptions only reinforce your need for control and your determination to take a rational approach to your emotional life. Your emotional potential is therefore limited, but your objectivity and reasonableness ensure you will be a fair person.

Psychosynthetic task: *Develop* your ability to be honest and fair in your emotional life. *Control* your tendency to over-analyse your feelings. *Harmonise* your feelings by sharing them with the world. Give space for the irrational when attending to your emotional needs.

Are you the cool, reserved feeling type that prefers a simple and practical emotional life?

The dedicated feeling type

Using the term "devotional" type, Assagioli (1983: 70) says of the dedicated feeling type: "As we can easily imagine, the devotional type is intensely emotional. His feelings are often passionate and extravagant. He loves a person or an ideal up to the point of veneration and opposes, and often hates, with equal force whatever is set against it."

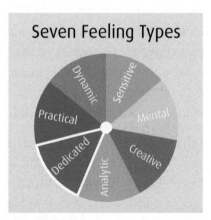

Seven Feeling Types

Basic temperament and love language: You have a potent and intense temperament, which makes for strong likes and dislikes. You can get carried away by passions that blind you. When you want something, your desire can turn into an addiction. You are loyal and persevering,

Temperament and love language	Intense temperament, either/or, loyalty, idealisation, dedicated, fighting spirit, supportive, happy, faithful.
Sensitivity and relationships	Powerful sensitivity, devoted, tender, caring, simple. *Distortion:* Fiery, violent, blind.
Desire strategies and defence mechanisms	Direct, resilient, focused, aspiring, devoted. *Distortion:* Primitive, idolising, unrealistic, thin-skinned, exaggeration.

with a fighting spirit. When your emotions are focused on an ideal, you feel confident, like an expert canoeist negotiating a wild river.

Your emotions are so powerful that sometimes you feel you are sitting on a volcano. But when you learn to master these strong emotional forces you will have great power at your disposal. Your enthusiasm and dedication infects those around you, lifting their spirits and giving them hope; being a powerful motivator is your greatest personal asset.

Sharing common goals with your partner is essential for your love life. You are focused on the future and are in search of a partner who can accompany you on this journey. You are devoted, passionate and appreciate clear expressions of love. You want to be your partner's sole focus, which means you will tend to avoid cool, distant types. Loyalty and fidelity are very important for you.

Sensitivity and relationships: You find it easy to show affection, tenderness and care for those who are important to you. You are highly sensitive, but unlike the sensitive and creative types, subtle nuances of emotion pass you by, however you make up for this with the depth

of your engagement. You are a friend for life who will risk anything for those you care for. You can also lose yourself by getting swallowed up in your concern for others. Your joy and enthusiasm energise and uplift your relationships, and this is your most precious gift.

You have a tendency to idealise your partner, so you need to remember that you are in love with a real person, not an ideal, which could lead to an unreasonable disappointment with your partner. Your tendency to relate to your ideal image of your loved ones is also potentially dangerous when it comes to children because children must be allowed to grow in their own image and not into your idealised image.

Desire strategies and defence mechanisms: You go straight for what you want and can be quite fierce about it, which can be an effective if primitive approach. You don't waste time cutting to the chase. Sophistication is not your strongest suit. Your interest is focused on whatever you see in your partner that is good and positive. You recognise potential in people and situations, and this allows you to grasp opportunities.

At times, you will feel crushed with disappointment when you have to admit that reality doesn't match up to your projected idealisations. When the bubble bursts you feel disillusioned, but you will always pick yourself up again: there is always a new cause worth fighting for or someone new to love.

Your devotion to what is good, true and beautiful is perhaps your most admirable quality. You are even willing to sacrifice yourself for the cause if necessary. You can handle extremes. The thing that hurts you the most is betrayal, which can turn passionate love into icy rejection in an instant.

You can become fiercely defensive if your values, freedom or love are threatened. You take things personally and are quick to feel offended. If you want to mature, you must learn to master your reactions, to think before you act. Your emotions are subject to stormy weather – if you want clear skies, you will need to learn how to accommodate your emotions.

You have a virile Arabian stallion at your disposal. The question is: who is riding whom?

Psychosynthetic task: *Develop* your capacity for sincerity and a pure heart. *Control* your tendency to be intense and fanatical in your devotion. *Harmonise* your emotional life by taking in other perspectives so that you can let go of your obsessions.

Are you a passionate feeling type who gets carried away with excitement?

The practical feeling type

Seven Feeling Types

Using the term "organisational-ritualistic" type, Assagioli (1983: 82) says of the practical feeling type: "He tends to be completely ruled by habit which he follows with complacent obstinacy, since he is often proud and over-sure of himself. Therefore, he tends to be emotionally arid and lacks tact in his relations with others. His overvaluation of ceremony and form makes him rigid and bigoted in religion as well. But in contrast to the devotional [dedicated] type, he has neither fanaticism nor apostolic zeal."

Basic temperament and love language: Your emotional life is well-organised and disciplined, as we would expect from someone of your type. Since the practical type also contains a sensitive element, you are more sensitive than the dynamic, mental and analytical types, but if the situation demands it you can override your feelings. Your emotional life is controlled and purposeful and your responses are usually appropriate to the situation – a good example of this is Japanese culture.

Your need for control keeps you on an even keel, with little variation in emotion, such that some may find you cool and calculating. Because you regulate your emotional life, you need rules, stability and predictability. You need to appear to be in control – having clear career goals and an orderly lifestyle, with all finances in place, suits you the best.

In your love life, you like relationships to be built on clearly defined boundaries and expectations. The legality of the marriage contract

Temperament and love language	Organised and practical temperament, disciplined, wilful, controlled, structured, focused on status, stability, formality, elegance, materialistic.
Sensitivity and relationships	Calm and balanced sensitivity, responsible, stable, faithful. _Distortion:_ Cool, formal, stiff, obsessive.
Desire strategies and defence mechanisms	Planning, strategic, practical, controlled. _Distortion:_ Repressive, calculating, rigid, unimaginative.

appeals to you – you enjoy the status and the stability that it brings. In your relationship, you are an attractive successful couple with a good reputation, and you want the world to know that you have these qualities. Formality is important to you, as are elegance and luxury, and you express your love with gifts that convey your sense of status.

Sensitivity and relationships: You are sensitive, calm and balanced. You act fairly based on agreed rules. Because you enjoy responsibility and the control it brings, commitment is not a problem for you.

You are a stable, faithful companion, able to deal with financial matters with your hand tightly on the purse strings. For some people, this will make you seem formal, cool and something of a bore.

You respond to difficulties in your relationship by adopting compulsive behaviour, such as rituals that you act out stiffly, with exaggerated correctness. This is how you control unwanted emotions. You have an eye for detail, which allows you to analyse emotions, but your approach tends to be overly rational, which is usually not appreciated.

Desire strategies and defence mechanisms: You tend to hide your desires and make plans to fulfil them without letting your true motives be known. You've learned to be practical and pragmatic in pursuing your goals.

To avoid complications, you like to keep things under control and suppress your emotions until you have reached your goal – then you can celebrate, though moderately, of course. Even when extremes are justified you will avoid them because it's simply not done.

You are cool, rational and stick to the facts when challenged. Rules help you to manoeuvre, and when they no longer work you find new ones. You operate well within any system and handle conflict by referring to the rule book, which will tend to make you rigid and unimaginative. You will go to any length to maintain your sense of control, and your emotional life must simply adjust to this.

Psychosynthetic task: *Develop* your elegant and courteous temperament. *Control* your tendency to be too attached to rules, routines and rituals. *Harmonise* your emotional life by giving yourself space to be loose and informal in your relationships.

Are you a reserved, elegant type who controls your feeling?

Exercise: How do you react in situations of conflict, especially when you think you're right?

The following statements will give you an indication of what type you are. Choose those you identify with the most, but ask someone who knows you well to verify your answers.

These statements have been carefully worded to include reference to the motivators that underlie the different feeling types, so please take care that you can agree with all aspects of a statement before selecting it.

1. I can become dramatic, creating chaos in my efforts to reach a balanced solution.
2. I can become enraged and show my anger because it's obvious that I'm right.
3. I argue rationally and sensibly in a way that highlights the fairness in my argument.
4. I look people straight in the eye and tell them, without emotion and with all my authority, that I will not give in.
5. I stick to facts. I can prove I'm right and that is why I stick to my argument.
6. I am friendly and empathetic when I listen to someone's point of view and hope we can arrive at a mutually-acceptable solution.
7. I'm an attentive listener but can respond with long arguments to prove I'm right.
8. I weigh the pros and cons and seek to reach a compromise.
9. I go directly to the heart of a conflict, control my emotions, and focus on the other person's weaknesses.
10. I'm sure I'm right and do not move an inch.
11. I listen to all the arguments then try to find a practical and pragmatic solution.
12. I gain an overview of all the opposing arguments then challenge the other person strategically.
13. I absorb the emotion of a conflict and try to hold it in, but I will start crying if this proves too difficult for me.
14. I focus on contracts, rules and routine, and use common sense.

Try matching each of the statements with the different feeling types before checking the footnote[1].

---

[1] Statements (the number in brackets is the feeling type, where 1-dynamic, 2-sensitive, 3-mental, 4-creative, 5-analytical, 6-dedicated, 7-practical): 1.(4), 2.(6), 3.(5), 4.(1), 5.(5), 6.(2), 7.(3), 8.(4), 9.(1), 10.(6), 11.(7), 12.(3), 13.(2), 14.(7)

Your physicality
– The seven body types

While many of us are mindful to look after our physical well-being, we may not be aware of our body's psychological and spiritual significance. But when we consider that human consciousness is structured like a pyramid (Figure 29), it can be seen that the body is the foundation upon which our whole psyche is built. Before anything else, our being and presence in the world relies on our physicality – our brain and nervous system. It is our physical being that is most prominent in our psyche when we come into the world, becoming the basis, or foundation stone, of all that we become. In developmental terms, our first learning experiences are centred on our body and how our body is treated. As we grow, our body retains its significance, with all of our psychological and spiritual qualities being expressed through the body in one way or another.

The body is our tool in the physical world; the body makes it possible for us to experience the outside world and to act in it. The degree of vitality in our body – meaning the amount of physical energy we can access, manifest and express through physical action – is part of what determines our impact in the world. By contrast, when we lack vitality – for example, when we are physically unwell – our capacity for action is limited, which affects our mental well-being.

Our body type is determined by which of the seven energies is dominant at the level of the body. It is through our body type that the four other psychological levels are able to manifest in the world through action and activity. The seven body types possess different degrees of vitality which means that, although all body types are prone to ill health, some body types are more resistant to illness than others. The seven body types affect us in other ways too. For example, for those with a *slow inert body*, it will take a lot of effort to try something new and giving up habits will be difficult; those with a *restless active body* will find it difficult to engage in peaceful activities, such as meditation; and those with a *weak vulnerable body* will find physically demanding tasks difficult.

Having bodies that are robust, flexible and active means we can take on creative and demanding

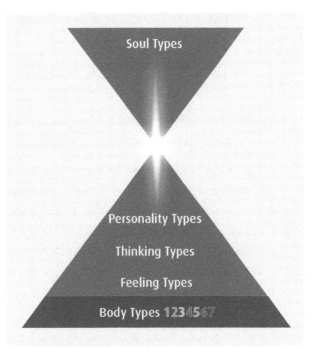

Figure 29. The Seven Body Types

tasks and create a materially secure life for ourselves. Also, having a body that can cope with the physical aspects of life is essential for the healthy functioning of the psyche at the other psychological levels (feeling, thought, personality, soul).

When we know our body type, with its qualities, strengths and weaknesses, then we can work to minimise the limitations of our physicality. Through coming to an understanding of our body type, we can know what we need to do to cooperate with our body and develop its potential.

Compared with the other psychological levels, our understanding of the level of the body is the least developed. However, our knowledge about the seven body types is growing. To date, our research has discerned the following three principles that we can identify and work with our body type:

1. **The body's constitution and appearance:** Each body type has a distinct physical presence.

2. **The behaviour of the body:** Each body type will function and behave in particular ways.

3. **The body's way of recharging (vitality):** Each body type will have preferred methods for restoring its energy.

The most common body types are the mental and the practical, both of which are robust and effective in dealing with the physical world. The dynamic body type also has a strong constitution. The sensitive, creative, analytical and dedicated body types are less common and are associated with a number of challenges, as will become apparent in the descriptions below.

An important point to note is that the body's constitution and behaviour can be greatly influenced – positively or negatively – by the dominant types at other psychological levels. For example, a rigid inflexible dynamic body can be softened by a flexible creative thinking type or personality type. This mixture of influences means we must be very careful when seeking to determine our body type.

As with previous chapters, I will draw upon Assagioli's wisdom in describing the types. It is important to note that Assagioli is not referring specifically to the body type, rather he is describing how the seven types express themselves in a general physical sense.

The dynamic body type

Using the term "will" type, Assagioli (1983: 19) describes how the dynamic type manifests physically: "At the physical level, the will type is characterised by *prompt and decisive action, courage, the power to conquer, rule and dominate* both physical surroundings and other men, with a tendency to *competitiveness* and even to *violence* and *destructiveness*."

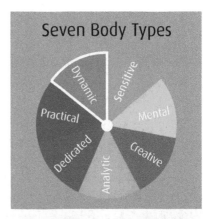

Seven Body Types

Constitution and appearance: Your body is often strong with long limbs. You will feel strong regardless of the size of your muscles. You are tall or of medium height, with a sinewy body and a radiance of strength. You rarely become fat or overweight due to your natural disposition for dynamic activity. You feel discomfort if you cannot move around freely. Because your immune system is strong you are able to shake off disease so you are rarely ill. Your physical radiance is intense, almost electric, and always ready to face challenges and struggles. Hugging you is like hugging a tree. You value your personal space and prefer not to be touched by strangers. You crave freedom of movement and don't like restrictive clothes or surroundings.

Your body's behaviour: Your body tends to be rigid, inflexible and a little uncoordinated. Your fine motor skills are not great. Your movements can be sudden and cause you to bump into things. Dynamic energy tends to stiffen, so your muscles will be tense and stiff unless you keep

Constitution	Strong, resilient, intense, sinewy, stiff, square.
The body's behaviour	Quick, dynamic activity, goal-orientated, resourceful, disciplined. *Distortion:* Rigid, uncoordinated movements, impatient, isolated.
Recharging vitality	Time alone, physical challenges, sunshine, fresh air, nature.

your body flexible. Your body is often in defence mode, which means your range of movement will be reduced to simple and basic gestures, such as giving someone directions by simply pointing a finger.

The head is the focus of your body because the will is expressed through the brain's frontal lobes. You act purposefully and instinctively. You tackle tasks head on and organise yourself efficiently to accomplish your goal.

Your body responds to directness, tangible results, routine and simplicity, but you don't like monotony or habits that restrict change and progress. You prefer order, but often create disorder because you have a tendency to ignore details. You are impatient, for example being the sort of person who would rip wrapping paper off a present rather than open it carefully.

Your body is inclined towards a simple way of life. Too much stuff slows you down, so you relinquish anything unnecessary to free up energy for action. In pursuing your goals, you can overlook your body's need for food and rest. Your body can be easily disciplined, responding well to hard work-outs. You eat fast, almost devouring food like a predator with its prey, but you can also be subtle when other sides of your nature help to moderate your dynamic tendencies.

Body's way of recharging vitality: You enjoy having time on your own to recharge your batteries, but you can also recharge in a public space as long as you can tune out of the environment. Challenging sports also invigorate you. Sunshine, fresh air and nature are other sources of vitality.

Psychosynthetic task: *Develop* your capacity for sustaining a vital and strong physical body through strenuous physical exercise. *Control* your tendency to become stiff and inflexible. *Harmonise* your body with stretching and gentle touch.

The sensitive body type

Using the term "love" type, Assagioli (1983: 28) described how the sensitive type manifests physically:

"On the physical level, the love type can exhibit strong sexual impulses. I say 'can' for it would be a great error to presume that it is always so. In many cases the element of love is directed towards physical objects such as money or property of all kinds; or else it is expressed through the mind or the emotions rather than the body. Because of this there are many people of the love type who are very little developed sexually."

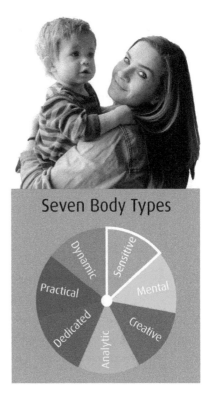

Seven Body Types

Constitution	Small, round, delicate, overweight, hypersensitive, need for protection.
The body's behaviour	Introverted, calm, resilient, loving. *Distortion:* Inactive, passive, lazy, fearful.
Recharging vitality	In company of people you love, sunshine, water, fresh air, nature.

Constitution and appearance: This body type is not particularly robust in dealing with practical life and is rather uncommon. The sensitive energy is related to fat and has a need for sugar and rest, so your body will tend to be round and perhaps a bit overweight.

You have a delicate hypersensitive body. The physical world is almost too much for you and you tend to be allergy-prone. Changes in the weather and environmental factors, such as traffic and noisy people, can deplete you. You need to feel protected in a soft and warm environment.

The body's behaviour: You tend to be passive and perhaps a bit lazy. The world is a bit too harsh to move around in. People with this body type tend to hide in self-made caves, usually a comfy bed with hot drinks and pets.

You do not like hard work or anything that requires a great deal of effort. You do not like strenuous exercise, preferring a walk in the woods, preferably by a stream. You have a need for comfort and comfortable surroundings where you can relax while working at a pace that is nourishing for you. Your body can be resilient to illness when the circumstances are right.

Physical intimacy is important and you love to touch and be touched. Your nervous system is receptive to tenderness, which helps to relieve stress. Your sensitivity causes you to fear pain, which limits your movement because you are afraid of getting hurt when moving around. You are receptive to bad energy in public spaces, which increases your sense of discomfort. The world can be too much for someone with your sensitivity.

You enjoy different kinds of food and take your time when eating. You are picky and concerned about food quality. It is important that food is prepared hygienically, and you drink a lot of water to help your body hydrate and detox.

You need to be careful with medicine. In particular, you are vulnerable to addiction so you should avoid painkillers and sleeping pills or using sugar as a form of self-medication. You would do well to access more robust energies from the other psychological levels to help overcome your vulnerabilities.

To avoid imbalances, your body needs the discipline of a careful diet, healthy habits and loving care.

Your body's way of recharging vitality: You recharge by being with people you love and by losing yourself in your studies. A good hug is healing for you, as is contact with water due to your body's affinity with this element.

Psychosynthetic task: *Develop* your capacity for a gentle and sensitive physical presence. *Control* your tendency to become lazy and addicted to substances. *Harmonise* your physical body through rituals and a healthy diet.

The mental body type

Assagioli (1983: 40) describes how the mental type manifests physically:

"Men and women in whom this specific quality predominates are intensely practical. They have an innate ability to manipulate matter and bend it to many uses. They often have a great manual ability and are clever and successful in constructing or repairing objects. They find themselves at ease in the external world which for them is 'real' and engrossing."

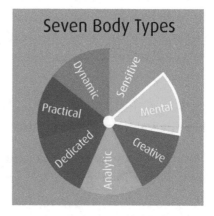

Constitution and appearance: This is one of the most common body types: an intelligent body, well adjusted for physical, practical life.

This type is adaptable and comes in all sorts of shapes and sizes, but tends to be strong, muscular, robust and not very refined. You are a workhorse, highly resilient, built to be on the move and active. Your appearance will often be "normal", meaning the "average" for your race and culture.

Constitution	Strong and robust, compact, muscular, adaptable, many shapes, grounded.
The body's behaviour	High level of activity, quick movements, craving variety, skilled at multi-tasking, getting things done. *Distortion:* Restless, doing too much, stress.
Recharging vitality	Hobbies, conversations, sunshine, fresh air, nature.

Your body is practical and interacts well with the physical world; you are grounded. You dress functionally and practically, not paying much attention to fashion or aesthetics unless you are influenced by other psychological types, such as the creative or practical. You prefer to blend in with the crowd so you follow the dress code most typical in your environment.

Many athletes, craftsmen and others who work with their body have this body type. Your coordination is good, you are adaptable, and the practical world of rituals, habits and daily routine is comfortable for you.

The body's behaviour: Your body requires a great deal of activity; you often feel restless. You benefit from moving around and being active in your environment. Being an active participant in your community gives you energy; like a worker bee, you are constantly gathering nutrients and coordinate your activities with the hive.

You don't like sitting down too much. Your movements are quick, and so are your gesticulations and speech. You need variety and change. You are probably good at multi-tasking, but have a tendency to spread yourself too thinly across many activities. Stress causes imbalances in your body.

You are grounded and can eat almost anything, which is good because you are curious about trying different foods and need variety in your diet. You don't have the same thing for breakfast every day.

You are well organised, but don't mind some mess as long as it doesn't interfere with your activities. Detail is not important providing things work out well as a whole. It doesn't matter much to you if something is beautiful, decent or well organised, as long as it works. Your intellectual and emotional life may need beauty, but your body can live without it.

Body's way of recharging vitality: You interact well with others and feel nourished by conversation and shared activity. You prefer doing things that are new, interesting or productive. Walking in the countryside, relaxing in the garden and other recreational activities are good for you.

Psychosynthetic task: *Develop* your capacity for perseverance and a durable physical life. *Control* your tendency to become stressed by resisting the temptation to plan too many activities. *Harmonise* your body by having mindful moments of stillness and inactivity.

The creative body type

Using the term "creative-artistic" type, Assagioli (1983: 52-53) describes how the creative type manifests physically:

"At the physical level, the individuals of the creative-artistic type demonstrate a fine appreciation of beauty and an excellent sense of colour and, in consequence, much

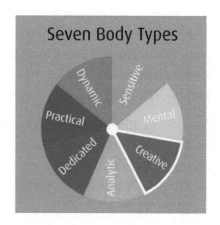

good taste. Their love for physical beauty and their desire to create tends to intensify their sexual desires and impulses. The manifestations of these impulses are generally refined; the expression of instinct is combined with a fascination with beauty and aesthetic qualities. This type tends to make a refined art of sexual love, and so of all other life processes."

Constitution and appearance: This body type is unusual and may present challenges unless it is tempered with different types at the other psychological levels.

Your creative energy makes your body petite, quick and thin. You may notice nervousness and tingling energies caused by your body's impressionability and changeability.

The creative energy is focused on harmony and beauty, and your body type can be beautiful with harmonic features and well-proportioned limbs. If you exercise and discipline your body it can become graceful, harmonious and beautiful. You probably enjoy decorating your body with colours and accessories that give you an unusual look.

Constitution	Petite, quick, beautiful proportions, sensitive, vulnerable.
The body's behaviour	Dramatic expression, musicality, dance, arts and crafts, balance, flexibility. *Distortion:* Restless, changing levels of activity, impulsive, chaotic, self-medicating to create harmony.
Recharging vitality	Routine, steady rhythms, beauty, colours, music, harmony, sunshine, fresh air, water, nature.

You are likely to face a number of challenges with your body unless you live a balanced physical life. The creative is one of the most fluctuating types and is vulnerable to stress, especially if you do not comply with your body's natural need for regular food, sleep and exercise.

You will be vulnerable to imbalances and disharmonies in your surroundings, which will affect your vitality and drain you of energy. Your body is not as robust as the other body types, especially the dynamic, mental and practical types.

The body's behaviour: Your body has great potential for drama and expressiveness. You love to dance and use your hands for doing something creative.

If your body is not disciplined or trained it may be prone to impulsive behaviour that can create chaos and disorder. Substance abuse is a real danger because your body wants harmony and will go to extremes to achieve this – and using substances to facilitate harmony can be an easy option, despite the dire consequences. Your body has the potential to express physical balance and flexibility or the extreme opposite, a worn-out depleted body.

A feeling of tingling restlessness and unease in your body is common, accompanied by quick movement, communication and gesticulation. These high levels of activity periodically cease – to be replaced with sudden physical fatigue, even paralysis, as a result of the conflicting needs of activity and rest.

You need balance but tend to lead an unstable and somewhat chaotic physical lifestyle that can cause your body to succumb to stress. When doing something new and exciting you will tend to skip a meal, which can cause you problems.

Your vulnerable and sensitive body type needs special care and a harmonious environment in order to function optimally and display its strength and flexibility.

Body's way of recharging vitality: Your body needs routine and a healthy and balanced diet to counteract an inclination towards impulsive behaviour that will waste your energy. Beauty recharges you, so colourful and beautiful surroundings, music and other harmonious influences are important. Sunshine, fresh air and nature are beneficial for you.

Psychosynthetic task: *Develop* your capacity for harmony and for having a graceful physical appearance. *Control* your tendency to favour restlessness and an irregular physical rhythm. *Harmonise* your body with a strict diet and discipline, setting boundaries for excessive physical activity.

The analytical body type

Using his own terminology of the "scientific" types, Assagioli (1983: 61) describes how the analytical type manifests physically:

"He is as fully alert to and acutely interested in the external world as

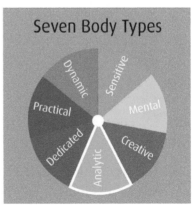

Seven Body Types

Constitution	Small to medium height, stiff, clumsy, uncoordinated, robust, resilient, isolated, compressed.
The body's behaviour	Slow actions, considered, methodical, ritualistic, habitual, hard working. *Distortion:* Rigid, obsessive, inflexible, keeping people at arm's length.
Recharging vitality	Withdrawn, stay in your cave, results give you energy, sunshine, fresh air, nature.

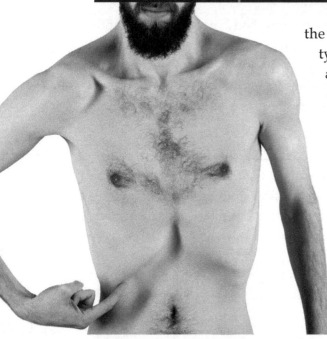

the active-practical [analytical] type but the motivations that arouse each one's interest are completely different. The motivation of the active type is to make good use of *things,* while the scientific type is interested in phenomena *per se,* in knowing the structure and function of the cosmic mechanism both in its broad sweep and in its tiny details."

Constitution and appearance: This is a somewhat uncommon body type. The analytical energy stiffens the body and impedes your freedom of movement.

Your body will probably be thin, small-to-medium sized and appear somewhat stiff, clumsy and uncoordinated. Your body type is compact and resilient but probably not typically beautiful. There is a tendency towards asceticism and simplicity, with a fondness for routine. You enjoy hard manual labour performed methodically.

As with the dynamic type, the analytical type tends to be hard, rigid and straight, but you lack the dynamic energy and athletic appearance of the dynamic, and have a tendency to withdraw or isolate yourself from your environment.

You are usually isolated and restricted in your body language. You don't like physical contact with those you don't know and find it difficult to open up to people and give hugs and physical comfort.

The body's behaviour: This body type tends to act slowly in a methodical, considered and mechanical fashion. You want to be in touch with the reality of the practical world. You are a creature of habit. Your body has a great capacity for hard work and concentration, but your dependency on rules and rituals can be obsessive – for example, you eat the same foods every day and go to bed at the same time. You thrive in predictable environments in which you can uphold your routines. You may have problems if your dominant types at other levels have different needs.

You like to have a simple diet – you could eat porridge with milk and sugar for breakfast for the rest of your life. The lack of variation in your diet may case vitamin and mineral deficiencies.

The body's way of recharging vitality: To recharge, you may need to withdraw into your cave, which could be in a basement or in a laboratory. You appreciate contact with nature, preferably in the mountains. You also recharge when you get work done.

Psychosynthetic task: *Develop* your capacity for a regulated and disciplined physical life. *Control* your tendency to become too attached to a minimalistic or rigid lifestyle. *Harmonise* your body through massages, hugs and close physical contact with gentle people.

The dedicated body type

Using the term "devotional" type, Assagioli (1983: 70) describes how the dedicated type manifests physically:

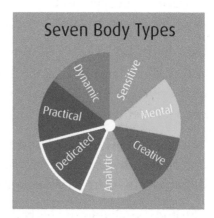

Seven Body Types

"The devotional type often has a severe and ascetic attitude to his body that, in many mystical devotees and religious people, is transformed into a hatred of it as an obstacle and an enemy to their spiritual ambitions. Consequently, they discipline and mortify it in the most drastic manner, at times to the extent of complete immolation."

Constitution and appearance: This body type tends to be large and plump, with weak muscle tone and a broad face. On the other hand, this type could sometimes have an ascetic body if the appetites have

Constitution	Large, plump, broad face, strong sexual desires.
The body's behaviour	Slow and uneasy movements, periods of passionate action followed by exhaustion, perspiring. *Distortion:* Conflicted impulses, hypersensitive, vulnerable, psychosomatic illnesses, addiction.
Recharging vitality	The countryside, by the sea, sunshine, fresh air, nature, dreams and fantasies.

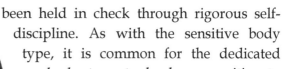

been held in check through rigorous self-discipline. As with the sensitive body type, it is common for the dedicated body type to be hypersensitive to conflict, noise and disharmony in the environment, which tends to prompt you to withdraw: too much activity exhausts you.

Deeply affected by your emotions, your energy levels can be erratic. On good days you will feel very energetic, on other days you will feel drained.

The dedicated body type is impacted by the sensitive and dynamic energies, and benefits in particular from drawing on the dynamic energy. The dedicated is an either/or type, with a tendency to polarise more than the other types. With so much fire in the system, this type tends to have powerful appetites – for food, sex, and so on – which can be difficult to control.

The body's behaviour: This body type moves slowly, giving up easily, losing breath quickly and perspiring heavily. This type is prone to addictions of all kinds. (It could be that some of those who use narcotics have this body type.)

The fire of desire in your constitution makes you move quickly, act passionately and, at times, behave compulsively.

Your body is hypersensitive to shifts in the physical and psychological atmosphere. You are strongly influenced by the dream world and the passions and longings that arise from your emotional life. You have a tendency to suppress emotions, which can lead to psychosomatic illnesses. Balancing your emotional life will have a positive effect on your body.

Body's way of recharging vitality: Water is your preferred element: you love the sea, lakes and rivers. You also enjoy the countryside and wide open empty spaces where you can lose yourself in dreams and fantasies.

Psychosynthetic task: *Develop* your capacity for handling an impressionable and sensitive physical life by creating a lifestyle based on clear and positive ideals. *Control* your tendency to be overly influenced by those emotional states that exhaust your physical vitality. *Harmonise* your body with an active physical life based on rituals and healthy habits.

The practical body type

In a discussion of the "organisational-ritualistic" type, to use his terminology, Assagioli (1983: 78) described how the practical type manifests physically:

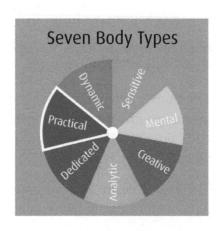

"At the physical level, he achieves his purposes by organising the cooperation and work of the group that is necessary to accomplish the desired end, and by assembling and ordering adequate materials for it."

Constitution and appearance: This is a common body type that is well suited to the challenges of an embodied physical life in the material world.

Constitution	Athletic body, resilient, sensitive, refined, beautiful proportions, coordinated, balance, controlled and elegant expression.
The body's behaviour	Graceful posture, elegant movement, wish for order and structure, easily disciplined. *Distortion:* Ritualistic, obsessive reactions to chaos and change.
Recharging vitality	Rhythm and structure, sunshine, nature, movement.

Your body type can be tall or short, but is usually slim and athletic. Your body is enduring, with good stamina, which makes it easy for you to function in the physical world. Your body type is delicate with refined features and beautiful proportions.

Your body is sensitive to the environment and needs care and attention, with healthy routines, in order to function optimally – however, this should be easy for you because you probably enjoy sport and exercise. Your coordination and balance are excellent: athletes, gymnasts and dancers often have this body type.

Your clothes are elegant and well-considered, but not too extravagant. You have an eye for detail, cut and quality, and feel comfortable in uniform, partly because this sends a clear signal that you appreciate a sense of order and control.

The body's behaviour: Your movements are coordinated, controlled and graceful, demonstrating kinaesthetic intelligence.

Your posture is straight and your attitude dignified. The practical type enjoys creating order, with an instinctive need to organise the physical

environment so that everything is in place. You experience a sense of physical well-being when the physical world feels organised.

Your body is sensitive to disorder, chaos and sudden changes in routine. When your body is out of balance it can compensate by adopting rigid patterns and through paying close attention to detail. As a result, as a coping mechanism, you are prone to eating disorders and other types of obsessive behaviour. Your body struggles to cope with extremes. You need a healthy and nutritious diet to thrive and, in contrast to the mental type, you need to be careful with what you eat.

Body's way of recharging vitality: Your level of activity is high, so it will benefit you to have an orderly lifestyle. You respond well to sunlight, which recharges your batteries.

Psychosynthetic task: *Develop* your capacity for leading an ordered and structured physical life. *Control* your tendency to become overly rigid and obsessed with detail. *Harmonise* your physical life with a careful diet, sunlight and gentle massages.

Which body type are you?

The following exercise will help you to identify your body type.

Exercise: How do you manage practical tasks?

Read the following statements and make a note of the ones you identify with most. Verify your answers by discussing your responses with someone who knows you well.

Note: These statements describe how the body types operate and have been carefully worded to reference the underlying motivators, so please check that you agree with all aspects of a statement before selecting it.

1. I have to do something intuitively, otherwise I lose energy.
2. I am active and practical and do what comes to me naturally.
3. I plan my day and do what needs to be done in the most efficient way.
4. I complete tasks quickly, with great energy, so I can move onto more important things.
5. I try to avoid practical tasks because they are boring, but I can cope better if my friends can join me.
6. I'm focused and able to get on with a task, but I prefer to get others to do it for me.
7. I wait until I feel ready to do something, then I'll do it slowly and carefully.
8. Before starting a task, I develop a strategy so I have a comprehensive overview of what I need to do.
9. I find the best approach to a task and just get on with it, focusing on the task in hand.
10. Being practical gives me energy, so I look forward to getting on with it.
11. I take time to build up the necessary energy, then I explode into action and keep going until the job is done.
12. I coordinate my activities and do what is necessary, looking forward to enjoying the results.
13. I don't enjoy practical tasks, but I will do them quickly and intensely just to get them over with.
14. When I have a task to do, I listen to music or think about how to do it in a fun way.

Try matching each of the statements to a different body type – select also the statements that best match your own experience, then check the footnote[1] below to discover your body type

---

[1] Statements (the number in brackets is the body type, where 1-dynamic, 2-sensitive, 3-mental, 4-creative, 5-analytical, 6-dedicated, 7-practical): 1.(2), 2.(3), 3.(7), 4.(1), 5.(4), 6.(1), 7.(2), 8.(3), 9.(5), 10.(5), 11.(6), 12.(7), 13.(6), 14.(4).

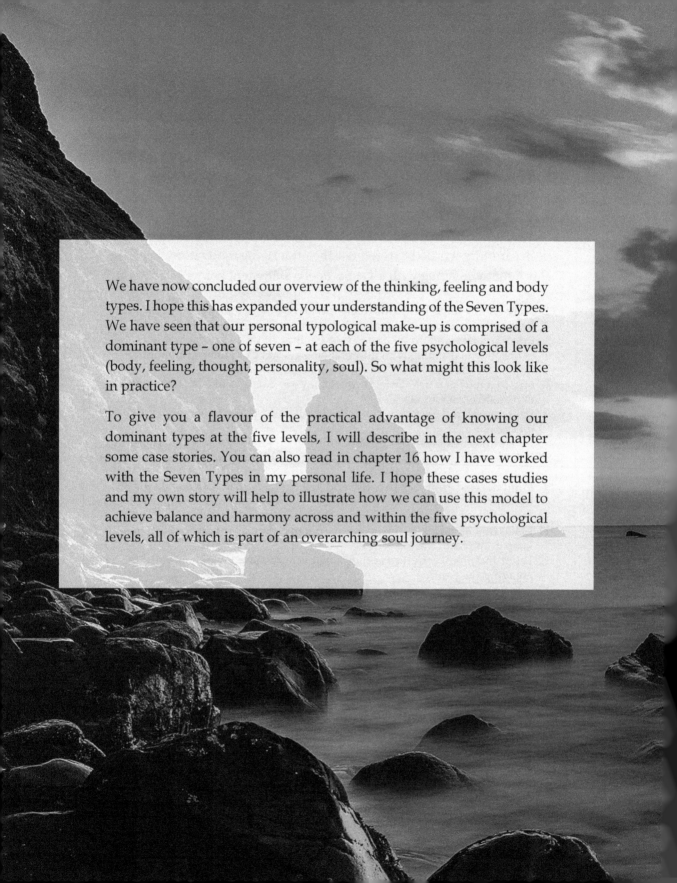

We have now concluded our overview of the thinking, feeling and body types. I hope this has expanded your understanding of the Seven Types. We have seen that our personal typological make-up is comprised of a dominant type – one of seven – at each of the five psychological levels (body, feeling, thought, personality, soul). So what might this look like in practice?

To give you a flavour of the practical advantage of knowing our dominant types at the five levels, I will describe in the next chapter some case stories. You can also read in chapter 16 how I have worked with the Seven Types in my personal life. I hope these cases studies and my own story will help to illustrate how we can use this model to achieve balance and harmony across and within the five psychological levels, all of which is part of an overarching soul journey.

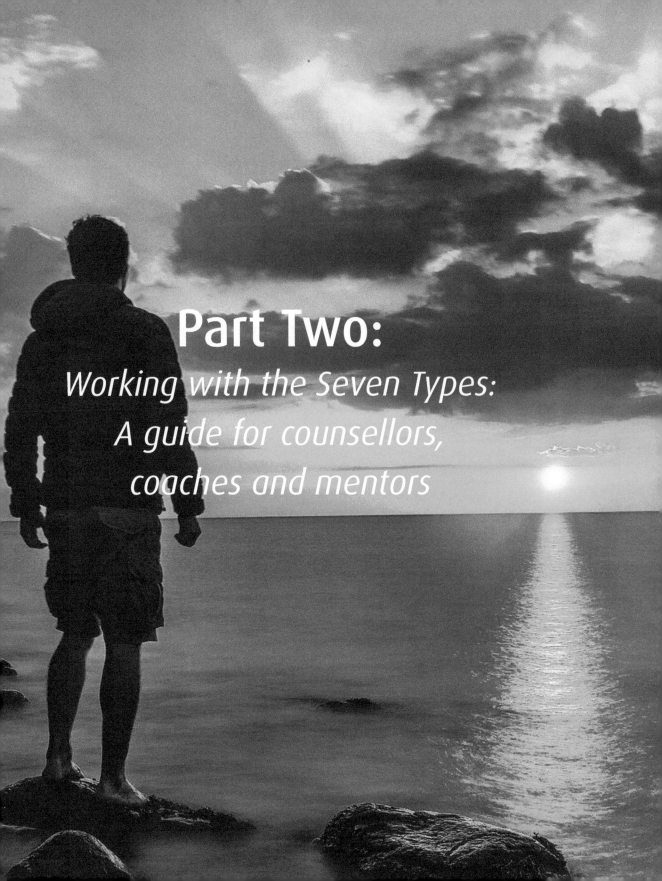

Part Two:

Working with the Seven Types:
A guide for counsellors,
coaches and mentors

Chapter 12

Case studies – Practical integration of the different types

In this chapter, we will take a closer look at the integration of the dominant types using examples from everyday life and the counselling room. The following case studies are taken from my own counselling practice (client permission has been given, with details anonymised).

The first three case studies concern the awakening of the soul type and its integration – or partial integration – with the personality type.

Mary: A creative personality type awakening to a sensitive soul type

When I first met her, Mary, aged 38, was in the midst of an existential crisis, feeling that many of her values no longer made sense. A creative personality type, she had lived her life dominated by a desperate need for attention and recognition, showing that personality integration was far from concluded.

Mary had been born into a privileged upper class family. Her upper class status opened many doors, as did her attractive looks. However, in pursuing this path, Mary had become attached to a superficial jet set lifestyle. All through her adult life, her primary focus had been on seeking in the world the beauty and harmony she clearly did not feel in her inner life. While growing up, she had received little care or attention from her parents, leaving an inner emptiness that she tried to fill through gaining recognition for her looks and happy-go-lucky attitude.

Mary had gone through many ups and downs – there had been broken relationships, an interrupted education and bouts of depression, mixed in with many amazing cultural and artistic experiences. She had tried to make a name for herself in the entertainment industry but when she failed she was left feeling unhappy, unstable and volatile. In retrospect, her life had been a series of joyful experiences of beauty, comfort or success, followed by feelings of emptiness and depression during which she felt unmotivated and disengaged from life.

Mary had a winning character, with a sense of humour and an openness and energy that made it easy for her to relate to others, so she was very popular. However, anyone who got close to her quickly realised she was only really interested in herself. Mary was self-absorbed and superficial, but a deep longing was growing within her to make a valuable contribution to life. Meanwhile, her sense of pain and emptiness had grown so much she started to avoid the parties and social occasions that had once provided her with so much sustenance and strength.

When Mary came to therapy, it was because her marriage to a rich elderly man had ended. She had not been able to communicate with him and grew tired of being a trophy wife and sexual toy. The divorce prompted a crisis – Mary felt as if all the doors that were once open to her had been slammed shut and she had been left alone to face the empty reality of her life and values for the first time. An inner voice kept telling her that there had to be a deeper meaning.

Mary started with intensive twice-weekly psychotherapy that revealed deep layers of her painful sense of emptiness, which also put her in touch with a deep longing for a profound interconnectedness. She asked herself: Who am I and why am I here? It was as if an inner void was calling out for wisdom, meaning and purpose. She was helped by reading numerous self-help books through which she was helped to find her inner soul nature, not as if it was something new but as if she was meeting a long lost friend. She discovered that meditation could fill the void from within. While acknowledging that transformation would take time, she discovered that the pain she had been trying to flee could become a resource, providing information on the road to greater insight. Most important of all, Mary started to understand how she could contribute to life: she wanted to work with others who were undergoing existential crises so she could help them to find their true vocation in life. During two years of psychotherapy, Mary's life changed dramatically. She made new friends, found new interests and started a university course in psychology. It was clear that her emerging sensitive soul type was influencing her life and providing her with a new set of values.

Mary still has much work to do to integrate her creative personality with her sensitive soul, but this is happening under the influence of a deep motivation to become a valuable instrument for wisdom in the world.

Mary found working with the Seven Types helped her to accept and understand her need for beauty and harmony, as well as the chaotic and unstructured elements in her life. Her sensitive soul type made deep sense to her: not only did it explain her need to understand life, it was also a source of wisdom, inspiring her to make a difference in life. Her need for beauty and harmony was still there, but now the emphasis was not on a superficial life but on a longing to see beauty and harmony unfolding in the deepest possible sense, both in her own life and in the lives of others.

Mary's story demonstrates that the personality does not need to be fully integrated before the deeper being and values of the soul are able to emerge. This corresponds with findings of Maslow and Wilber which show that people in real life situations are far more complex than theory will allow for.

Mary continues the journey of personality integration, now motivated by a desire to make a difference in the world. Through her psychological work, she is attempting to become an effective and purposeful creative personality who is able to express soul wisdom. The next phase in her journey, where the soul type starts to take charge, will produce what is termed the "soul-infused personality", which comes about as the result of transpersonal psychosynthesis.

Peter: An analytical personality type awakening to a dedicated soul type

Peter was a classic analytical personality type. He had spent his adult life pursuing an interest in engineering, specialising in bridge construction, and was recognised as an expert in his field with a sharp eye for detail. His manner was low-key and somewhat dry. His movements were measured as if he was controlling his body with mathematical precision.

Peter came to therapy because of the devastating impact of meeting and losing a woman he had felt was the love of his life. He couldn't focus on his work, he felt empty and his life was in chaos. Susan, the woman in question, had been a very different type to any of Peter's previous romances. In particular, she was clairvoyant and a healer, something Peter, with his analytical mindset, would have previously dismissed as nonsense. But, through spending time with Susan,

Peter started to take a great interest in the paranormal. Susan had an uncanny ability to know and intuit things about Peter that amazed him and awakened a desire to undertake a scientific study of this hitherto ignored area of life.

When Peter arrived for therapy he seemed highly unbalanced. He idealised Susan, whom he attributed with awakening in him a desire to experience an ideal spiritual world in which everything was in perfect order. Indeed, to his surprise, he had discovered he could sense the presence of angels and felt he could communicate with enlightened masters and cosmic beings in the spiritual dimension.

Peter's passionate desire to connect with the spiritual world had arisen partly due to Susan's influence and partly due to the deep grief of losing her. As therapy progressed, it became obvious that two things were happening: in part, the crisis in his love life had caused Peter to regress to a primitive emotional stage where magical thinking predominates, but it was also clear that Peter's dedicated soul type was emerging. Understandably, this brought a great deal of imbalance into his life, but the experience was also an opening into a rich new area of experience that would change his life forever.

There were transpersonal energies visible both in Peter's sorrow and in his desire to access the spirit world. Clearly, he was not just seeking personal gratification – he wanted to study and engage with psychic and paranormal phenomena so he could write a book and give lectures to help others.

An essential part of the therapy for Peter was to examine what he was projecting onto Susan. In his idealisation of Susan, Peter was projecting onto her his spiritual archetype, which not surprisingly meant that, for him, she had a bedazzling unearthly quality. As we worked together, Peter came to see that Susan was not the saint he had initially thought her to be, for example she had been very unkind at times, especially in the way she ended their relationship. At the same time, Peter started to reality test his paranormal experiences and discovered that not all of the 'messages' he had been receiving were expressions of wisdom, but were in fact often quite ordinary thoughts.

Through making analytical and reality-based investigations, Peter started to feel more grounded. However, he didn't lose his passion or his fire: he realised that many of his psychic experiences were real and he retained a deeply felt call to understand these experiences and to assist others by helping them to build bridges to the spiritual dimension. Through therapy, he accepted that his relationship with Susan was over, but the overwhelming love the relationship had awakened could be transferred to the paranormal realm.

When therapy ended after one year, Peter was still working as an engineer, but he felt his job played a secondary role in his life, with his spare time now consumed with pursuing his spiritual interests. His relationship with Susan had caused pain, but it had also changed his life.

Peter's story is a good example of a typical soul awakening. At first, the new soul energy overwhelmed the personality and expressed itself in a highly unbalanced manner. Secondly, this crisis was exacerbated when an incident in the external world – in this case a new relationship –became the catalyst for a deeper and lasting awakening to the soul's vocation. In Peter's case, Susan carried the soul energy that Peter's personality was awakening to, which threw him out of his familiar routine and out of his safe conceptual framework. Thirdly, the qualities of the personality type helped to anchor the emerging energy from the soul. In Peter's case, his analytical abilities helped him to test and validate his psychic experiences.

It is important to note that awakening often comes like a thief in the night, in Peter's case in the disguise of an ordinary love affair. It took the experience and insight of a transpersonal psychotherapist to discern and disentangle ordinary heartbreak from a spiritual crisis. Though it brought great pain, Susan was in a sense perfect for Peter because her presence enabled him to discover his latent spirituality. Peter didn't have the love affair he was hoping for, but he received from Susan something far better: an awakening to a new and more meaningful life.

Hanne: A sensitive personality awakening to the practical soul type

Hanne was clearly a sensitive personality type. She was calm, gentle and centred. The years she had spent teaching social and community psychiatry testified to her concern to help others. Hanne thrived on making life comfortable for her husband and two children and those she worked with. However, something had changed. Hanne had lost her concern to be the all-loving mother – she had given so much and felt she had nothing left to give – tending to others needs no longer gave her the satisfaction it once had. She also felt dissatisfied that, despite all the care she continued to give, little seemed to change. She wanted more – in her work life and in her private life. She was in a crisis.

When Hanne started therapy it quickly emerged that she didn't feel she was utilising all of her resources and potential. It was as if she had become trapped in the role of a carer. She longed for freedom and to let go of her emotional caretaking. In her own words, she was a "problem-magnet", but far from solving problems she felt she was only fire-fighting; she sensed she wasn't tackling the core issues.

When Hanne meditated on the needs of her heart, she felt a deep wish to leave her job and find a new role that was less hands-on. She had acquired a great deal of experience in community and social psychiatry and now she wanted to help implement better practice in a wider general sense, perhaps by working for a relevant organisation or getting involved in legislative work. It became clear in our sessions that Hanne was done by being *the mother*, whether professionally or in her personal life. However, this insight challenged her self-identity and prompted a crisis – she feared that if she changed her life she might find herself unemployed or might be abandoned by her family. But despite these fears, she knew it was a case of sink or swim: if she didn't change her life she knew she would become ill.

The more Hanne sat with the crisis, the more the thought of becoming the conductor of her own life started to make sense. Also, as we worked together, there was a distinct sense of transpersonal energy in the room whenever we focused on her life purpose and will. Indeed, in time, Hanne got in touch with a powerful field of *strong will* and a desire to take control over her life – this was the awakening of her practical soul type. Hanne started to experience an influx of ideas around how she could make use of her work experience to create a new holistic vision for what social psychiatry could be; Hanne sensed she could change the future if she was to apply her energy and dedication. Rather than working hard to simply sustain a system that was barely working, Hanne wanted to build a more effective system. This emerging desire demonstrated how the dynamic and inspirational nature of the soul can become a creative fountainhead for a better future.

Hanne also realised she needed to reform her personal life. Rather than focusing solely on her family's well-being, she wanted to spend time developing relationships at home so that instead of being the mother hen with a brood of chicks, she could be one of a collection of individuals who were able to cooperate and share different views.

Hanne was surprised at the strength she found in herself. She realised she had to develop the skills she had been using to organise her family and her work, and start using them in a new way. Rather than being the "fixer", working hard on the frontline, she took a step back so she could take an overview, see the big picture, and start working in a more general and detached manner.

Of course, this transition to a new way of being is not easy – it can take a long time for a new idea to fully manifest. And, as part of the process, Hanne knew she would have to face her fear of hurting or disappointing those around her, at home and in the workplace. She was afraid of being unpopular and afraid that people might think she was failing – the two biggest fears of the sensitive personality type. However, at the same time, Hanne knew her new path better reflected her true identity. She had awakened to the call of her soul, not in a "spiritual" sense of seeking oneness with the divine, but in the sense of discovering an inner *will to do good* that would not compromise on her vision. There was also a longing for freedom. In the workplace, for example, Hanne wanted to be free to work at a director level so she could devise new working practices and frameworks – the result of which was that clients with mental health problems were also set free, being liberated from the imprisonment of a failing system and, ultimately, liberated from their own mental disorders.

It is hard to tell whether it was the practical or the dynamic soul type that had been awakened in Hanne – Hanne felt it was the practical soul type, but an argument could be made for the dynamic soul type, especially because of the power displayed at the beginning of her transformation.

When Hanne ended therapy, she was reforming her life with a set of clearly formulated goals and felt she no longer had time for "rumination" in therapy. Clearly, she wanted to take care of things herself and get on with her life, which are features that characterise both the dynamic and the practical soul types.

In therapy work, the transpersonal dimension often reveals itself through the type of motivation that starts to emerge and dominate. In Hanne's case, it was a strong motivation to create freedom through creative activity. This vocation, or inner call, impacted Hanne at all levels of Maslow's Hierarchy of Needs, including her relationship to her family.

In the next case study, we will explore a different sort of integration, namely the integration of the dominant types at the levels of thought and feeling.

Hans: Integrating a sensitive emotional life

Hans was an influential figure in the field of marketing, but he had never managed to reach the top in his profession. As he said: "I am way too soft to make unpleasant decisions." This softness and vulnerability was causing him great pain.

When I met Hans, I could see he had the direct tough radiance of a leader, but I could also sense an underlying sensitivity, especially in his eyes. The dynamic personality type was clear – he was someone who got the job done – but, according to his own understanding, his emotions repeatedly obstructed his impact.

When he came to me for coaching, he had already thoroughly analysed his situation. He was clear and precise, factual and objective, and it was clear that his mentality was characterised by the analytical thought type. He was also extremely critical, almost merciless, in his condemnation of his inner "weakling", which was the name he had given to his sensitivity. This weakling stood in the way of his ambitions for personal and professional success. There was a clear and strong division between his sensitive emotional life and his critical thought life.

As coaching progressed, it became clear that it was not Hans' sensitivity that was his biggest obstacle, but his *relationship* to his sensitivity (Hans was a sensitive type at the level of feeling).

Hans was trying to block out his feelings by focusing on his thought life – but coaching revealed that his prejudice against his feelings had its roots in the way his father had handled emotions. In his father's world there was no room for emotions – and this had deeply impacted Hans' self-understanding, with Hans learning to despise his vulnerability because he felt it was unmanly. This discovery sparked in him an understanding that he needed to accept his sensitivity as an integral part of his personality. Hans realised his feelings were something he had to live with and get the best out of. Far from making him a bad leader, he realised that sensitivity would help him to cooperate, to empathise and to develop his skills in networking.

Hans also realised that his ability to predict market trends was not only due to his goal-oriented drive and analytical skills, but also due to his intuitive sense of public opinion, which was a quality of the sensitive feeling type.

Ironically, it was clear from Hans' relentless self-criticism that, far from blocking out his sensitivity, he had in fact become more timid and over-sensitive than he needed to be – which is a distortion of the sensitive feeling type which will manifest when the type is being blocked. However, as Hans gradually came to accept his feelings, his hypersensitivity lessened because he had less to hide or defend against. By the time Hans ended coaching, it was as if something had fallen into place inside. He still had a long way to go to fully include his feeling nature, but he had made an excellent start.

Hans' story demonstrates the value of vertical integration between personality, thought and feeling and shows how understanding the qualities of the types can lead to a more rounded and harmonious personality.

Horizontal integration between types

So far, we have been looking at examples of *vertical* integration between different psychological levels. Now we will look at what could be called *horizontal* integration.

This type of integration emphasises that each of our dominant types – at each of the five levels – needs to integrate qualities from the other types in order to become fully balanced and manifest. For example, a dynamic thinking type will tend to be one-dimensional in their approach to life, so they should strive to develop the qualities of the creative thought type – such as spontaneity and the desire for open dialogue, which would challenge the tendency of the dynamic thinking type to act in isolation.

Horizontal integrations often take place when there are interactions between people of different types which necessitate that we must evolve different ways of functioning to make cooperation possible.

George: A dynamic thinking type meeting an analytical thinking type

With great enthusiasm, George started to gather everything his spiritual role model had ever written on a particular subject. George's idea was to publish a book so he could share all of these writings with the world, and he had a publishing company lined up. George loved to work like this – gaining an overview, trying to see the big picture, having an impact in people's lives. And, as with all of his ideas, George had a tendency to rush into action. The project suited him perfectly: as well as sharing the big picture described by his favorite author, he could also put a dynamic plan into action by sharing his guru's message with a large audience.

George's dynamic mind was obvious to everyone – he always spoke with great authority and confidence. Another essential quality of the dynamic thinking type is the ability to delegate, letting others do the hard graft while you direct and take an overview. Accordingly, George organised a group of like-minded enthusiasts to gather up all the relevant material, while he set about making the final editorial decisions. The texts were collected swiftly – the dynamic mind loves rapidity – and George organised them into a single document to hand to the publisher. By this stage, George anticipated that the final result – the printing of the book – would be merely a formality and he looked forward to receiving the finished publication. However, George got a surprise.

The publisher was a meticulous man whose passion was to create books that were works of art, where every small detail had been considered. He was an example of the analytical thinking type – so the inevitable clash happened because George hated attending to the nitty-gritty, which he considered to be mere triviality. George's concern was only with the message of the book and the riches it contained, offering meaning, essence and core purpose to the world. So when the publisher returned George's manuscript along with many painstakingly-made notes describing all the points that needed attention, George was furious!

George's first reaction was to ignore the publisher and have the book printed himself. But then he realised that if he did that the book would reach fewer people and therefore have less impact. So, following a brief analysis of power dynamics – something the dynamic mind does very well – George realised he needed to get on with the detailed work. He could not wait for others to do it – time is precious for the dynamic mind – so he took it upon himself to accomplish the task.

It was tedious, dragging work. Following his initial burst of energy, George now had to sit down and pay attention to aspects of his manuscript that he hadn't previously considered. But, as he made progress, he started to realise how perfecting the details brought a clarify that would make the book more effective, with both content and presentation greatly improved. For example, George came to see how the design of the book was as important as the content because, unless the book looked good and was easy to read, no-one was likely to buy it.

For the first time, George realised the detail was as important as the bigger picture, and that sometimes it was important to slow down and deal with small painstaking tasks. It was not the aesthetics of the book that inspired him, but by the fact that paying attention to detail had helped to reinforce the message he wanted to convey. This is exactly what motivates the dynamic mind: to make strong messages that will have an impact in ways that influence people and change perspectives. Thanks to an officious publisher, the next time George writes a book he will put more effort into preparing it. The dynamic thinking type had learned from the analytical thinking type.

Stine: A dedicated feeling type lives with a creative personality type

Stine was elegant in her appearance, with stylish clothes in discrete colors. She was known for being a skilled organiser and facilitator who had worked for many years in the shipping industry. There was no doubt she had a practical personality type, but behind her effective and slightly cold personality lay a dedicated emotional life that gave her a passion for her work and family life. She loved her husband and children and would go to great lengths to make their lives peaceful and tranquil. She had a clear image of the *perfect* family that was able to blend quality family time with social gatherings.

But her life was not always peaceful. Her husband, Torben, was an unpredictable person, an actor, which is a profession marked by uncertainty. While Stine strived for stability, her husband thrived on upheaval, drama and spontaneous emotion, all qualities of the creative personality type. It was never boring being around Torben because the unexpected usually occurred, whether in the situation or in his moods which fluctuated between exhilaration and depression.

Torben's lifestyle challenged Stine's image of the perfect life of order and balance. Yet, she loved him for the fun he brought to the family – at least, when he wasn't away working. Stine hated it when they quarrelled about finance and household chores. When they argued, Stine told Torben he was like a child because he refused to take responsibility in practical matters. What she hated most was when Torben would storm out of the house in the middle of an argument, leaving the whole matter unresolved – this tore Stine apart, leaving her feeling as if her world had collapsed. Whenever he did this, Stine believed her husband had walked out on the family for good. By contrast, Torben was fine with drama and felt their quarrelling was a good thing because it helped to bring issues out into the open and clear the atmosphere. Torben also liked quarrelling because it broke up the monotony of the family idyll which, while appreciating its stability, Torben felt spoiled his ideal image of himself as an untraditional bohemian. For Torben, normality was a graveyard populated by the living dead.

When Stine started therapy, she was upset because she had just had an argument with her husband. I encouraged her to consider the opposites inside her: on one side was her ideal image of the perfect family, with its values and needs, while on the other side was her strong attraction to Torben's unpredictable and spontaneous nature. She had both sides, but she only saw creativity in Torben while ignoring her own creative side: it was as if there wasn't room for two adult children in the family.

Through analysing her ideal world of peace and her tendency to devote herself to only a few people, Stine realised it was important that she had more space in her life for play, spontaneity and joy. It also became clear that she had taken on her parents' norms for the perfect family life and still felt a need to be "correct" in her parents' eyes.

When we explored the Seven Types, Stine realised she could learn a lot from Torben's creative approach to life, while also understanding she had a great deal to contribute to his life, such as order, efficiency and devotion. Stine understood that she would always be a deeply dedicated and organised type, but that life needn't to be so serious. If she opened up to a more playful element, through her husband, she could start to build a wider network of friends and associates outside the home – something she realised she craved. It is a common imbalance with the dedicated type to become too focused and thereby isolate themselves within a few areas of interest – to put all their eggs in one basket – which leaves them vulnerable when emotional conflicts arise since there is so much at stake; ideal situations – in Stine's case the family nest – are simply too uncomfortable to lose. However, through integrating the creative type, Stine was able to learn that emotional conflicts are not necessarily a disaster but can bring new life when you steer the drama in positive directions.

It was obvious that Torben had much to learn, but Stine could at least change herself and, by embracing Torben's creative nature, develop emotionally. As a result, she could more easily accept Torben's differences and even see the value in these differences.

I hope these case studies have given the reader a sense of how the types can play out in real life situations, and how they can be worked with to resolve conflicts and crises. Let us now investigate how to work with the types.

How to work with the Seven Types

This chapter is written for counsellors who would like to work with the Seven Types as part of their professional practice.

The first and most important step is to undergo the same training as the one you would like to offer your clients. As with any model or mode of therapy, the best education is to have undergone the process yourself so you know the theory from an experiential point of view. Undergoing the work will involve studying the Seven Types, but will also ideally involve undergoing training and/or consultations with a qualified Seven Types typologist. There is, of course, no problem with applying the theory of the types yourself when you feel ready but, as you might realise after reading this book, the Seven Types is a vast typological system which needs deep understanding to apply properly.

As you begin to explore working with the Seven Types, the ideas in this chapter will help you. I will not be touching upon the areas of auto-psychosynthesis (working on yourself), couples counselling, social work, teamwork or education – even though these are all fruitful areas for the application of the Seven Types. Rather, my focus will be entirely on psychotherapy, counselling and coaching. In particular, I will describe a five-step approach for basic work – first in brief, then in more detail – then I describe two more tools for the counsellors – the Circle of Integration and the seven glamours – and, finally, I will conclude with a summary of the many ways that the Seven Types can be used to help clients.

A five-step approach to using the Seven Types with clients

1. Describe the benefits of the Seven Types: The client must understand the benefits of the Seven Types. We must therefore explain the basic theory and explain how the Seven Types can offer new insights as part of the psychosynthesis process.

2. Identify the client's types: A counsellor trained in the Seven Types will be able to formulate a hypothesis about a client's dominant types at the five levels. You can also make use of various online profiling tools (our own website, JivaYou.com, offers a range of profiling tools – see conclusion of this chapter for more information).

3. Verify and calibrate the types: If you are working with an online profiling tool, it is important to remember that the client's results will, at least in part, reflect the client's distorted and false self-perceptions – as is inevitable with any form of self-assessment. It is therefore necessary to work with the client to match their profile results with reality – and the trained typologist can do this by making a deeper exploration of the client's life (looking at areas such as their education, work and interests). In this way, the typologist can generate a more accurate five-digit type-combination for the client. Note: at this early stage of counselling, this type-combination is a *hypothesis* – the ongoing counselling is likely to shed new light on the client's combination of types.

4. Goal-setting: Having established a hypothetical type-combination, the client is ready to reflect on the particular developmental needs and goals for his combination of types. In this regard, the counsellor might like to proceed with the work making use of the four cardinal areas and seven perspectives (as described in chapter 14). The aim of the work at this stage is to help the client formulate a vision for their developmental goals. The therapist can also make use of *ideal models* (self-images, or visions, of what one might be) – these will naturally emerge as the work proceeds and will inform the direction of the counselling.

5. Psychosynthetic work: Having worked through the first four steps, the deep work of counselling will be well underway, and the client will be aware of the particular psychosynthetic task facing their type-combination. At this point, the therapist can work in a number of ways:

- Draw on different methods and techniques according to the client's type-combination and goals, and the approach can be updated as the work progresses.
- Hold in mind Assagioli's (1983: 13) three developmental concepts: expression, control and harmonisation of the psychological qualities.
- Always acknowledge and mirror the qualities of the types as they emerge in the client via subpersonalities, personality traits, longings and expressions.
- Adapt your approach and communication style to fit with the client's dominant types (whichever of the five dominant types is most present in the session). For example, a dynamic personality type should be addressed in a direct style (see chapter 14 for the seven counselling styles).

Let's now look at each of these five steps in more detail.

1. Describe the benefits of the Seven Types

I will begin by highlighting some of the key points regarding the Seven Types that the counsellor needs to share with the client.

- The Seven Types offer an in-depth understanding of a person's *essential qualities*, motivations and developmental patterns.

- Knowing a client's dominant types at the five psychological levels offers a profound insight into our *natural way of being* – and knowing this can help us begin to disidentify from external and inauthentic influences that can trap us.

When we work with the core of our being, we will start to understand how we can:

- *Own* ourselves;
- *Express* our natural qualities;
- *Control* our natural tendencies to create imbalance;
- *Harmonise* our natural qualities with the complementary qualities of the other types.

- In short, the philosophy of the Seven Types offers a unique way for being *in tune* with our natural energies as they manifest at the five psychological levels. There is no stronger foundation than being aligned with our natural DNA – biologically, psychologically and spiritually.

- The importance of the soul type should be emphasised. Our soul type reveals our particular way to the soul, revealing our most valuable creative resources and showing us how to express them in service to the world. Our soul type connects us with our life purpose and with the meaning we are here to unfold. Our soul type directs us to our *service group* (for each of us there is a specific community that we are called to nurture, develop and cooperate with). We need to understand about our soul type so we can work on transpersonal psychosynthesis (which is the integration of our soul qualities with our personality qualities, a process during which there may be an existential crisis due to conflict in the dynamics of the energies, values and motivations of these two types).

- It is crucial for the client to identify their *personality type*. Knowing our personality type means we will know which qualities and personal resources we need to develop in order to realise our ambitions and goals; the personality type is the vehicle through which we can be a success in the world through making an impact and having an influential voice in our chosen field. In particular, unfolding our personality type will enable us to identify the quality of our *will-to-be-self* – be it dynamic, sensitive, creative, etc. – and this will help us to integrate our inner resources and outside support so we can achieve our goals. To fully manifest our personality type means becoming a *self-actualised* person, to use Maslow's term. However, the integration of our personality type is not an easy task – it entails utilising the guidance of a strong and loving self to harmonise and align conflicting forces under the rule of the strong and loving self. The most common conflicts are those that arise between our body, feeling and thinking types, and those that are due to the impact of the environment on our inner well-being.

2. Identify the client's types

The trained typologist is advised to make use of online profiling tools to start the process of identifying the client's type-combination. Clients can be assessed in other ways – for example they can be assessed directly by an experienced typologist – but an online tool is a useful way to start the process.

If working with the JivaYou online profile, the client's answers will have suggested some typological preferences (top of the iceberg), while the online system will have generated a comprehensive profile of the deeper underlying typological system, which are a magnification of the client's self-perceptions. In this way, the JivaYou profile mirrors the consequences of the clients' choices and offers an image of how clients see themselves. The process is valuable because it focuses the client's self-awareness – while the online system generates ideal models for them to emulate by identifying the archetypes that are related to the client's particular personality type and soul type. However, as valuable as this is, it is not enough to create a valid

hypothesis of the client's types because the online profiles rely on the accuracy of both the client's self-evaluation and the system's validity, neither of which can be 100% accurate.

What do I mean by the system's validity? The system is a work in progress. The results it gives are based on gathering data from the client that can be accurately matched with the types. However, we are still in the process of fine-tuning our questionnaire in order to ensure accurate matches. The more the questionnaire is used, the more we will be able to fine-tune the questions. For example, with a statement such as "I am a strong and courageous leader", several types will be able to identify with such a statement, especially the dynamic, dedicated and practical types. Hence, we have been working hard to discover unique statements that can be matched only to one particular type. This is an ongoing process, which requires a lot of research and experimentation involving many types of people.

Let's take a closer look at the phenomenon of the client's distorted self-image, which reflects a lack of self-awareness. Assagioli has described how it is possible to develop a self-model (self-perception) that represents a false self (false self-image) in that it does not reflect who we truly are. Indeed, most of us have, to some extent, an inaccurate, or false, view of ourselves. In fact, we can each hold a number of false self-models which could be in conflict with each other – these form the many subpersonalities and inner voices that compete for our attention. In my book The Soul of Psychosynthesis I devote an entire chapter to these self-images and how to work with them.

Among the variety of false self-models, Assagioli (1965: 167) mentions the following:

1. Who we *believe* we are. These models come in two classes according to whether we *over*-evaluate or *under*-evaluate ourselves. In the first category, we magnify qualities and make them more prominent than they are, perhaps imagining certain qualities are dominant energies, whereas they are in fact secondary energies. In the second category, we neglect or are unaware that we have significant qualities. Both of these errors in self-perception will affect the client's online profile results.

2. Who we think we *should* be. This refers to our identification with an idealistic, unrealistic or unattainable model of self, the effect of this is that any online profile results will confuse these idealised qualities with our dominant types.

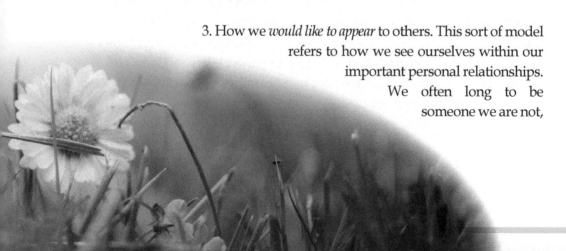

3. How we *would like to appear* to others. This sort of model refers to how we see ourselves within our important personal relationships. We often long to be someone we are not,

perhaps fooling ourselves into believing that's what we are. When under the influence of this sort of false self-model, we would create an online profile that makes us look good in the eyes of others.

4. Images which others *produce* in us, i.e. self-images evoked by others. We are often unconsciously identified with this sort of false self-model. In technical language, this is called "projective identification". These self-models can be very damaging. For example, someone brought up in a harsh military setting might consider himself to be soft, weak and sensitive because he is comparing himself with those around him and has internalised their negative judgements. According to this distorted self-perception, he might consider himself to be a sensitive type, but he might in fact be any of the other types. Alternatively, in a situation like this one, a person could overcompensate for his perceived sensitivity by making himself appear tough and courageous, which would also be a false self-model, this time falsely conveying the idea of the dynamic type. On this topic of compensation, Assagioli (1983: 12-13) offers the following interesting observations from history:

> In fact, we often have the tendency to over-estimate precisely the quality that we lack. Two famous examples of hyper-compensation are those of Nietzsche and Tolstoy. Nietzsche originally had a sensitive, passionate but rather weak nature and, in his frantic efforts to conquer his limitations, he over-emphasised the value of power and of a stern and unyielding will, coming in the end to justify cruelty itself.
>
> The case of Tolstoy is at the opposite extreme. By nature a man of great vitality, Tolstoy was impulsive and violent, with strong instincts and a great love of beauty and physical well-being. He tried to master himself and in his struggle against his exuberant nature, which we may read in his diary – a human and psychological document of

great value – he arrived at the glorification of non-resistance to evil and of celibacy and eventually came to an excessive depreciation of art and a total condemnation of modern civilisation.

Apart from these well-known examples, we have many cases, half amusing and half pathetic, of weak, timid and unsuccessful men who affect to possess Napoleonic qualities.

The counsellor must therefore help the client to distinguish between their *inherent natural types* and qualities that have been created by their environment, which may include qualities and behaviours that are based on the client's fear, guilt or shame in response to the context of their environment.

It should also be noted that a person might semi-consciously repress certain aspects of themselves because they don't like those particular qualities, which would make the self-model category something like: what one really is but tries to repress. To give an example, I worked with a client who'd had a long career as a computer programmer but whose profile results suggested a very low analytical function. When we discussed his profile results and reflected on his dominant types, the client admitted he was tired of his analytical qualities and had deliberately devalued them when answering the questionnaire. He was no doubt an analytical thinking type, but his concern was to develop new qualities.

Clearly, it is not an easy task to discern a client's dominant types at the five levels. This is why we always recommend that client's work with a professional counsellor who can test any online profiling results: we call this verifying and calibrating the types.

3. Verify and calibrate the types

The aim of the counsellor working with the seven Types is to help the client to establish a clear and accurate picture of themselves – to acquire a realistic self-image that can form the basis of an authentic self-identity. When this has been established, the work of integration can begin.

Working with the client and their online profile results, a trained typologist can implement the process of verifying and calibrating the types. The counsellor will be able to compare the client's profile results with the qualities the client radiates in the counselling room. As well as working with the client's online profile, the counsellor can explore aspects of the client's life in detail – such as type of education, work and interests – all of which will generate additional information to help identify the client's types.

By gathering all this information, and working through any apparent contradictions or mismatches in the data, the counsellor can help the client to generate a more accurate profile by adjusting the answers to the questionnaire, so a new profile is generated of their dominant types. The result will be a *valid hypothesis of types* which can then be tested and adjusted repeatedly by observing real life situations.

During this period of the counselling, the counsellor must consider what Assagioli referred to as *the age of the soul*, which means a person's level of development. Assagioli (1930) explained: "If we consider, even superficially, the various human beings who surround us, we soon discover that they are not equally developed from the psychological and spiritual standpoint".

Clearly, some clients are further ahead on the spiritual path having undergone a change of values, shifting from a personal to a transpersonal value-system wherein altruistic and idealistic motivations start to emerge. For such people, transpersonal psychosynthesis is a relevant issue because their soul type has started to influence their personality type.

However, some other clients are still focused on their need for status and recognition. Such clients might not be interested in ideals or spiritual values, but only want to live a good material life and take care of their relatives. In these cases, it is the personality type that is in the driving seat, pursuing personal success and well-being, and personal psychosynthesis is the relevant therapeutic work.

Yet another client might be struggling simply to manage their lives and meet their basic needs – such clients aspire no higher than to live a normal life and feel a sense of acceptance. Such clients don't hold any conscious ambitions or idealistic inclinations, they only want to be safe and to get through the day. For these clients, the therapeutic work will centre on their body, feeling and thinking types. This kind of therapy is dealing primarily with the pre-personal.

So, as we can see, the focus of therapy will vary according to the client's level of development. This is how Assagioli (1967b), quoting Jung, differentiated between these different types of psychotherapy:

> There are many, specially among the young, whose disturbances have been produced by psychic traumas, by conflicts rooted in the personal unconscious, or by strife between the individual and other people, above all members of the family and the social environment. Jung maintains that in these cases, treatment mainly psychoanalytical and certain methods that he included in what he called "little therapy" may suffice (see *La Guérison Psychologique*, p. 239). However, these cases often require also the application of active techniques that Jung neglects.
>
> On the other hand, there is a broad group of patients whose disturbances are the product of crises and deep conflicts of an "existential" kind, which involve fundamental human problems about the meaning and purpose of life in general and about the

individual's own life. It is to be remarked that not infrequently the patient is not aware of these deep-seated causes of his illness, and it is the treatment that renders him conscious of them and then helps him to eliminate them.

Therefore, we can see that the counsellor working with the Seven Types must be able to differentiate between three levels of counselling, i.e. the pre-personal, personal and transpersonal. Being able to work at all three levels will ensure that the counsellor is able to cover all aspects of the client's life and psychic journey – and, as a result, it will be possible to identify which of the types have unfolded at the different stages of development.

As this process proceeds, the client will sense a lot of new questions. As their self-awareness and knowledge of their types grows, the client will start to question their present needs and start to imagine new ambitions and goals.

4. Goal-setting: Where do we go from here?

The task at this stage of counselling is for the counsellor to help the client to set realistic goals that are in line with their dominant types. There is no fixed way of working. Rather, the client's unique existential situation will determine the most appropriate way to proceed. For example, if we were to track the developmental stage of the client's psychological functions, we could find that each one is in a different place on a developmental line that runs from the pre-personal, through the personal to the transpersonal (I explore this idea in detail in my MA dissertation, *Integral Psychosynthesis*). The developmental task facing each function will generate different conflicts or crises which can be analysed through the lens of the Seven Types. Remember that whenever we wish to develop new qualities in the personality, we must work with the underlying psychological function in order to discern where a function is being impeded and is in need of development – hence, objectives, or goals, can be set to allow for each function to develop.

At this stage, we can also work with the four cardinal angles and the seven counselling strategies (as described in chapter 14).

5. Psychosynthetic work

For the psychosynthesis practitioner, it can be helpful to consider organising your counselling work around Assagioli's three concepts of expression, control and harmonisation. To explain:

- *Expression:* The client needs to understand what the best possible expression of his types would look like and, accordingly, he must be encouraged to work with the most appropriate ideal model (ideal self-image) to help him develop his natural types.
- *Control:* The client must be aware of the possible distortions that can afflict his dominant types and learn how to *control* such distortions.
- *Harmonisation:* The client is called to harmonise his dominant types because very often qualities from other types will help in balancing the distortions of this dominant types.

Circle of integration

The Circle of Integration is a useful tool for the counsellor who is seeking to support the unfolding of the dominant types through the balancing of opposite, and therefore conflicting, types. The Circle of Integration shows which psychological functions are in opposition and how they can be integrated to create balance within the types. For each type, at every level, there is a Primary Developer that needs to be integrated. The Primary Developer is our 'opposite function', so called because it contains the qualities we find most difficult to access. The two functions which are on the left and right of the Primary Developer in the circle are called Helpers because they provide further opportunities and perspectives for establishing the harmony required for the type to fully unfold.

Let me give an example of how to use the Circle of Integration. I will be using the sensitive soul type, whose archetype is the Illuminator. The Circle of Integration for the Illuminator is shown in Figure 30. As can be seen, it is through the psychological function of feeling that the soul type will primarily unfold.

As can be seen in the circle diagram, the Primary Developer for the Illuminator is the **Explorer**, an archetype derived from the psychological function of **logic**. The development and integration of

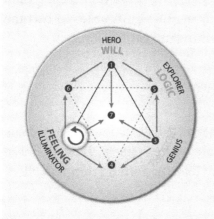

How to work with the model:

The arrow symbol for your Soul Type is under your dominant psychological function.

On the opposite side of the circle you will find the Soul Type and psychological function you need to develop and integrate in order to fully unfold the potential of your type. The Helpers can be found either side of the opposite Soul Type and function.

Figure 30. Circle of Integration for the Illuminator

the Explorer will give the Illuminator the ability to prioritise and discern what is true and false. Through developing the Explorer, the

Illuminator can learn to take a detached and objective position that is not caught up with feelings or a sense of dependency. Through integrating these qualities, the Illuminator will learn how to make objective use of factual information rather than getting caught up in subjective values. This will make the Illuminator better able to analyse a situation.

In addition, the Illuminator can draw upon two Helpers – the **Hero** and the **Genius** (**will** and **thought**). The Hero is a guide with a strong sense of power and authority – the Hero gives the Illuminator the freedom and courage to explore new opportunities in life. The Genius, meanwhile, provides the ability to take an overview of a situation and the mental flexibility to discern intelligent energy-efficient solutions – the Genius helps the Illuminator to devise, communicate and implement new ideas, building on the Illuminator's natural ability to work with empathy and practical compassion.

This example shows how a client's weaker psychological functions can be developed (a core concept in psychosynthesis) in order to become more balanced and harmonised in their overall expression.

The seven glamours and shadow work

Shadow work involves addressing the many distorted ways (conscious or unconscious) in which a type can express itself. Indeed, these distortions generate the sort of material that very often prompts a client to seek counselling.

When the client who is working with the Seven Types comes to understand that their problem is related to a particular type – whether a natural dominant type, qualities from overcompensation, or a false type that has been projected onto the client – this often generates a feeling of acceptance and gratitude that their problem is natural or due to false self-images. For example, for the strong dynamic or dedicated type it is natural to have anger management issues. Understanding their issues in this way will help the client to either accept the situation as a natural condition or to recognise that the issue is the result of a false self-image that they can reject – either way they are able to develop.

In his writings on meditation, Assagioli (1970b: Year 3) described some of the distortions that can arise from the seven types to hinder personal and transpersonal psychosynthesis. He terms these distortions "glamours" because they distort spiritual reality; in the language of the Seven Types we call these distortions "limiters" because they limit higher expressions of the types. Table 11 offers an overview of these glamours/limiters, but I would advise the reader to look at how Assagioli (1970b) defines the glamours and describes how they can be managed.

The Glamours related to the seven types according to Assagioli

Dynamic	Sensitive	Mental	Creative	Analytical	Dedicated	Practical
1. Power	1. Fear	1. The glamour of "being busy"	1. The glamour of vague artistic perception	1. The glamour of intellectuallity	1. Personal devotion	1. The glamour of law and order of organisation of ceremonial and ritual of the mystical and secret of magical powers
2. Imposition of authority	2. Loneliness	2. Constant planning	2. The glamour of beauty	2. The glamour of analysing and dissecting	2. Possessiveness	2. Psychism, mediumship
3. Ambition	3. Inferiority complex	3. Scheming to bring about desired ends	3. Tendency to diffusion	3. Criticism	3. Rigid adherence to an existing form or model	
4. Pride and conceit	4. Sense of futility	4. Deviousness and manipulation	4. Impracticality	4. Insecurity	4. Idealism	
5. Physical strength	5. Frustration	5. Self-interest	5. Lack of objectivity	5. The glamour of cold mental assessment	5. Fanaticism	
6. Self-centeredness	6. Depression	6. Preoccupation with practical matters at the expense of Spiritual Efficiency	6. Dissatisfaction with existing conditions because of a sense of that which is higher or greater	6. Over-emphasis of form	6. Narrow vision	
7. Surety of being right	7. Self-pity		7. Inner and outer conflict		7. Sentimental attachment	
8. Impatience and irritation	8. Anxiety					
9. Separativeness, isolation, aloofness	9. Inertia					
10. Independence	10. Self-effacement					
11. Freedom	11. Self-sacrifice					

Table 11. How the Glamours relate to the seven types, according to Assagioli

Next steps:
A whole range of possibilities in counselling work

Let me conclude this chapter by summarising some of the many themes and aspects of life that be addressed when working with the Seven Types in counselling.

The following list is based on the information that can be generated by completing the online profiling tools available at JivaYou.com. To begin with, the client can complete profiles to help discover their personality type, soul type, five top talents, and top limiters. This gives a lot of information that can be used as part of the counselling process. Let's consider some of the themes that can be drawn out of the information generated by these profiles and then worked with:

Life purpose and meaning: This theme is related to the seven ways to the soul and the development of the qualities of the soul type.

Soul motivation: This theme concerns our essential motivation for living a meaningful life, which is linked to our soul type. This motivation could be power, love, intelligence, creativity, knowledge, faith or results.

Soul integration: This refers to the harmonisation of the soul type with its opposites and with the qualities of the primary developer, helpers and integrators. This involves learning to control the distortions of the types, or limiters.

Ambition and self-esteem. This is related to the development of the personality type and our path to material and personal success.

Personality motivation. This concerns the discovery of our primary drive to success, be it power, love, intelligence, harmony, know-how, faith or results.

Personality integration. This concerns the development of the highest and most positive expression of our personality by integrating qualities from other types and transforming distortions.

Soul-personality integration. As discussed in chapter 8, the client needs to balance their outer life with their inner being, which involves combining the qualities of the personality type and soul type in service to the world.

Communication issues. Work in this area will be primarily focused on finding ways to unfold and develop the best qualities of the client's dominant thinking type.

Love issues. This theme involves working with the client's dominant feeling type, which will provide insight for developing relational qualities and tackling relational problems.

Grounding. This theme involves working with the body type to help a client relate to the material world and generate sufficient physical energy to accomplish what is needed.

Balancing the psychological functions: The JivaYou profiles show how the seven psychological functions can be balanced by highlighting where there is an insufficient development of the functions.

Top talents and their development. The JivaYou talent profile identifies a client's most developed talents based on their self-perception and experience. The profile identifies how these talents can be developed and balanced and how distortions can be addressed. The profile also identifies the three developmental keys for each talent that needs working on, these are the imbalance, the imbalance trigger, the primary developer and helpers that could be utilised to address the imbalance.

The talent balance. The degree of development of each of the 63 talents that we all possess can be identified. This will reveal potential talents and emergent talents we can nurture and develop.

Top limiters and their development. This aspect of profiling identifies a client's top five limiters (i.e. shadows or distortions) and describes the difficulties they create and how they can be worked with to achieve harmonisation.

Limiter balance. This theme concerns the relationship between the 56 limiters, identifying which of the limiters need addressing.

Being-Doing balance. This concerns the balance between being (soul) and doing (personality), as discussed in chapter 8.

Introvert-Extrovert balance. This theme concerns our introvert/ extrovert preference at each of the five levels. This information is generated when the JivaYou personality, soul, talent and limiter profiles have all been completed.

Intelligence balance. This concerns the balance between the renewing types (dynamic, sensitive, mental) and the manifesting types (creative, analytical, dedicated and practical).

The five elements balance. This concerns how the elements can be balanced across the five levels of body (earth), feeling (water), thinking (air), personality/will (fire) and soul (ether).

Masculine-feminine balance. The JivaYou profiling can identify how the client is balance across the more masculine energies (dynamic, mental, analytical, practical) and the more feminine energies (sensitive, creative, dedicated).

As can be seen from the above list, the counsellor working with the Seven Types has a great many options and angles from which to work with the client. Given this vast range of options, it can be helpful to gain a sense of clarity at the beginning of the work. Asking the following questions will help:

What does the client want? What are the client's fundamental needs, longings and goals?

Why does the client want this? What are the values and motivations underlying the client's desires?

What limits the client? What makes it difficult for the client to realise their needs?

What supports the client? What resources – inner and outer – can the client call on for support while journeying towards their goal?

How will the client do it? What are the client's first and next steps?

Chapter 14

The seven counselling strategies and styles

"If each of us interpreted his or her problems in terms of the ray energies, of their interplay, their conflicts and their harmonisation, we should receive much light on our problems and would find the keys and the ways to their solution."
Roberto Assagioli [1]

One of the key aims of this book is to show how the Seven Types can be applied very effectively in counselling, coaching, psychotherapy and mentoring. Working with the types is particularly useful for counsellors who take a holistic perspective that seeks to integrate the personal and transpersonal aspects of human nature – as with the

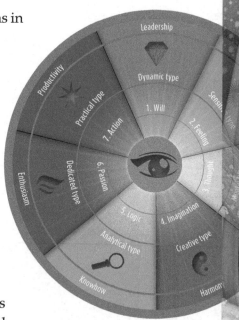

Figure 31. The seven core talents and functions.

psychosynthesis model, where the aim is to cooperate with the client to facilitate holistic development.

Four cardinal angles of therapy

In my book *Integral Meditation* (in chapter 12) I propose *four cardinal areas*, which are four angles from which to approach holistic work with a client. These four areas are covered in detail in my book, but in brief the counsellor is urged to work with the client from the following four angles:

---

[1] Assagioli quoted in The Seven Rays of Energy, by Michal Eastcott,1980, Sundial House, p. 82

1. *The Identity and being of the client.* Focus on answering the question: 'Who am I?' Explore the needs and values of the dominant types at the five psychological levels.
2. *The authenticity and autonomy of the client.* Focus on the will and its expression through an authentic and powerful identity in which the dominant types are manifesting.
3. *The social skills and community life of the client.* Focus on the client's love life and relationships and the development of empathy in line with the qualities of the dominant types.
4. *The creative expression of the client.* Focus on the development of the specific talents that arise from the client's dominant types and their contribution to greater wholeness.

These four areas constitute a general overview of the typical life journey, and this process is reflected in the journey of counselling. At each stage of this evolutionary process, it is vital that the seven psychological functions and their respective types are developed so that the corresponding skills and talents can manifest fully.

Seven counselling strategies and styles for developing the psychological qualities, functions and talents of the types

The Seven Types offers a psychological key to understanding the individual. For the counsellor, the Seven Types also offers seven counselling *perspectives*, or approaches, from which it is possible to address each of the types effectively. The challenge facing the counsellor is to identify and work with the client's dominant types as they arise in the work at any of the five levels. Adopting the appropriate perspective from which to work will help the counsellor to tackle whatever is obstructing the development of a particular type and its corresponding talent, function and qualities.

Each of the seven counselling perspectives has an associated style, strategy and a set of techniques. When working with a particular type, the counsellor is urged to adopt the appropriate perspective and style, and implement the relevant strategies and techniques.

We will now look in detail at how these counselling perspectives, styles and strategies can be called upon to develop the talents associated with the seven types (Figure 31). These seven talents are:

Leadership: the talent associated with the function of will and the dynamic type. From this perspective, the counsellor strengthens the client's autonomy and authority and ability to live an independent life.

Empathy: the talent associated with the function of feeling and the sensitive type. Here, the objective is to expand the client's ability to hold a loving space so they can gain insight into whatever arises in their consciousness and improve their social life.

Ingenuity: the talent associated with the function of thought and the mental type. The focus here is to strengthen the talent for intelligent, inventive and strategic thought that can make use of all resources in the client's network.

Harmony: the talent associated with the function of imagination and the creative type. From this perspective, the client's talent for conflict resolution is developed through an ability to play with opposite desires – both in their own psyche and in the environment – in order to reach a unique harmonious balance.

Know-how: the talent associated with the function of logic and the analytical type. Here, the client's objectivity is trained through rigorous reality testing of subjective feelings and belief systems.

Enthusiasm: the talent associated with the function of passion and the dedicated type. Here, the client's core values and ideals are brought into focus, which will ignite the motivational fire of enthusiasm.

Productivity: the talent associated with the function of action and the practical type. The client's organisational powers are harnessed, ideas and insights are put into action, and real physical change is effected.

These seven talents can be addressed independently of each other and in any order. The counsellor is called on to adopt whichever counselling strategy is most relevant according to whichever talent or aspect of the client's development is most present in the work.

Over time, the aim is to develop all of the seven functions *no matter which types dominate our nature* – this is because each psychological function generates a core talent, or competence, that needs to be mastered for us to become fully integrated and functional. During the counselling, different blind spots, weaknesses and blockages will emerge – these belong often to an undeveloped function and will indicate which function requires work at that moment.

Most counsellors tend to work from the perspective of *empathy and insight*, so, correspondingly, the client will come to master those issues associated with the feeling function and the sensitive type. It is therefore essential that the counsellor calls on other counselling perspectives, strategies and styles so that the other talents and functions can also be addressed. Furthermore, a tendency to focus on empathy might be contra-indicated in some cases, for example, some masculine types might become irritated and resistant if the counsellor comes across as *too* empathic and "motherly". By making use of the seven counselling perspectives, rather than following a habitual style, the counsellor can adapt their style so they are able to empathically meet the client in their world.

Table 12 shows the relationship between the seven psychological functions, the seven types and the seven core talents. We are all called to develop our talents – clients and counsellors alike – and the counsellor is encouraged to call upon all of the talents as part of the work, and the next section will explore what this might look like in practice. But while the following section has a focus on counselling, the reader is encouraged to consider how the same principles could be applied in other areas, such as teaching and parenting.

The seven psychological functions and core talents

Functions	Will	Feeling	Thought	Imagination	Logic	Passion	Action
Types	Dynamic	Sensitive	Mental	Creative	Analytical	Dedicated	Practical
Talents	Leadership	Empathy	Ingenious	Harmony	Knowhow	Enthusiasm	Productivity

Table 12. The seven psychological functions and core talents

One of the primary objectives in psychosynthesis counselling is to develop the weaker psychological functions. According to Assagioli (1967a):

Psychosynthesis has evolved naturally, and I would say spontaneously, from the ground, or out of the main stem, of psychoanalysis, as a method of psychotherapy – or, more precisely, as a body of techniques and methods coordinated and directed towards the achievement of a complete and harmonious development of the human personality. Its principal aims and tasks are:

1. The *elimination* of the conflicts and obstacles, conscious and unconscious, that block this development.

2. The use of *active techniques* to stimulate the psychic functions still weak and immature.

Adopting the right counselling style

A different style of counselling will be suitable for each of the seven types. Each style suggests the best approach for how to sit with the natural energies of clients. In each case, the key is empathy. The art of empathy is the art of stepping into the other's world – and sometimes out of the comfort zone of our own natural environment. Of course, it is not always possible to be 100 per cent present with a client, especially when we encounter types whose qualities are very different from our own, but we can always take a step in the client's direction. I am not suggesting that we overly identify with the client, only that we learn to empathise through consciously accessing the qualities within us that best match the qualities of the client. Assagioli speaks about it in this way: "Truth is One – but its presentation is diverse and so different levels, according to the kind of people to whom we address ourselves. One has to talk to each in their language. We have to be polyglots psychologically and spiritually, learn to be translators." [2]

When I speak about types I am usually referring to a *personality type*, but the same principles apply when working with a dominant type at any of the five levels. Sometimes the types appear in the guise of subpersonalities – so the same client might express a range of different types – the trick is to change our counselling style in order to mirror the particular subpersonality we are working with.

---

[2] From a paper prepared for students of his Leo and the Will Project class in 1963 (Assagioli Archive, Florence).

Counselling is an art form – a dance with energies – so having an insight into the Seven Types will provide us with flexibility and creativity in the moment. When we can mirror the client's different energies, we can empower that particular aspect of the client and encourage it to manifest more fully in its natural state. Your insights into what motivates a particular energy of the client – its longings and desires, its highest expression, its imbalance and potential for harmonisation – will help guide the client towards finding their own unique expression of that energy.

Whenever a significant obstacle to development of a talent has been identified, *active techniques* can be adopted to unlock the potential in the corresponding psychological function. The principal way of doing this – which applies for all the types – is for the counsellor to *radiate* the quality that is being blocked by adopting the counselling style associated with that talent.

As mentioned, counsellors can become accustomed and comfortable with a particular counselling style because it is *convenient* for us. We feel safe when adopting our familiar style, but when we do so we might not be attending to what the client really needs. In fact, we could be working against our clients' best interests because we are not addressing the whole range of talents. The Seven Types is an approach that provides us with the necessary flexibility.

Let me give an example. If a client is lacking the quality of will, then the counsellor should choose a will-based counselling style if the client agrees. (there is a chapter on this style in my book *The Soul of Psychosynthesis*). This style of counselling style will bring forth the qualities of will by helping the client to clarify his core needs, which means *identifying*, *owning* and *taking responsibility* for them. The counsellor will supervise and support the client through this process, and help the client to evaluate the results of his actions. The aim in this approach is to help the client to recognise themselves as the sole authority of their life – perhaps helping the client to identify with their inner king, queen, director, leader, etc. Role-play with chair work can help. The client must *feel* the will as a psychological force – the *will-to-be-self*– and this is facilitated through an awareness-based counselling (presented in full in *The Soul of Psychosynthesis*). This approach involves the counsellor encouraging the client to adopt the inner attitude of the observer and to tune into the felt sense of will energy, which is the particular *purpose* and *intention* behind a need, the will to make something happen. At the same time, the counsellor will change their style of counselling by becoming more demanding of the client, directing the focus of the work towards meeting the client's needs. The counsellor's tone of voice will become sharper and there will be a focus on the client's responsibility and strength, alongside an *expectation* that the client will rise to the occasion. Active techniques that can be made use of include meditation, role play, and physical movement exercises to do between sessions whereby the client is encouraged to practice stepping into their authority.

Assagioli called the above counselling style "father therapy". In an interview, Assagioli (Miller, 1972) explained:

> The therapist, you see, has two major roles: *the motherly role and the fatherly role*. The motherly role of the therapist is in order in the first part of the treatment, especially in the more serious cases. It consists in giving a sense of protection, understanding, sympathy and encouragement. What a wise mother does. It is a direct *helping* by the therapist of the client.

> The fatherly role, on the other hand, can be summed up as the *training to independence*. The true fatherly role, as I see it, is to encourage, to arouse the inner energies of the child and to show him the way to

independence. Therefore, the fatherly function is to awaken the will of the client.

A will-based counselling style looks more like business coaching: training the client to become a competent leader of his or her life. Let us now look in detail at how we can develop and strengthen a weak psychological function through particular counselling perspectives, strategies, styles and techniques. These are effective for developing the seven psychological functions and their respective qualities and talents.

Development of leadership and the dynamic type

Assagioli defines the self as "*a centre of pure consciousness and will*". Another way of saying this is that we is the conscious observer – the conscious "I" – who is continually making choices. This centre is not identical with the contents of consciousness – i.e. our thoughts, feelings and sensations – but is a neutral presence behind the mind, emotions and body. In other words, we *have* a body, emotions and a mind, but we are not our body, emotions and mind, we simply make use of them as we act in the world.

By developing the client's ability to observe rather than identify with the contents of consciousness, the client will come to realise that they can take charge of their lives through conscious choice and the application of the will. The client can learn to choose what to identify with and how they want to act in the world – and this is the foundation of an independent life. When clients discover this centre, they can begin to choose who they are and how they want to live through the use of conscious intention. In terms of the Seven Types, they can choose which types and qualities they want to express. In this way, the client becomes the leader and creator of their own life.

The will and the dynamic qualities urge us to become the independent leader of our own lives through the authentic expression of our unique qualities as we seek to achieve self-initiated objectives. Through the function of will and the qualities of the dynamic type, we can develop authority and take full responsibility for our lives. In doing so, we can stop playing the victim and become a purposeful *leader* who is living an empowered life.

Therefore, to encourage leadership, the primary task for the counsellor is to help the client disidentify from limiting roles and self-perceptions, and to identify instead with the conscious "I". This is how Assagioli (Keen, 1974) describes the process:

> At the heart of the self there is both an active and a passive element, an agent and a spectator. Self-consciousness involves our being a witness – a pure, objective, loving witness – to what is happening within and without. In this sense the self is not dynamic in itself but is a point of witness, a spectator, an observer who watches the flow. But there is another part of the inner self – the will-er or the directing agent – that actively intervenes to orchestrate the various functions and energies of the personality, to make commitments and to instigate action in the external world. So, at the centre of the self there is a unity of masculine and feminine, will and love, action and observation.

Many methods can be used to help the client to access what Assagioli calls the "directing agent", including dialogue, the disidentification/ identification exercise, meditation on the wilful observer, visualisation, and chair work.

Through making use of these various techniques, the client is encouraged to develop the qualities of will, which are one-pointedness, courage, attention, responsibility, initiative, organisation and discipline. [3] The client is encouraged to practice acts of the will between sessions, such as setting boundaries, cutting ties, taking action, and stepping into authority. Evolving the will and dynamic type of the client will reduce his dependence on the therapist and strengthen his ability to realise his vision.

Let's look in more detail at how we might use chair work. The counsellor informs the client that the chair he normally sits in is the seat of the directing agent (leader, instructor, director, captain, etc.) – this chair represents the client's core identity as consciousness and will. From there, the client directs the therapy session, making decisions regarding what to work with – this provides the client with an opportunity to practice leadership and autonomy in their own life. As the session proceeds, whenever a significant pattern of behaviour or subpersonality emerges, the counsellor invites the client to give it a name and place it in another chair in the room: in this way, the subpersonality becomes an *employee* that the directing agent can observe, contain and negotiate with. The qualities of the subpersonality are felt and analysed so that its type can be determined. Continuing in this way, the client will be able to become the leader of his various subpersonalities as they emerge and are placed in the other chair. All the while, the client is enacting being the leader who can identify and integrate his subpersonalities so they become active co-creators of the life he wants to live.

The dynamic style of counselling when you encounter a dynamic type

Your style of communication: Get straight to the point. Cut to the chase. Help your client define their objectives with first, second and third

---

[3] See Assagioli (1974: 19) for a full list of the qualities of the will.

priorities. Be direct in your communication. Be demanding, have high expectations, and count on your client's strength.

When giving feedback, start with your conclusions before illustrating with anecdotes. Stay with the main focus and don't get lost in detail. Have a clear direction for the counselling and invite feedback on progress. Expect the client to act and hold themselves responsible for whatever they decide to do. Don't hesitate to be confrontational when naming their defenses.

It's important to meet this type strongly and directly. You must demonstrate you have mastered your skills, which promotes confidence and is a prerequisite for accessing the client's more vulnerable parts.

Show authority and authenticity by being yourself. Communicate feelings coherently in a contained manner that is not too emotional. Avoid nursing the client, as this can be perceived as pity. Take for granted that this type can manage themselves and expect them to take responsibility. Accept that this type often has difficulties accessing their emotional nature in a nuanced way.

Your body language: Hold boundaries. Shake hands firmly. Don't hug the client immediately, and perhaps never. Look directly in their eyes. Show high energy and vitality if possible.

Client's expectations towards the counsellor: Looks for strength in your clarity, understanding, presence and authority, especially via eye contact. Wants to be challenged with a clear set of goals and suggested actions, and your ability to do this will determine whether you receive their respect, which is not a given but something you must earn. If you lack clarity, generalise or fluctuate, it is highly probable you will be perceived as weak.

Active techniques to develop leadership: Devise a relevant meditation on the will and record it on the client's phone for use at any time. Help the client to create a vision board displaying their core objectives. Design images or signs with evocative words that the client can put up at home or in the office – words could include 'courage', 'attention', 'focus', 'leadership', 'initiative'. Role play using the director's chair. Challenge the client to engage with their difficulties and submit to consequences, however harsh, because this will develop assertiveness.

Development of empathy and the sensitive type

An important focus in counselling is to strengthen the client's ability to hold and accept painful material with self-empathy. This will involve containing energies and subpersonalities that arise in consciousness, then seeking to understand their needs and strategies through empathic presence. This ability for compassionate containment, of both ourselves and others, is acquired through the development of the sensitive type.

The development of *empathy* creates an internal loving space that will grow as the client comes to accept all aspects of themselves, both personal and transpersonal. The result is an ability to stand in sensitive contact with the vast inner world of consciousness at all five levels, with respect to both the self and others. For the developed sensitive type, all human feelings can be tolerated, including destructive energies from the lower unconscious and the unifying energies of wisdom and love from the higher unconscious.

Through empathy, the client can stand in their own light with a sense of loving-acceptance towards inhibited and rejected aspects of themselves that emerge from the shadow – as Assagioli stated above, the client will be able to adopt a *"pure, objective, loving witness – to what is happening within and without"*. As the client gradually develops the core talent of empathy, the capacity to be a loving witness will unfold.

The sensitive type primarily develops and unfolds within the context of relationship, whether inter-personal or intra-personal. Because of this, the *quality* of the counselling relationship is immensely important. In working with the sensitive qualities, the compassion and wisdom of the counsellor becomes an outer image of the client's soul which the client can internalise through the relationship. The more the counsellor can demonstrate wisdom, insight and compassion, the more she will be able to mirror the sensitive qualities of the client's soul.

In working with the sensitive qualities, the intention of the counsellor is "to love everything that is". The client will, in turn, acquire this attitude and be able to make empathic connections with their pain and, as they do so, the challenges and conflicts they face will start to resolve. The therapist assists this process by transmitting their empathic intention through feedback and, more directly, by allowing a sense of acceptance to embrace the client – the counsellor can enlighten the client through the radiation of love. This ability to hold the client in a bifocal awareness of both *who they are* and *who they can be* is crucial for helping the client to develop empathy. There is a need to see the client as a soul that is evolving through the challenges of life and learning to find meaning in pain. The counsellor must therefore hold a compassionate understanding of human pain.

Part of this deep work will involve exploring the dynamics of the client's personal relationships: family, partner, friends, colleagues, social network.

The sensitive style of counselling when you encounter a sensitive type

Your style of communication: You need to connect with this person with a distinct kindness, listening and creating space for the client to open up. You are dealing with a highly sensitive person, so seek to generate a warm, gentle and relaxed atmosphere. Communicate in an inclusive way. Avoid jumping to conclusions. Adopt a calm communication style that allows for the client's subconscious elements to emerge gradually without being forced. Give yourself plenty of time to relax into the client's material so that deeper content can emerge and reveal itself.

Point out possible solutions, but don't be overly goal-oriented and do not push. Emphasise the client's core values and themes and illustrate them with relevant anecdotes. It is through connecting and being with the client in his or her sensitive field that your counselling will have the best effect. It is your radiance of a calm open strength that will nurture and heal, and that will help this type to prosper.

Show authenticity by showing your personal reactions to the client's content. Create comfortable conditions. Develop a situation where trust can grow and where it is natural to be personal, relaxed and open to vulnerability.

Your body language: Offer a warm handshake, perhaps a hug or touch on the shoulder. Smile to show kindness. Create a warm soft physical environment, perhaps offering something hot to drink.

Client's expectations towards the counsellor: The client will look to you for kindness, warmth and availability, and an ability to interact personally. If you are too direct and goal-oriented, or too generalising and impersonal, you could be perceived as cold and insensitive.

Active techniques to develop empathy: The relationship between client and counsellor is crucial because the empathic role and function of the counsellor will be internalised. Recording a meditation focused on the loving-witness will be a resource for the client to work with between sessions to help expand their sensitive awareness. Chair work involving dialogue with unacceptable parts or people in the client's life will help to develop a sense of acceptance. The client should learn to express genuine openness, appreciation and love towards significant people in the client's life because this will improve the client's love language. The counsellor can support the client with dating and relating, in particular with learning how to be vulnerable in a contained way.

Development of ingenuity and the mental type

Ingenuity is the talent for coming up with ideas that prompt practical change. In the context of counselling, ingenuity shows itself in the capacity for turning insight into action, which strengthens the client's ability to learn new behaviour. For this to happen, the counsellor needs to help the client to gain new perspectives and evolve realistic strategies for action.

When life is seen from the perspective of the mental type, the focus is on learning to thrive in a social network. The client must realise he is an integral part of a social community and that his growth is dependent on his ability to access and utilise the resources of the network (including his own resources) for the benefit of all. From the mental perspective, knowing our position in a social structure and how we fit into the social organism is crucial because it is through the exchange of our mutual resources at the five levels that we learn to thrive and succeed in life.

Many of our clients lack a healthy perspective on how life works. The counsellor can help the client by offering psycho-education and by describing various maps of reality, focusing on human growth and social change. The counsellor could draw on their own experience of studying and working from a range of conceptual frameworks, which will help the client to examine their core values, social history and ongoing concerns. The effect will be to help the client to put their life and circumstances into perspective and create clarity in the areas of work, family, finance and hopes for the future.

Developing the core talent of *ingenuity* will ensure that the client has the ability to keep life in perspective and to adopt a strategic outlook so that their energies can be used wisely in their social network. In this respect, the mental type has the advantage of "network-awareness", meaning the ability to assess where they stand and how to act from the perspective of their social groups.

The counsellor needs to help the client to view their challenges from different perspectives – and this will create space for fresh insights to emerge. Techniques that will help the client include reflective meditation, brainstorming, role play, speaking from the diverse viewpoints of subpersonalities, creative drawing, and studying a range of conceptual frameworks, such as psychoenergetics, the Seven Types, psychosynthesis and Ken Wilber's integral psychology.

With regards to role play, it can be transformative to see oneself through the eyes of one's mother or father, or even God, simply playing the role and speaking to oneself from this position. Another effective technique is Ken Wilber's 3-2-1 method whereby the client is invited to take the position of the first, second and third person with respect to a person or life challenge – this means, firstly, describing the person/situation in question from the perspective of an outside observer; secondly, engaging in an imaginative dialogue with the relevant parties; and, thirdly, identifying with the person/situation by talking from that perspective.

The counsellor can help the client to observe the content of their inner life, noticing in particular how thoughts are often a regurgitation of what we have internalised from our family or culture. Indeed, it could be argued that most of our inner life is merely a reflection of the collective life, which means there is very little that can be said to be authentically our own. Training the client to observe their relationship to people and society in an objective way will help them to detach from the influences of the collective and find their own voice. To this end, making use of systemic therapy, family constellation work and role play will help to unfold the talent of ingenuity and the qualities of the mental type.

Having acquired the ability to adopt a strategic perspective and social awareness, ingenuity then provides us with the ability to implement action using skillful will. There will be a focus on accessing social and economic resources in the individual's network through establishing better connections, working collaboratively and exchanging of information and resources with family, friends and society. To this end, the counsellor and client should devise plans for tackling specific challenges that will lead to growth – with an agreed process for monitoring and evaluation to ensure that results are achieved. When insights can be continually tested with practical experiments, a creative flow will emerge between the client's inner and outer reality that will help to ground the client in daily life.

The mental style of counselling when you encounter a mental type

Your style of communication: This type needs to know that you are intelligent and competent, so your communication style will be very important. You must first connect with the person in the mind by sharing a clear agenda and a comprehensive overview of how you work and why.

This type tends to be impersonal, so don't be too personal in your style. Don't set a rigid frame for how you work; allow for flexibility and experimentation. This type loves to explore many avenues, so keep doors open and help the client to conclude at the close of the session. This type tends to have insights in terms of patterns, taking an overview and devising strategies. They reach conclusions cautiously, so don't offer interpretations too soon, allow the process itself to generate mental clarity, which is what this type needs more than anything. This type changes their behaviour when they start to comprehend patterns mentally, so be smart and strategic and support them by showing you have a masterful command of theory.

Help the client to remain focused on action rather than words, because this type needs to be held accountable for their practice, not what they talk about. This type can be slippery and avoidant when confronted with their pain, so watch out for rationalisations and excuses – if you can detect their manipulations and call them out, they will respect you. If they can outsmart you, they will leave.

Help the client to connect with the emotional aspects of their problems, and offer helpful explanations for why you are doing this. Radiate calmness and quiet strength and resist the temptation to get lost in their mental associations. When you hold them accountable and keep them on track, they will let you to take over their thinking function for a moment and allow themselves to drop into the irrational abyss which they fear, but which they need to do so they can experience catharsis.

Your body language: Be calm and relaxed but alert, and give the client plenty of space.

Client's expectations towards the counsellor: The client will focus on your mental skills, CV, achievements and language skills. They will appreciate it if you can hold onto the bigger picture and adopt a flexible approach. They will expect you to keep track of all the threads of their material and synthesise them in clear ways. They may withdraw if you become too personal or if they perceive you as stupid or if you adopt a limited focus.

Active techniques to develop ingenuity: Brainstorming. Drawing maps of social networks and economic and social resources. Invite the client to stand on a chair and view a wheel of life that has been placed on the floor. Encourage the client to debate their life and needs, with the counsellor playing devil's advocate or playing other useful roles. Develop the client's social and communication skills by playing with words, concepts and strategies. Learn to negotiate needs by implementing experiments between sessions so that the client can learn better ways of engaging with the important people in their lives. Experiment with social roles to practice getting what one needs.

Development of harmony and the creative type

Conflict and change have always been a part of humanity's life and experience. So how do we create harmony in an unpredictable world? The counsellor will pinpoint that conflict keeps us on our toes and prevents life from stagnating into routine. At the same time, we all have a longing for harmony. Indeed, there is within each of us a permanent centre of harmony that does not change: this is the centre of pure consciousness and will. In our discussion  of the dynamic type, we referred to this centre as the *loving observer* – no matter what happens in our lives, the observer is a resource that is always available to us and does not change. This centre is our "I Am-ness" – it is and has always been constant, even though our *interpretation* of who we are – our self-identity – changes from child to mature adult.

When we connect with our centre, an openness and creativity starts to unfold: we are no longer so afraid to be ourselves, we do not feel the need to constantly defend who we are or our point of view, we can access a calm centre amid the chaos of life. The creative type is able to access this centre intuitively due to a natural desire to be in the present moment – but all types need to develop this mindset. When we are identified with this calm centre, we are able to accept complexity and conflict and leave things to interact and combine in new and creative ways so that beauty and harmony can emerge. From this perspective, the vision of the creative type is primarily to achieve an integrated personality that accepts all of our facets and talents – producing unity in diversity.

From the perspective of the creative type, the counsellor will "go with the flow", working in creative and experimental ways that leave room for surprises. There will be a focus on working with conflict in the client's life – whether between parts of the self or with other people. Conflicts always arise in the absence of a third balancing factor, which is the wholeness-oriented, loving observer – the still calm centre. Most conflicts can be resolved by adopting this observer stance and empathising with the needs of the conflicting forces, then seeking to find a position that can satisfy the opposing needs to some degree.

Very often during work with the creative type, a resistance will arise in the client – but this resistance can itself become a cooperative partner in the work if it can be seen as another aspect of the client's psyche that needs to be heard and included in the larger picture. However, acceptance is only the first stage: we must also investigate the subpersonalities if there is to be deep transformation. We need to discover the strategies being adopted by the subpersonalities and how their needs can be met. Dramatisation can help with this, using role play to explore the underlying forces that drive the subpersonalities; we can also use visualisation and drawing exercises that encourage the client to play out the needs of the different parts. This "'play" brings to the surface the various energies that are engaged in the conflict, which provides opportunities to work with the conflicting energies to find creative solutions.

The act of engaging with a conflict will itself release creative energy. Indeed, while conflicts cannot always be resolved, the simple act of exploring tensions will release creative possibilities for new attitudes and courses of action. For example, two people in a campaign group might want the same thing but disagree over how to achieve this shared vision; in working with this tension, the conflict may remain unresolved, but the work itself will release energy and creativity, allowing for a third balancing perspective and creating space for at least mutual respect and appreciation for different perspectives. This is a description of what often happens in a democracy that is working at its best.

It can be seen, therefore, that harmony is not necessarily an absence of conflict, but an attitude in which polarities can be held in balance around a shared higher value. When we embrace this higher value, conflict may remain, but there will be a sense of order, direction and harmony that exists *despite* the chaos. In other words, our task as counsellors in helping clients to develop the core talent of harmony involves encouraging the client to play with opposites, embrace chaos, and trust in the process – and out of this a sense of balance can be achieved as old patterns break up and reassemble to produce new patterns, possibilities and liberation.

The creative style of counselling when you encounter a creative type

Your style of communication: This type needs a lot of space to experiment with emotional expression, so create an open atmosphere where there is room for improvisation, with few rules and regulations. It is important to explore the client's emotions and fantasies and what you are experiencing while you are with them. They need your feedback and authentic presence and need to feel you can pick up on all the emotional currents in the room.

Be prepared to use creative interventions to support the work, such as drawing, body work, role playing, visualisation, meditation. Make space for the full range of emotions and accept the client's chaotic elements. A good sense of humor is often essential and helps to create trust, so be lively and full of situational awareness. You might offer psycho-education using imagery or lived examples from your own or other people's lives.

Let the client feel your acceptance. Create room for opposites and extremes. Make space for an informal, joyful and relaxed relationship that allows the present moment to reveal what needs to be explored.

Your body language: Be loose, allowing space for eye contact, even body contact if appropriate. Maintain situational awareness. Adopting these approaches will help to create a sense of comfort and wellness.

Client's expectations towards the counsellor: This type will expect you to be vibrant and authentic and to encounter them both in the here and now and in the extremes that may be characteristic of their personal life. At the same time, the client needs you to be a solid rock-like presence as they travel the emotional roller coaster, so show an authority and calmness that will reassure them that you can handle chaos and drama.

Active techniques to develop harmony: Visualisations, dream work, free drawing, role play and dramatisation in which conflicting voices can be acted out and appreciated. Explore and accept taboos, abnormalities, darkness and weirdness within an integrated whole.

Motivate the client to experiment with doing the unexpected, playing with new roles and different social environments. They might also benefit from strengthening their grace, beauty and harmony through yoga, meditation or decorating the home with beautiful art and colour.

Development of know-how and the analytical type

The content of our experience is one thing, how we *interpret* our experience is another. The analytical type is pre-occupied with how we interpret reality, and in seeking to distinguish what is real from what is false. This is a challenge because none of us sees reality as it really is, rather we perceive the world through our particular lenses or interpretations. Hence, for the analytical type, the challenge is to constantly reassess  how we are perceiving the world, testing perceptions against the best available data. This is how we develop the talent of *know-how* – which is the ability to acquire and make use of objective knowledge through experimentation and verification. If we want to develop the talent of know-how, we need to develop our analytical qualities and apply them to life in a practical manner.

The analytical strategy of counselling involves gathering factual and objective data about the client. For the counsellor, this means adopting a neutral perspective regarding the client's material and history. This requires a balancing act: listening with empathy to the *experience* of the client, while adopting a neutral stance towards the *interpretation* of that experience.

The analytical type believes that the truth will set us free, so he wants to see reality as clearly as possible. This clear, cool quality of intellect tends to cut through all kinds of romantic notions and delusions. To give an example, the analytical type does not take the word love for granted, but wants to analyse the different kinds of love: possessive, abusive, altruistic, fatherly, motherly, romantic, impersonal, etc. Because of this discriminating tendency, when seeking to develop analytical qualities in the client, it is helpful if the counsellor can be specific in how they ask questions and gather material, and in how that material is examined. It can be helpful to come at the same material from many different angles in order to achieve as accurate an understanding as possible. It is due to the quality of discrimination and the clear cold light of the intellect that the client can learn to see things as they are. All counsellors know the magical effect of finding the right words to describe a client's condition – when these words are heard, there is integration between thought and emotion and something that was fragmented can become whole. In such moments, we see that words can redeem.

To develop the client's analytical skills, the counsellor needs to model and teach the stance of the neutral observer who is able to detach from feelings and circumstances and hold them instead in the light of consciousness, where they can be examined dispassionately and in detail. In this respect, the technique of *disidentification* will be a helpful tool to work with.

This stance of the neutral observer can evolve so that it becomes possible to engage in *penetrating reflection,* wherein a thorough examination can be made of all thoughts, convictions, emotions, desires, images, bodily sensations and meanings that might arise for the client – whether in the moment or as reported from their lives. It is during such meticulous examinations that interpretations of life experience – such as "Mom doesn't love me" – can be updated and finessed.

When using this strategy, the counsellor might adopt techniques such as journaling, questionnaires and personality questionnaires, all of which can gather data. This is a focused approach that uses scientific testing to reach reliable conclusions. In this regard, counsellor and client are working together on a fact-finding mission to discover the truth about the client's life, generating insight into what is real and what is not real.

Interestingly, it is the analytical perspective that the counsellor is required to draw upon when seeking to develop an effective professional practice, for example ensuring that supervision, therapy and meditation are in place to help ensure that our own interpretations and projections of the client are as clear and accurate as possible.

The analytical style of counselling when you encounter an analytical type

Your style of communication: From the beginning, show you are professional by creating a structured environment and by outlining how you work and your expectations, all of which will create a sense of security. This is important because this type of client will often be well out of their comfort zone when they show up for counselling because their typical approach in life is to solve problems on their own.

This type needs clear boundaries, so don't be too personal. You need to win their trust through a professional mental understanding. You need to demonstrate your competence and knowledge so the client can see you are reliable and in control of what you are doing.

Be factual and keep track of important details in the client's life. They may get lost in detail, so help them to see the bigger picture. Work from a position of common sense in which material can be evaluated, compared and measured by results. When exploring the emotional and irrational aspects of their nature, allow plenty of time for putting words to all the nuances of their experience because this will help them process uncomfortable experiences. Be specific and factual with a sense of timing to create noteworthy milestones and results.

Meet the client with calmness and an objective focus with the aim of getting to the heart of the matter. It is important to motivate the client to be courageous in dealing with their emotional nature. Help them to feel their emotions instead of just talking about them and rationalising. Be focused and show patience when they allow themselves to become absorbed by emotional content. Be a calm and problem-orientated listener, keeping the focus on the essence of the matter and leaving out secondary details.

Your body language: Respect boundaries. Be serious, contained and focused. Show courtesy and be quietly reliable.

Client's expectations towards the counsellor: The client will expect a high degree of reliability and a professional attitude. They will look for a highly competent counsellor with an ability to work methodically and to focus on experience. They want a counsellor who can help them to achieve tangible results in a structured setting. It is not enough for this type to be in a pleasant and loving atmosphere: they need to see practical changes in their life. They need you to formulate clear goals and a reliable strategy for them to accomplish.

Active techniques to develop know-how: Gather and test data through questioning and personality tests. Use reflective meditation, the disidentification exercise, and role playing with the objective observer (invite the client to stand behind their chair and look down at his situation from an objective bird's eye perspective). Invite the client to write an objective autobiography and/or go on a fact-finding mission, seeking to verify assumptions through collecting information about her life from family and friends. The client should be encouraged to practice stating the truth as they see it and to discriminate between priorities so that their values and needs can become clear.

Development of enthusiasm and the dedicated type

With enthusiasm and energy and a clear direction, we can cope with most of life's challenges. We can establish a clear direction when we are able to discern what makes our lives valuable, good, true and beautiful. From an evolutionary perspective, adopting a goal-oriented life, with our energies gathered around a positive focus, is enormously stabilising and beneficial in terms of our psychological health and well-being. Establishing such goals, and pursuing them with enthusiasm, is the perspective of the dedicated type.

In working from the dedicated perspective, the counsellor is helping the client to develop the talent of *enthusiasm* – which first requires that the client discovers what they are most passionate about. The aim of counselling is to bring these interests into play, which will give the work direction. The client could be asked: What do you long for? What is your dream? What excites you? Such questions will activate the fire of enthusiasm, or what Assagioli called the *joyful will* (1974: 199). Through exploring these questions, the client will be able to distinguish between what is important and what is *urgent* – which will help to cut through surface material and get to the heart of what really motivates them; alternatively, these questions will reveal that the client does not yet know what they want, in which case their journey can begin by discovering a valuable need. When they discover their passion, the client can begin the process of taking a stance in life and accepting responsibility.

An effective technique in this work involves the use of *ideal models*, which are *realistic images of what we might become and attain*. These models encapsulate our needs and values in any given area. We can develop ideal models for every aspect of our lives, though as counsellors it is important that we only work with a few at a time because having too many goals can become overwhelming for the client. We can establish ideal models for our professional role, our company, and our roles as friend, father or mother, and this will help us to develop an integrated personality.

An ideal model contains a reservoir of powerful motivational energy that is characterised by joy and enthusiasm. Reflecting and meditating on these ideal models will help bring them to life, making it easier for us to steer our thinking and action towards specific goals, with less risk of being distracted by our daily routines.

Using ideal models with our clients will help bring into consciousness whatever is preventing them from achieving their goals – whether internal resistances or external barriers. We can invite the client to use the quality of desire to purify their focus. Blockages and resistances can include laziness, fear, and negative self-images. As the client works through these resistances, they will begin to develop a clear and sharp focus. For us, as counsellors, rather than "digging up the whole backyard" looking for traumas and early life material, the focus is on encouraging our clients to set their sights on pursuing their dreams.

Working with ideal models largely involves visualisation to call forth an inner image. Sometimes it can take a client a while to envisage an accurate image of what they are seeking, but at other times the image will appear fully formed, perhaps in the client's dreams. Sometimes, images enter consciousness with such power that they can become life-long guides. (In my book *The Soul of Psychosynthesis*, I dedicate a chapter to working with ideal models.)

Working with ideal models is highly directive and purposeful – it avoids meandering on the surface of consciousness. This method encourages the client to take responsibility for seeking and realising their life goals.

The dedicated style of counselling when you encounter a dedicated type

Your style of communication: Approach the client with a wholehearted engagement, creating a positive and optimistic atmosphere in which there is a clear focus on core issues. This client is on a quest and holds high ideals, so allow them to set the bar high. Make sure there is direction and a clear purpose. They need you to share some of their ideals, so be aware of those values you share and express this: they need a personal and loyal relationship.

This type needs a counsellor who can understand their sincerity, romantic sentiment and explosive temperament, so be prepared for an intense and extreme encounter with idealisations and aggressive emotions. You must be able to stay present and open whenever the highs and lows of their experience come to the fore.

You must be able to express your emotions and share your commitment to the client's process. Don't become too dry, theoretical or analytical because this type needs action, so help them to set goals – and celebrate when these goals are achieved. It is ok to be receptive, warm and accepting, but this type will become bored if you just listen without helping them to feel their passions and pains.

Help the client to loosen up using humor and a relaxed tone, which will help to disarm the seriousness that they use to block out feelings. It's important to help this type see alternative perspectives, which will help them to avoid becoming compulsive or trapped in unhealthy desires.

Your body language: Radiate positivity, warmth and strength by showing them your dedication to counselling. Be sincere and direct in your eye contact.

Client's expectations towards the counsellor: This type needs high ethical standards and will judge your behaviour according to their system of values. They will tend to idealise you if you perform well and be very disappointed if you perform badly. They will expect 100 per cent, so don't be superficial: they want a counsellor who can help them to reach heaven. If you are too talkative or theoretical it will weaken the connection.

Active techniques to develop enthusiasm: Encourage the client to meditate on desired goals. Explore the client's passions, desires and longings through visualising their ideal future self. Focus on the client's romantic life, including their fantasies and passions. Use drawing and role play to help the client express their dream. Set goals and focus the client's enthusiasm on ideal models, working to conquer any resistances and opposing energies. Encourage the client to use imagination to relive former successes and peak experiences.

Development of productivity and the practical type

Some people have a knack for making things happen, while others seem to wait in vain for something or someone to intervene and make their dreams come true. The difference between these types of people is the ability to access the talent for productivity.

The practical type knows how to organise energies and resources around a realistic goal. This type is effective in life because they are able to synthesise all their inherent qualities through an orchestrated effort and bring them into action. *The perspective for this type of counselling is to support the client to become a self-directed individual*

– a leader who can achieve his goals through the talent of productivity.

The counsellor seeking to develop the quality of productivity in a client can draw upon all of the counselling strategies and styles for the different types, albeit selecting the strategy and style that will be most effective and practical in terms of the client's material and level of development.

For example, if a client is strong in leadership but lacking enthusiasm, the counsellor should adapt to the client's unique situation and adopt the dedicated strategy and style of counselling, because this will empower his productivity.

In selecting a counsellor strategy and style, the counsellor must be able to identify the client's least developed qualities, then choose methods that will help to strengthen those qualities. Being aware of all aspects of the client's life from the perspective of all seven types is therefore crucial. The goal in working in this way is to support the client's productivity, which means developing the leadership and organisational skills required to complete valuable tasks in a systematic and skilful way through accessing the most relevant qualities.

It takes effort and discipline to implement change, so the counsellor needs to strengthen the client's ability to remain strong when the going gets tough and challenges arise. As counsellors, we can help by modelling the practical qualities of strength and discipline, while avoiding the temptation to give in to pampering the client or being overly-sympathetic.

To work from a practical counselling style, we start by taking an overview of the client's purpose, goals and resources and the degree to which the client can be a competent leader in his own life. From this perspective, which might be shared with the client or not (it is a big responsibility to take on), the work can proceed.

While there is no rule of sequence in counselling, because each client's existential situation is unique, it could be argued that the three first and most important steps are to work with leadership, empathy and ingenuity – three qualities that help to build authenticity. These qualities build the *dimension of being*, which refers to an authentic self-identity and a sense of purpose. The next four steps – which involve building harmony, know-how, enthusiasm and productivity – are more concerned with goals and how they can be attained – or, in other words, the *dimension of doing*, which is the practical unfoldment of identity and purpose.

The above counselling philosophy is held within the mind of the counsellor and will guide interaction with the client. Remember, the primary focus here is to help the client manifest his needs in a practical and organised way, and to achieve this we will begin the work where the need is greatest, no matter where it fit into the above sequence. The practical type acts from an overview, a purpose and a plan, which will be brought into action in a systematic way. So it might be a good idea to share your perspectives, strategies and styles with this type of client because it will foster a sense of healthy collaboration.

Speaking generally, this means the beginning of the therapy will tend to involve building a trustful therapeutic relationship that can take an overview of the client's life situation and hold their pain with empathy. From this starting point, the client can explore self-identity and explore their underlying desires and motivations. Then, at a certain point, there will be a practical shift as the focus turns towards putting plans into action in order to realise their goals and dreams. Assagioli (1974) proposes a similar a model in his book *The Act of Will*, in which he identifies six stages of will.) This method is effective for helping all types to turn ideas into reality.

The practical type wants to get on with life. Therefore, the client will not benefit from being put into a kind of therapeutic incubator in which problems are endlessly processed. Rather, with this aspect of counselling, the focus is on strengthening the practical will of the client. While working with ingenuity is very open and explorative, investigating numerous perspectives and scenarios, the counsellor who is focused on developing the talent of productivity is more concerned with gathering information in a systematic way and creating focus and action. Through working on productivity, the client will discover that real change is only possible when resources can be applied.

It is through implementing practical action that the client will gain an experience of responsibility, independence, competence and *freedom*. As a result, the client will finally experience the fruit of counselling, which is the power to make things happen, in big or small ways, through the application and utilisation of all of their skills and resources, drawing upon all of the types.

The practical style of counselling when you encounter a practical type

Your style of communication: This type needs you to be elegant and structured, so be ready with a plan. You need to be professional and show that you are in control of the counselling setting. Offer a sense of predictability by offering a clear overview of how you work and what you expect from the client. This type enjoys being in the hands of a professional who has authority.

Be result-oriented in your approach, helping the client to clarify issues and objectives, and deciding together how you will approach the work in terms of setting homework and evaluating progress. You must help this type to test and experiment with theory in the real world so they can find out for themselves if it works.

When a professional setting has been established, this type will let go of their control and start to experience their underlying emotional issues. They will need to go back and forth between times of dropping into emotional experience and times of mental processing. You must help them to maintain a balance between chaos and order. Remember that this type is highly disciplined and can accomplish a lot through a strong and skillful will.

This type is pragmatic and doesn't need to explore every emotional nuance, they just want to fix their problems and get on with life. So be a competent guide who can offer practical steps to help them overcome their issues. Don't psychoanalyse the client too much but rely on their strength, remembering the client is a do-it-yourself type.

Your body language: Be relaxed and a little formal without becoming cold or detached. They will appreciate it when the counsellor dresses well and when the therapy room is attractive, or at least clean and simple.

Client's expectations towards the counsellor: This type will look to your practical skills to help them accomplish goals, so a well-structured approach is essential. Your own achievements will create respect because it is crucial for the client to experience someone who can "walk the talk". They will test your competence and be on the lookout for times when you relinquish your authority.

Active techniques to develop productivity: Work with Assagioli's six stages of the will: defining objectives, planning, and taking practical steps to realise goals. Help the client to set goals and targets, then evaluate progress, calibrating and fine-tuning objectives in the light of experience. Strengthen the client's discipline and work ethic by drawing on the qualities of the other types.

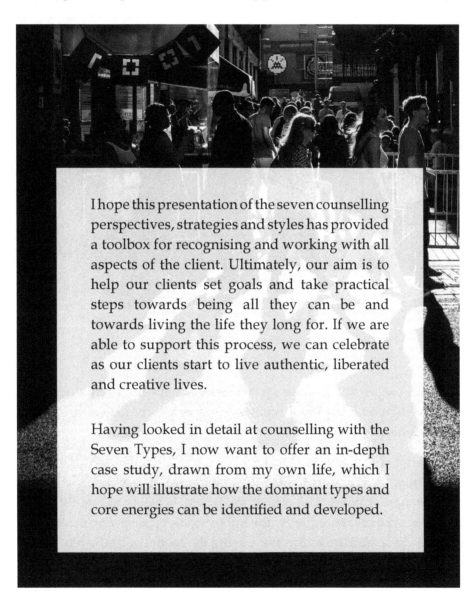

I hope this presentation of the seven counselling perspectives, strategies and styles has provided a toolbox for recognising and working with all aspects of the client. Ultimately, our aim is to help our clients set goals and take practical steps towards being all they can be and towards living the life they long for. If we are able to support this process, we can celebrate as our clients start to live authentic, liberated and creative lives.

Having looked in detail at counselling with the Seven Types, I now want to offer an in-depth case study, drawn from my own life, which I hope will illustrate how the dominant types and core energies can be identified and developed.

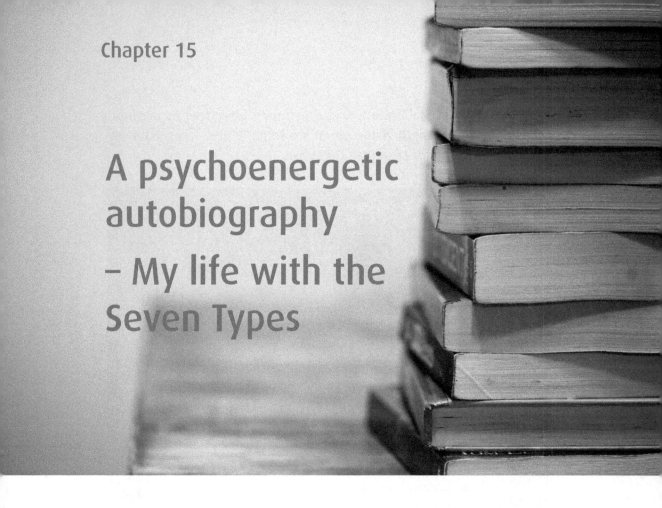

Chapter 15

A psychoenergetic autobiography – My life with the Seven Types

The purpose of this chapter is to illustrate with my own story how discovering your dominant types at the five psychological levels can revolutionise your understanding of yourself and others.

We do not see reality as it is, but as we are – we perceive ourselves and others through a coloured filter made up of our own particular combination of types. The aim of the Seven Types is to fine-tune this lens so we can see more clearly the full psychological spectrum for what it means to be human. In this way, using the model of the Seven Types, we can develop our understanding, increase our sense of acceptance, and act in the world with greater wisdom and authenticity.

By telling the story of how I came to know my types – and the enormous benefits I derived from this – I hope I can inspire you to do the same. I hope to demonstrate that the model of the Seven Types has both substance and valuable practical application. Studying a theory is not enough: it must be put to the test and confirmed through observation and experimentation.

So please come with me on a journey through my life to see how I came to an understanding of my types, which seems to be a sensitive soul (2), dedicated personality (6), dynamic thinking type (1), dedicated feeling type (6) and dynamic body type (1). This combination can be expressed as in formula "2-6, 161" and, as my story develops, you will see how my body, feeling and thinking types were the first to emerge.

1968, pre school aged six.

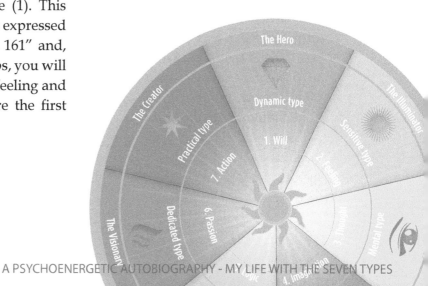

Early life: My emerging personality

Growing up, I used to read stories about war and the Wild West. These stories offered clear cut black and white images of good and evil, with the good strong man always beating the bad guys. It is no wonder that this particular stereotype appealed to me – it embodied both the passion (dedicated) and bravado (dynamism) of my own emerging personality.

With the conflicting dedicated and dynamic energies emerging, it is not surprising that, as a boy, I had a difficult temperament. Inner conflict was a major theme for me. I resented it when anyone tried to dominate me or treat me unfairly – but my need for self-control (dynamic) would often win out and prevent me from acting out my emotions. That said, I often fought with the other boys at school, largely because it was part of the core beliefs in my upbringing that men were meant to be fighters: it felt natural to fight, it was something that boys did – but this only increased my isolation.

I was strong and a good fighter, which is reflected in my **dynamic body type**, which can put up a good fight. However, this inclination to fight ended when I lost to a stronger boy when I was 11 years old and was badly humiliated. So I started looking for less dangerous, ways to be the best, and one way I found – which is typical of the dynamic thinking type – was to become quick-witted to score points and win recognition. But all the time, I had a fear of humiliation, which is one of the great fears of the dynamic type, who always wants to be the strongest and best, no matter at what level the dynamic type is being expressed.

Closed off from other people and from my feelings, it is little wonder that in my early teens I was an insecure and vulnerable young man. I was bottling up the passionate emotional life of the **dedicated feeling type**. I had learned to hide my feelings behind a tough and cool masculine exterior. With considerable effort, I had suppressed my emotions, vulnerability and sensitivity. In hindsight, I realise that I had been able to do this because of the qualities of the **dynamic thinking type**, with its capacity for self-control, with which I could suppress my deep fear of feeling humiliated by showing my emotions.

Another key aspect of my early personality was a sense of isolation: I didn't have a real friend until I joined the army. Friendship was out of reach when I was growing up, perhaps due to the many fights I got into. From an existential point of view, it could also be that growing up in a working class environment offered little to stimulate my true nature, hence my frustration. There was an inner conflict because my lifestyle was at variance with my core nature. Feeling at a loss, the patriarchal nature of my family environment served to stimulate the dynamic aspect of my typological make-up. Today, knowing that the dynamic type needs time alone, my isolation as a boy and young man makes sense. Furthermore, I can recognise in my younger self the dynamic type's need for freedom and refusal to compromise.

Joining the army and finding a cause

At 17, with little interest in my school subjects, I decided to join the army as a professional soldier. I subsequently spent five years in service, first in the infantry, then as a gunner, and finally as a battlefield scout. I also spent a year with the United Nations as a soldier in Cyprus. My time in the army shaped my budding personality.

I was in my element in the army due to my **dynamic thinking type**. I had found a self-identity as a right-wing nationalist whose goal in life was to defend his country (Denmark) from the Communist threat coming from Russia. This was when the Cold War was at its height, before the fall of the Berlin Wall, and this provided me with a cause I could engage with wholeheartedly: my **dedicated personality type** had been awoken. It felt as though I had finally found a cause I could fully engage with and believe in.

In later years, when I discovered the Seven Types, I was able to identify that, at this stage of my development, my overall combination of types at four levels was 6-161, which means a dedicated personality type (6), dynamic thinking type (1), dedicated feeling type (6) and dynamic body type (1). (Note: At this stage, my soul qualities – at the fifth psychological level – had not yet emerged.)

It can be noted that, in my earlier life, the will – which characterises both the dedicated and dynamic types –

1982 – Promoted to Corporal and joined UN's Peacekeeping force at Cyprus

was very dominant in my combination of types. Will generates a lot of aggression, together with frustration when the energies are blocked, which they were during my upbringing in a strict, almost military-like, family structure in which physical punishment was the norm when rules where broken.

The army allowed me to channel my aggression and frustrations constructively. The discipline was important for me. Even learning how to use weapons was helpful because it gave me an opportunity to manage my dedicated and dynamic energy. Learning to use firearms can teach us how to trust the assertive and combative energies in our personality through learning to be calm and focused. For example, when handling a live hand grenade you have to trust it won't blow up in your face, and when firing a tank gun you have to both access and control primitive destructive energies.

However, I don't want to glamorise life in the army – indeed, most of us would rather we didn't need armies at all. However, for me, while being in the army didn't solve my problems, it was a good experience because it gave me direction. Looking back now, equipped with the knowledge of the Seven Types, I can identify and accept how the army helped me in my struggle to harness the basic energies within me. I understand now that there was a battle going on between my positive qualities – focus, idealism and industriousness (dynamic and dedicated types) – and my shadow qualities – self-sufficiency (dynamic), fiery temperament (dedicated), and dissatisfaction at failing to meet high ideals (dedicated).

The army gave me something to believe in. By becoming a good soldier I learned to discipline my nature and direct my resources toward a goal. My time in the army enabled me to start synthesising the different energies in my personality through idealism, commitment and activism: I believed in defending my country and the free world. However, my personality was still developing and immature, and this showed in my distorted and unbalanced emotional nature.

Breakdown and break-up

Until my 20s, I had never attempted to reflect on my deeper nature and, for a stereotypical man, psychotherapy was out of the question. However, I was deeply unhappy, primarily because I had no love life. I was going through life alone. I had a friend in the army but I was unable to talk to him about my worries and feelings. But, as is typical with the dynamic thinking type, I found answers in my own time under my own initiative.

My defences were impenetrable (dynamic), and no woman could reach my vulnerability (dedicated feeling type), but behind this tough facade

there was a devotional and romantic heart (dedicated feeling type). I felt as if a wall separated me from my surroundings, making it impossible for me to open up to love, even though I had plenty of opportunities. I had also been badly affected by the experience of having severe acne in my teens, which had served to increase my deep sense of vulnerability and fear of humiliation when it came to romance.

So, aged 21, I was dealing with a personality composed equally of the dynamic and dedicated types, which inevitably led to violent inner tensions: my need for self-control (dynamic) was in opposition with my need for a passionate romance (dedicated). Then I met my first serious girlfriend and the lid came off the pressure cooker! Out came years of repressed emotions: powerful romantic desire and all the frustrations I had been keeping at bay. This turned my life upside down. These strong emotions came out, overwhelming any sense of self-control, and almost destroyed my self-perception and self-identity overnight.

This first relationship lasted a couple of years and, when it ended, I had my first major existential crisis. I came to realise I could not carry on living in isolation behind the tough facade I had created (dynamic). Something had to change. Shortly after the break-up, I left the army and moved to Copenhagen to enrol at a Folk High School. During the next few years, my identity underwent a total transformation.

From soldier to New Ager: Personality 2.0

A new energy came into my life that was focused on understanding and developing my emotions (dedicated personality type). While becoming more aware of the repressed feelings and social phobias that were making me depressed, I also found a new direction. I realised I had to break out of the shell I had been hiding behind. I made new friends and developed a social life centred around my emerging interests in astrology and self-development. This was an important shift for me because I started cutting ties with my old life. I sensed I had to free myself from old influences so that something new could emerge – and

I was able to do this because, having a dynamic mind, I possessed the ability to let go and cut ties in service of achieving greater freedom.

Taking courses in astrology and parapsychology ignited a fire in me that I had not felt before. When I first heard about astrology, I realised I could spend the rest of my life studying it. Astrology helped me to understand who I was and what I could become. The types in my personality structure were helping me: my passionate dedicated qualities were motivating me, while my dynamic mentality made me ambitious and helped me to focus. Through astrology I discovered a cosmological wisdom that helped me to see that I was part of a greater whole – and, for the first time, I started to experience the energies of my sensitive soul type.

At this point, I was still largely focused on myself – I had not fully embraced a sense of the yearning of the whole world. My focus was on self-improvement and, in particular, on learning how to jettison my various insecurities and inner conflicts, and I started to do something about it. I spent the next few years, from 1986 to 1991, studying astrology, attending high school to gain some general qualifications, meditating and undergoing psychotherapy. Meanwhile, having no formal qualifications, I earned a living working in construction and as a cleaner. I had ambitions which my upbringing had not satisfied, but the dynamic energy gave me the will to be financially independent and to work hard to achieve it. Unskilled physical labour humiliated my dynamic thinking type because I was at the bottom of the social hierarchy, but the new world I was discovering held many compensations – I was engaging with the mindset of spirituality, which was completely new to me. It suited me and, for the first time, I started to feel confident in myself and with how my life was going.

It was in 1988, at the age of 26, that I sat down and meditated for the first time. I immediately felt I had come home. Through meditation, I discovered I could dissolve my unhappy emotions by visualising a sun in my chest that held me in a loving embrace. I had discovered an inner source of love. From this point on, meditation became a daily practice of self-healing and transformation.

Initially, my mediation was driven by a need to experience love (sensitive and dedicated energies) and to be completely free to be myself (dynamic). Meditation also activated the introverted part of my dedicated nature and my inner mystic emerged. I also opened up to the energy of unconditional love, which helped me to feel less vulnerable. After a year of meditating I developed a deep love for Christ, as I understood him, which seemed quite natural to me, despite growing up an atheist. I had discovered a space in my personality that was open to energies that until this point had lain dormant in me.

From New Age to social psychiatry

My dedicated personality was focused on meditation, psychotherapy, astrology and spirituality. But in 1991, this focus changed when I started to study social work. Suddenly I found myself in a relatively left-wing environment, which was a culture shock for me. Not long since I had been a soldier with nationalistic leanings who hated communists and the left-wing. My younger self would have been horrified and accused me of joining the enemy, but my identity had changed and I had cut ties with my past – indeed, now I was a vegetarian and tee-total, someone who meditated and read New Age philosophy. So, education in social work felt like a natural next step in my transformation. I was transitioning from one extreme to the other, which is typical of an immature dedicated personality.

During the 1990s, my personality stabilised. I settled down, had a family and dedicated myself to my work in the field of mental health. I started a national magazine for mental health service users, written and produced by the users themselves. My work, together with my growing interest in theosophy and Eastern traditions, was the focus of my life. Indeed, I had become an activist and a missionary for two causes – mental health and spirituality – my dedicated personality type was very much in the driver's seat. My approach was admittedly single-minded and somewhat fanatical, but good things came from this.

As the millennium approached, I had a daughter, which once again changed everything. Overnight, I had to develop a new identity as a father, which helped me to become less rigid and more receptive.

Around 2001, I dropped my identification with theosophy after a crisis in the group I was involved with. I had become deeply disappointed and disillusioned with the group's inability to put our ideals into practice, and I vowed that I would never again identify myself solely with one religion or philosophy. While appreciating many of the values and insights offered by theosophy – not least the philosophy of the Seven Rays – I realised that adhering to a single philosophy was limiting. I needed the flexibility to think for myself. But while the missionary in me died, the activist was still very much alive. Both archetypes – the missionary and the activist – are aspects of the dedicated personality type, which needs to be a passionate advocate for a cause.

The missionary dies, but the Illuminator is born

At this time, my identification with the dedicated personality type started to lessen and in its place I started to derive my primary motivation from the sensitive energy in my awakening soul via the archetype of the Illuminator. I decided to start an intensive training in psychotherapy and enrolled on a four-year diploma in psychosynthesis that later turned into a Master's degree. As a result, I became the first person in my family to gain an academic degree – an example of both the ambitious nature of the dynamic energy and the ground-breaking nature of the dedicated energy.

This training led to another career-change. I left social psychiatry and started my own business as a coach, teacher and psychotherapist. Now more fully under the influence of the sensitive energy, my focus had changed. Psychotherapy introduced me to a calmer, more intimate and spacious inner world. My philosophical outlook became less rigid as I became more grounded and more focused on experience rather than ideas. My sensitive soul type had paved the way for my work as

a psychotherapist and teacher in psychology and meditation. I was now more in control of my passionate energy. To use an analogy, I was now mostly riding the horse rather than it riding me. In terms of my combination of types, this was the final piece of the puzzle: I had started to integrate my sensitive soul type (2), meaning my combination was: 2-6-161.

The sensitive energy of love-wisdom gave me greater awareness and insight into the psychological universe. Aligning myself with this sensitive energy, I found an inner connection with myself and my surroundings. Of course, this is not as easy as it might sound: abiding in this calm, loving and observant presence remains a daily struggle – frequently the fire from my other dominant types temporarily upsets the balance.

Let me give you an example of the tension between my types and how I harmonise them to make my body, feelings and thoughts cooperate with my soul.

When I write, I am often influenced by the reactions of my dedicated and passionate emotional life. I can get so excited about ideas and insights that I cannot continue writing. My solar plexus starts bubbling and I have to get up and let off steam. Clearly this can interrupt the creative flow. I also practice breathing to calm my emotions. I observe them in a loving and impersonal manner and ask them to relax. This is an example of how to use the sensitive energies to calm the disturbing passion of the dedicated type.

Another problem when writing is that I can overlook signals from my body and emotions. I write intensely with absolute focus then, after a few days of this, I notice stress symptoms: irritation, tension and general annoyance. This is an example of how the dynamic mind can use sheer will power to push through its agenda, which is ultimately unproductive because, at some point, I have to stop writing for a few days to allow my depleted nervous system to recharge. I can also get agitated or irritated if the words come too slowly, then I will push myself too hard with an intense discipline. To avoid this, I am learning to control my impatience and limit the hours I work. Spending time in nature is one of the best ways I have found to help balance out this intensity.

These are examples of how the excessive intensity and power of the dedicated and dynamic energies can cause problems. They are also examples of how I have learned to balance my energies. I often say that my life project is to learn to express my wise and sensitive soul nature through a personality that is like a battle tank. This is not an easy project.

Humour, spontaneity and openness

This brings me to my last point, which is the need to integrate all the types – with all seven energies at our disposal, not just the dominant types – a process that Assagioli called *harmonisation*.

To give an example, in 2012, I realised I was still too stiff, inhibited and one-sided in my expression as a consequence of my particular dominant types (dynamic and dedicated). I decided I needed to become more spontaneous, easy going and relaxed. To accomplish this, I realised I had to strengthen my contact with the creative type, with its sense of creativity and spontaneity.

Knowing the model of the Seven Types, and its methods for working with the energies, can help us to consciously shape our personality. Within the framework of our types, we can integrate aspects of the other types. How much progress we make depends on how much effort we are prepared to put in.

Whenever we experience an energy and immerse ourselves in it, we will slowly integrate its qualities. In this way, we can create a new inner atmosphere and change our behaviour. This concept is at the core of Eastern yoga, or from a Christian perspective we could say: "As a human being thinks in his heart, so he is". Accordingly, I changed my style of meditation so I could start to focus on the qualities of the creative type. I started visualising images of beauty and harmony, and slowly I started to feel a sense of grace and playfulness.

However, changing habits is costly. In my case, the shadow side of the open and playful energy started to manifest. In my encounters with the world, rather than expressing this emerging sense of creativity, I instead noticed a stiffness and a fear of people getting close to me. Psychotherapy helped, once again. I was reminded of a wise teaching: *the opposite will emerge whenever we endeavour to bring in new energies.* The way to tackle this is to clear the way so the new energy has space to manifest. I started attending yoga classes three times a week. My body was stiff and inflexible, but yoga, which expresses the creative energy, helped me to establish physical and mental balance and harmony. I practised yoga for two years, with amazing results. My body changed significantly. I became far more flexible and coordinated. Also, being with other yoga practitioners affected my emotions as I absorbed their energy – my fellow practitioners were lithe and gracious and radiated the ease and grace I needed.

I also attended classes in dance, authentic relationships and intimacy. This was challenging, but the combination of inner work and participation with others who are on the spiritual path can hasten transformation. I was spending time with people who exhibited a strong creative energy and who were more physical and intimate than I had ever been. For me, the result was a whole new way of life.

Integrating the qualities of the creative type helped me to express my sensitive soul type. I became more expressive and interested in relationships, and my teaching started to focus more on experience and the body, rather than on ideas and head knowledge. It also affected my love life: in 2015 I met Karianne, who became my wife, soul mate and life partner. Our love and her feminine radiation have strengthened my ability to be present, vulnerable and strong.

I am still on a journey to balance my energy composition with the other energies, but I have found the colour palette with which I know I can learn to express myself more fully. This has enriched my life immensely – and I feel I have even more to give. I believe the greatest gift we have to give in this world is to simply be who we truly are.

Studying psychoenergetics – and the four quadrants

We are now coming to the end of this book, but perhaps you would like to continue exploring the world of the Seven Types? So, what are the most important tools to help you to do this?

I have observed, studied and experimented with psychoenergetics since the mid-1990s and would like to share what I believe is important if we are to put this teaching into practice.

I have read a lot of literature to ensure I have a solid theoretical grounding in the principles of psychoenergetics, specifically the seven energies, the seven psychological functions, the five psychological levels and the seven types. But theoretical understanding is not enough – we also need a direct and felt experience of the energies. Both of the following statements are true: theory provides a language with which to interpret our experiences; experience determine how we interpret theory. Understand these twin principles, we can learn to connect theory and practice.

For me, meditation, psychotherapy and teaching are the particular pathways that have informed my understanding of the Seven Types. This has been my unique way, but others will find a different path, depending on their dominant types. But, regardless of our individual approach, the same basic principles apply.

We must learn the language of the Seven Types. First, we must study the theory so we know how to identify the energies through felt experience, that is, to distinguish one energy or type from another when we experience them in ourselves or in other people.

The energies we *notice, observe and register*, i.e. study through analysis and discernment, are:

1. Our own subjective reactions and psychological qualities (Wilber's upper left quadrant).

2. Our special pattern of behaviours (upper right quadrant).

3. The qualities, norms and behaviours of the different groups to which we belong: family, friends, work and interest groups (lower quadrants).

The observation of the energies as they manifest in our lives through the four quadrants will reveal important patterns. It will help us to identify the energies that shape us.

The skill of observation

Observation refers to the ability to neutrally observe our inner and outer worlds – and this requires an awareness of the conscious "I". We must learn to be vigilant, present and observant in relation to what is happening, without analysing or judging. The trick is to step back and observe what's happening without getting involved in what's going on. As we do this, we will become aware that we are not what we observe, but that we are the one who observes. In terms of psychosynthesis, we must learn to practice disidentification and identification with the Self (i.e. pure consciousness and will).

Identifying our dominant energies at the level of thought, feeling and body can be difficult. We can become so identified with our thoughts and emotions that we can struggle to distinguish between the observer and the observed, between the conscious "I" and the psychological content of our consciousness.

Awareness-based meditation and mindfulness can help us to be present with our experience and to become aware of ourselves as a conscious "I". That said, some types can develop the ability to be consciously

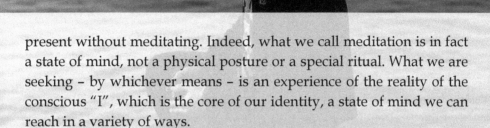

present without meditating. Indeed, what we call meditation is in fact a state of mind, not a physical posture or a special ritual. What we are seeking – by whichever means – is an experience of the reality of the conscious "I", which is the core of our identity, a state of mind we can reach in a variety of ways.

Observation or awareness – however we attain it – is what is necessary if we are to understand our energies. Awareness will shed light on our unconscious experiences and make them conscious. We can learn to experience our experiences – we can learn to go in and out of an experience.

Observation makes it possible to "taste" and reflect deeply on the energies, helping us to understand the energies of an experience. Let's take an example. When we learn to swim, we can observe how others do it and study the theory of swimming. We can acquire a theory of what it means to swim, but we will not understand how it feels to swim, the actual experience of swimming, until we try it ourselves. We need to dive in! Likewise, while it's helpful to read about and study the energies, we will not truly understand them until we dive in and experiencing them as they manifest in our own lives.

Mastering the energies through action

It is possible to learn to master the energies. To do this we have to throw ourselves into life with an intention to allow *who we truly are* to unfold through our action in the world.

It's only when we are tested in the real world that we can begin to truly manifest our being, or essence. Life's many challenges transform our identity, resulting in inner realisation (soul) and external action (personality) – this balancing act was described in chapter 8 where we examined the integration of soul and personality.

Whichever energy we resonate with most deeply in our soul, that is the energy we must express through action in our lives. This is our duty and responsibility, no less; if we don't do it, we are failing ourselves. We have an opportunity to work on ourselves to organise all of our qualities and energies – and, in this way, we will manifest a life that truly reflects what we understand and believe ourselves to be. It is through this authentic self-expression that the energies are brought into action. As we do this, the strength of our "will-to-be-who-we-are" will be tested and challenged by the resistances that arise as a natural part of the creative process.

No work of art is more noble or beautiful than the creation and expression of our authentic identity; this is what we are here to accomplish and manifest. When we commit ourselves to this work, the will and love we require to complete the project will become available to us and we will learn to master our energies. We have to master the fear, the inner imperfections and the resistances that emerge when we start to consciously create our lives. This is the journey which the Greek heroes undertook and survived. Like them, we must fight monsters and treacherous circumstances – whatever it is that blocks our path. As we do so, the school of life will gradually teach us the art of mastering the energies.

I warmly wish you
a wonderful journey
so that you may
unfold a rainbow
of possibilities and
qualities for the
benefit of yourself
and the world.

Old wisdom, new insights

By Søren Hauge and Kenneth Sørensen

It has been our intention from the start to present a modern version of the philosophy of the Seven Rays. As with many exponents of Western mindfulness, we have focused our exploration into the psychological element, choosing to omit underlying cosmological considerations. But, in a book focused on psychoenergetics, it would be reasonable to briefly cover the historical roots of the Seven Types.

The ancient wisdom traditions evolved throughout history across many cultures, with a core of teachings that have been expanded, maintained and held sacred by countless practitioners. A key aspect of these traditions is an attempt to encapsulate and understand the diverse range of types that we find expressed in humanity. Indeed, the primary focus of the Seven Types, which is an updated version of the ancient philosophy of the Seven Rays, is an attempt to explain human diversity. In modern psychology, this study of types is referred to as *differential psychology*.

With the ancient traditions, astrology, which examines the zodiac and its astrological signs, is both a typology and an example of profound psychological wisdom; in its esoteric form, astrology has a close association with the philosophy of the Seven Rays.

Another ancient typological system is the teaching of the four temperaments associated with the elements earth, water, air and fire. Invaluable insights can be also found in the ancient Indian understanding of the three basic forms of energy that are reflected in consciousness – the *Gunas* – namely *tamas* (inertia), *rajas* (motion) and *sattva* (rhythm).

In recent times, Carl Gustav Jung reformulated the wisdom of the four temperaments with his archetypal psychological types (sensation, intuition, thinking and feeling – each with an introverted and extroverted expression), which he presented in his book *Psychological Types* in 1921. An expanded version of Jung's theory was later developed as the Myers-Briggs Type Indicator, which describes 16 possible psychological types. Another modern attempt to understand the spectrum of human nature is the Enneagram, which was developed primarily by George Gurdjieff, Oscar Ichazo and Claudio Naranjo, and which also has references to ancient wisdom. Also in recent times, medical science has developed a typological system to categorise pathology; in the field of psychiatry, the ICD-10 and DSM-IV manuals are attempts to categorise pathological symptoms to assist in the treatment of personality disorders.

These are just a few of the numerous systems and methods for understanding the spectrum of human nature, with each of them offering valuable insights and practical tools.

Why just seven energies?

Given the variety of systems that have been proposed throughout history, why have we settled on a model that proposes we are comprised of seven basic energies, not more or less? To answer this question, it will be helpful to see how teachings about seven energies, or rays, have arisen in perhaps all cultures throughout history, with each different expression offering unique perspectives on the same spiritual wisdom[1]. Let's look at some of these models of seven.

There are old Persian's teachings about the seven *Amesha Spentans* which penetrate the universe and characterise all of life. These teachings have a close correspondence with the esoteric Kabbalah of the Jews, which describes the universe as a tree of ten *sephirot*, or names, of which the first three form a foundation out of which the other seven unfold.

In Greek mythology, Zeus takes the form of the bull Taurus that shines with "seven rays of fire". In the Chaldean oracle of the second century, the Seven Rays are understood to be the cleansing rays of the sun Helios. In the Hindu tradition, we find teachings about the seven *rishis*, or seven-fold lotus. The Indian mystic Sri Aurobindo refers to the seven rays and to the seven heavenly rivers that created the universe. Hinduism also teaches us about the seven *lokas* (planes of existence) and the seven *chakras* (energy centres), as well as describing seven horses that pull the sun god Surya's sky carriage.

In Christianity, we have the seven archangels, as well as the seven angels that gather around the throne of God to oversee creation. There are the seven deadly sins (pride, greed, lust, envy, gluttony, wrath and

---

[1] See Wikipedia for descriptions and references: https://en.wikipedia.org/wiki/Seven_rays

sloth) and the seven virtues (prudence, justice, temperance, courage, faith, hope and charity/love). The Bible is filled with symbolism of the number seven: the seven days of creation, the seven-branched candlestick, the seven congregations, the seven gifts of the Holy Ghost, the seven lean years and the seven plentiful years, to mention a few.

Other historical references include the seven stages of life, the seven liberal arts, the seven classical planets, the seven-part diatonic scale, the seven-day week, and the seven colours of the rainbow. Pleiades is referred to as the Seven Stars or Seven Sisters, and the seven largest stars of the Big Dipper are well-known. We have the "seven-mile boots" and seventh heaven. The cult of Mithras had seven altars and seven mysteries. The seven wonders of ancient times are another example... we could go on. These examples all serve to show that the seven-fold division is not a new invention but seems to illustrate a number and constellation that has been universally perceived to be of profound significance.

With the rise of theosophy in the late eighteenth century, the philosophy of the Seven Rays reached a wide audience. H.P. Blavatsky, the founder of the Theosophical Society, describes the rays in her book *The Secret Doctrine*. Later, other well-known theosophists explored the subject, but it was primarily through Alice Bailey's extensive work that the philosophy of the Seven Rays became widespread in esoteric circles.[2]

You can read more about some of the esoteric pioneers in chapter one.

_____

[2] See literature list in Appendix.

How the types interact with each other

In this section, we will explore how each type relates to all the others, including their own type. It can be noted that these relationships apply not only in everyday life but also in the interactions between counsellor and client. Indeed, the dynamics described are a useful resource for the counsellor who is making use of the counselling strategies and styles described elsewhere in this book.

No-one is only one type, rather we each have a dominant type at each of the five psychological levels. That said, we will each tend to express ourselves through one principle type, from any of the five levels, at any one time – for example, someone might be the dynamic leader at work, then the sensitive parent at home. This means the relational dynamics described here will play out with respect to whichever type is dominant in a person in the moment.

The Dynamic type

The Hero and The Leader

Likely partners: Dynamic, Mental, Analytical, Practical

Unlikely partners: Sensitive, Creative, Dedicated

Best friend: Practical

Relationship with other dynamic types

Connection: When dynamic types meet, they will respect each other's authority, strength and reliability. They will appreciate the chance to cross swords without feeling they need to hold back. This competition is seen as healthy and a chance to bring out the best ideas and solutions. Dynamic types can learn from each other about the nature of power and how to use it, which will make them stronger, sharper and more willing to step outside of their comfort zones in order to achieve excellence.

Challenge: Power struggles can ensue when dynamic types get together. The competition for honour, status and competence can lead to power play for dominance and "life and death" struggles, bringing out this type's most brutal tendencies and the capacity to play dirty.

Relationship with the sensitive type

Connection: The dynamic type will appreciate the sensitive type's psychological insight and their ability to cooperate, make relationships, and work with empathy to foster well-being. On closer inspection, the dynamic type will realise that the sensitive type's capacity for vulnerability is a strength rather than a weakness, and that their gentle and calm nature can heal broken relationships and create new relationships that bring out the best in people.

Challenge: The dynamic type will often interpret the gentleness of the sensitive type as a form a weakness. Because of the dynamic type's belief in power, autonomy and self-discipline, the sensitive type's empathetic style can appear to the dynamic type as soft, compliant, whining, fearful and dependent.

Relationship with the mental type

Connection: The dynamic type will admire the mental type's capacity to reflect then take strategic action that will translate ideas into concrete results. The dynamic type can learn from the mental type's ability to communicate in an intelligent and persuasive way that incorporates many points of view and can help to build bridges around a shared purpose. The dynamic type can learn from the mental type's flexibility and ability to work across a wide network to consider many possibilities for action.

Challenge: The dynamic type will feel frustrated by the mental type's tendency to spread themselves thinly, which means they can lack focus and consistency and fail to achieve concrete results. This tendency of the mental type will often be accompanied by excuses and deceptions, which will infuriate the straight-talking dynamic type, as will the mental type's tendency to talk in circles without making a point.

Relationship with the creative type

Connection: The dynamic type, with their tendency to stick with familiar routines, will be intrigued by the creative type's ability to generate change through unorthodox means, such as using improvisation, imagination, humour and the arts. The creative type's ability to bring social disharmony to the surface so that issues can be resolved and human potential released will also be appreciated. The dynamic type could also learn from the creative type's ability to help people to relax so that relationships and cooperation can blossom.

Challenge: The dynamic type will become frustrated by the creative type's tendency to become distracted by anything that seems to offer novelty, entertainment or an opportunity for self-promotion. The dynamic type will also struggle with the creative type's mood swings, which will be perceived as immature and a sign of unreliability.

Relations with the analytical type

Connection: The dynamic type will appreciate the analytical type's skill, reliability and efficiency, as well as their objectivity, thoroughness and sound judgment. The dynamic type can learn from the analytical type's ability to adopt a critical distance and to not be seduced by the temptations of ambition that can derail a project. The analytical type's ability to work with detail in a competent and serious way will also be appreciated.

Challenge: The dynamic type, in their desire to see quick results, will become deeply frustrated by the cautious, critical and sometimes pessimistic attitude of the analytical type, whose elaborate explanations and focus on detail will only seem to impede the dynamic type's plans.

Relations with the dedicated type

Connection: The dynamic type will appreciate the enthusiasm and loyal support offered by the dedicated type, whose determination and willingness to go the extra mile matches the dynamic type's own sense of commitment to fulfilling their purpose. The dynamic type can learn from the dedicated type that it is important to hold onto core values, which is a reminder that the end does not justify the means, especially if this means losing one's integrity through the use of dishonest tactics and power play to achieve one's goals. The dedicated type's ability to unite people around a shared valuable goal will also be appreciated.

Challenge: The dynamic type will be unable to relate to the dedicated type's emotional nature, which will come across as naïve and as lacking in self-control. Furthermore, the dedicated type's extreme adherence to ethics and values will seem to the dynamic type to be fanatical and a needless distraction to getting the job done.

Relations with the practical type

Connection: The dynamic type will appreciate the practical type's efficiency and ability to organise and implement action to achieve concrete results. The practical type's controlled and elegant behaviour will also be appreciated. The impulsive dynamic type can learn from the practical type's sense of control and their ability to work in an efficient and cooperative manner in which results are achieved through patient and thorough preparation and execution.

Challenge: The dynamic type will become frustrated by the practical type's insistence on sticking with routines and well-tested systems when what is needed is a radical new approach. In contrast to the conservative practical type, the dynamic type will find it easy to let go of ideas, processes and relationships to create space for something new to emerge – for this reason, the dynamic type will be challenged by the practical type's adherence to tradition, history and ritual.

The Sensitive Type

The Illuminator and The Altruist

Likely partners: Sensitive, Creative, Dedicated

Unlikely partners: Dynamic, Mental, Analytical, Practical

Best friend: Creative

Relationship with the dynamic type

Connection: The sensitive type can learn a great deal from the dynamic type's authority, strength, reliability and personal sense of greatness. The sensitive type's focus on empathy and understanding means they can get lost in feelings, so they could learn from the dynamic type's insistence that people take responsibility for their actions – which is a kind of generosity because this is giving others the space and freedom to be autonomous. The sensitive type, who often holds a false perception that people are all the same, would benefit from acquiring the dynamic type's ability to recognise differences in intelligence, skills and moral capacity. The dynamic type's ability to fight for crucial principles and ideas would also benefit the sensitive type.

Challenge: The sensitive type will experience the dynamic type as authoritarian, insensitive and self-indulgent. Rather than taking time to explore feelings, the dynamic type tends to adopt an attitude of tough love that can brutally "cut through" and break down resistance, indecisiveness and moral ambivalence – a relational style that is unheard of for the sensitive type.

Relationship with other sensitive types

Connection: The sensitive type feels warm and at home with other sensitive types because they are able to relate with openness, empathy and appreciation. It is possible to share vulnerabilities and receive mutual care and support. For this reason, the sensitive type often has another sensitive type for their best friend.

Challenge: A distortion of the sensitive type is a tendency to adopt the role of helpless victim – so, when sensitive types meet, this can result in a co-dependent attachment between helper and victim in which both can get lost in emotionalism and lose their sense of individuality. Both types tend to understand and accept a lack of discipline, strength and responsibility, which means these types might end up reinforcing immaturity in each other.

Relationship with mental types

Connection: For the sensitive type, who has a tendency to explore personal feelings and look for emotional depth, the mental type offers a refreshing cool, rational and practical perspective on life. Rather than exploring feelings, the mental type uses intelligence, looking at the big picture, and is able to come up with ideas and solutions and simply get on with life, even in complicated situations. The mental type's ability to master the concrete world and fix things and circumstances is also appreciated by the sensitive type.

Challenge: To the sensitive type, the mental type's pragmatic approach to life can feel impersonal, cold and superficial. The mental type will seem restless, almost hyperactive, in their concern to do what is necessary to get things done – and this will disturb the sensitive type's need for presence and calm. Indeed, the sensitive type may experience the mental type as opportunistic and untrustworthy.

Relationship with creative types

Connection: The sensitive type, who is concerned with the quality of relationships, can learn a great deal from the creative type's enthusiasm to deal with situations of conflict in order to establish harmony. The creative type can teach the sensitive type that it can be helpful to explore conflict and use the energy to create new relational dynamics. While the sensitive type tends to focus on feelings and empathy, the creative type makes use of humour, play and spontaneity – qualities that will help the sensitive type in their efforts to facilitate authentic relationships. The sensitive type can also learn from the creative type that embracing new experiences can expand and renew the emotional life.

Challenge: The calm and stable sensitive type may be shocked by the creative type's approach to life: their mood swings; their wish to be the centre of attention; their tendency to focus on conflict in the hope that a resolution can be found; and their tendency to seek out new emotional experiences, sometimes through reckless behaviour.

Relationship with analytical types

Connection: The sensitive type will appreciate the analytical type's ability to remain calm and sober in emotionally challenging situations. They will also be impressed by the analytical type's reliability and honesty, and their ability to be practical and objective in a way that supports relationships by offering a refreshing counterbalance to subjectivity. The analytical type's ability to be precise in communication will also be appreciated by the sensitive type, especially when it helps to express emotions and improve relationships. The analytical type's ability to look at people and the world with a critical eye, but without judgement, is a quality that would benefit the sensitive type.

Challenge: To the sensitive type, who has a focus on feelings, the analytical type's objective and practical focus on relationships will seem distant, cold and impersonal – and this difference between the objectivity of the analytical type and the subjectivity of the sensitive type will make it difficult for these types to establish intimate relationships with each other.

Relationship with dedicated types

Connection: The sensitive type will be drawn to the dedicated type's emotional warmth, enthusiasm and sense of loyalty. The sensitive type will be impressed by the dedicated type's determination to fight for a cause and to refuse to compromise core values, even when faced with obstacles and difficulties. The sensitive type can learn from the dedicated type how to be focused and persistent, despite any challenges, while holding a positive and optimistic attitude that focuses on growth and potential.

Challenge: The calm sensitive type, who thrives in positive relationships, will be alarmed by the extreme emotions of the dedicated type, whose passion for a cause can lead them to adopt an "all or nothing" attitude in which the cause is all that matters, even if this means causing upset and forsaking relationships.

Relationship with practical types

Connection: The sensitive type will appreciate the practical type's talent for identifying people's strengths and then inspiring and organising people in such a way that they can work together to achieve results. The sensitive type can learn from the practical type's ability to put emotions to one side and to remain focused and disciplined, creating a sense of order and safety. The practical type's reliable rhythm and discipline, and willingness to take responsibility and leadership, will also be appreciated by the sensitive type.

Challenge: The sensitive type will struggle with the practical type's focus on efficiency and achieving an end result, which can seem mechanical, insensitive and cold because it leaves little space for subjective values, such as kind manners, vulnerability, and sensitivity in relationships. The practical type's focus on appearances – such as attractive clothing, expensive status symbols and extravagant food – can be considered superficial by the sensitive type.

The Mental Type

The Genius and The Innovator

Likely partners: Dynamic, Mental, Analytical, Practical

Unlikely partners: Sensitive, Creative, Dedicated

Best friend: Analytical

Relationship with the dynamic type

Connection: The mental type, who has a tendency to get caught up in investigating every angle, can learn from the dynamic type's ability to take a stand on principles and focus on their goals without denying core values. The mental type, who has a tendency to give up easily, can be inspired by the dynamic type's ability to resist pressure and remain determined, honest and focused despite opposition. The dynamic type's ability to face conflict, set boundaries and be authoritative will also be appreciated by the mental type.

Challenge: The mental type, who is drawn to open debate and conversation, will experience the dynamic type as inflexible, restrictive and over-bearing because of their reluctance to engage in discussion and reflection. The dynamic type's desire to gather excessive personal power is a great challenge to the mental type, who thrives on democracy and debate.

Relationship with the sensitive type

Connection: The mental type, who will often put relationships second in order to pursue a practical or financial agenda, can learn from the sensitive type's skill at fostering positive relationships, rooted in trust, in which people feel appreciated and therefore thrive. Incorporating this capacity for deeper empathic relationships will enable the mental type to gain more benefit from their interactions with people while in the pursuit of their goals. The mental type can learn from the sensitive type's ability to understand people's need for deep meaning and intimate relationships.

Challenge: The mental type will become frustrated by the sensitive type's slow pace and apparently endless need to explore subjective feelings, which seems irrelevant to the mental type because feelings offer no practical benefit. The sensitive type's somewhat impractical approach to life will also be a cause of irritation to the mental type.

Relations with other mental types

Connection: The mental type will enjoy lively and intelligent conversation with other mental types. Together, they will be in their element as they explore the world of knowledge, exchanging ideas and making links, perhaps doing so at a furious pace. They can teach each other how to finesse their communication style. They can help each other to find practical solutions to problems and can teach each other how to prosper financially.

Challenge: The mental type has so many thoughts running around their minds that engaging with another mental type can leave them feeling overwhelmed by ideas, leading to more stress. This type is so proud of their intellect that they can become distressed when they suspect another mental type is smarter or trying to steal their ideas.

Relationship with the creative type

Connection: The mental type can be entertained and impressed by the liveliness and quirkiness of the creative type, who appears to have a similar thirst for knowledge but who seeks it in unexpected ways, with a focus on relationships, spontaneity and humour. To the mental type, this approach can feel like a welcome relief from their relentless thinking and activity, yet they will see the value in this approach if it can generate new information and perspectives. Creative types, who have a tendency to get so caught up in endless activity that they forget what life is for, can learn from the mental type how to relax and enjoy life. The mental type can learn from the creative type how to spend time with people without needing to fulfil strategic or practical goals, and to be present in the here and now without the need for planning.

Challenge: The mental type can be left feeling distracted, disorientated and unable to think clearly due to the emotional nature of the creative type. To the mental type, the creative type's playful approach to life can seem impractical, selfish and childish, while the creative type's work will seem like a waste of energy and resources on activities that don't lead to anything worthwhile.

Relationship with the analytical type

Connection: The mental type can feel highly stimulated by the analytical type, who has a similar curiosity but who investigates the world from a different perspective. While the mental type is focused on the big picture and on gathering up as much information as possible, the analytical type is able to tune into the fine detail and acquire specialist knowledge that has real practical value. The mental type, who can become overly theoretical and unrealistic, will be impressed by the analytical type's ability to conduct experiments that establish solid facts and practical know-how. The mental type will appreciate the analytical type's concern to investigate, test and experiment with ideas in practical ways before sharing them with others. The mental type will also appreciate the analytical type's concern to check what they are saying is true and sensible and not just a product of their enthusiasm.

Challenge: The mental type will feel frustrated with the analytical type's cautious, sceptical and time-consuming approach to life, which they feel narrows the focus and stems the flow of ideas that the mental type thrives on. The analytical type's critical sense can be toxic to the mental type who will feel their ideas are being dissected and dismissed before being given a chance to mature in the mind.

Relationship with the dedicated type

Connection: The mental type will be intrigued by the dedicated type's capacity to see potential and work diligently towards concrete goals while upholding core ideas and values. The mental type will benefit from integrating the dedicated type's discipline, focus and reluctance to compromise, even when in a situation that is boring or personally challenging.

Challenge: The mental type will struggle with the dedicated type's emotional temperament and mood swings, which will seem like a waste of energy and resources. The dedicated type tends to take things personally and lack a sense of detachment, which means conflict will be difficult to resolve without the dedicated type flaring up in anger. Because the mental type has a focus on facts and is willing to change their mind when new facts emerge, the dedicated type's unswerving and idealistic faith will seem illogical, even delusional.

Relationship with the practical type

Connection: The mental and practical types make for an effective team. Both are interested in ideas, but while the mental type can get lost in countless possibilities and options, the practical is able to select the most useful ideas, and then organise resources in a coordinated and orderly manner so that targets can be set and concrete results achieved. The mental type will appreciate the practical type's elegant, controlled and flawless physical appearance because it gives the impression of order and predictability.

Challenge: To the mental type, the practical type is so focused on the end result that the process can feel rushed, leaving no room for ideas to mature. This tendency of the practical type to control and systematise goes against the mental type's wish for mental freedom and exploration. The need of the practical type to be direct will limit the mental type who likes goals to emerge organically while taking time to explore options, environments and strategies from many angles, even if this means changing their minds.

The Creative Type

The Artist and The Reconciler

Likely partners: Sensitive, Creative, Dedicated

Unlikely partners: Dynamic, Mental, Analytical, Practical

Best friend: Sensitive

Relationship with the dynamic type

Connection: The creative type will be impressed by the dynamic type's ability to.remain calm and focused despite any conflict or drama that might arise. The creative type can learn from the dynamic type's ability to stay true to themselves and their core values and principles no matter what obstacles or external influences threaten to block their path. The dynamic type's ability to be independent and detached in their relationships, and to do without recognition, will be appreciated by the creative type.

Challenge: To the lively, colourful and relational creative type, the dynamic type will feel serious, solitary and even authoritarian, so it will be difficult for these two types to create a close personal bond. The dynamic type's tendency to be solitary and make decisions alone will be deeply frustrating to the creative type. The dynamic type's somewhat colourless "back to basics" lifestyle and ability to eschew aesthetics, spontaneity and relaxation will be a challenge to the creative type.

Relationship with the sensitive type

Connection: The creative type will be impressed by the sensitive type's warmth, empathy and concern to foster healthy relationships. To the often emotional and volatile creative type, the sensitive type's serenity and sense of acceptance is greatly appreciated. The creative type can learn from the sensitive type's relaxed and stable qualities, which are in contrast to the creative type's restless need to seek out new experiences and resolve conflict. The creative type can learn from the sensitive type how to hold emotions in relationships instead of always expressing them. The creative type can also learn from the sensitive type that is it important to seek wisdom and understanding in relationships rather than looking for a "quick fix" to personal problems in the form of hedonistic pleasures, entertainments and other forms of avoidance.

Challenge: For the adventurous creative type, the peace and serenity of the sensitive type will seem boring, even deadening. Similarly, the sensitive type's need for intimacy can feel like co-dependence and will stifle the creative type's need for freedom and autonomy. Due to their hyper-sensitivity, the sensitive type will often feel hurt by conflict, which will challenge the creative type's preference to clear the air with an argument.

Relationship with the mental type

Connection: The creative type will be impressed by the mental type quick intellect, comprehensive knowledge, and ability to remain cool and objective. The creative type, who has a tendency to get caught in emotional complexities, can learn from the mental type's ability to act with a strategy and focus and to organise people in a professional way to achieve concrete results. The mental type's ability to build comprehensive knowledge and take a broad overview as a result of their focused studies will be admired by the creative type, whose preference is to improvise rather than study.

Challenge: The mental type's seemingly insatiable desire to gather and process information will feel stressful, superficial and nerdy to the creative type. The mental type's tendency to talk about superficial or practical matters, instead of relating from the heart, will frustrate the creative type. Similarly, the restless activity of the mental type will challenge the creative type's need for an emotional depth and intimate connection. The creative type, who enjoys being in the moment and who can find inspiration in chaos, will feel constrained by the mental type's rational mindset.

Relationship with other creative types

Connection: When creative types meet, their playful and joyful personalities will inspire lively and honest communication, helping them to stretch their imaginations. Creative types are rarely bored in each other's company because they become sparring partners able to explore new ideas and possibilities. They can help each other to identify unhelpful patterns so they can work on them together. They can also help each other to explore taboos and the darker aspects of the human psyche because these are places where they can find beauty and harmony. This type will be highly creative together because they love to explore unchartered territory and renew their creative agenda.

Challenge: When creative types meet, their combined sense of fun and adventure can lead them into an infertile waste of time and resources. Their unstructured and impulsive behaviour means they will struggle to maintain their focus, which will serve to magnify their sense of chaos and disorientation. Meanwhile, this type's strong need for attention and praise can lead to conflict – as if they were celebrities vying for top billing in a movie.

Relationship with the analytical type

Connection: The creative type, with their flights of fancy, can be astounded by the analytical type's ability to remain grounded, logical and practical. While the creative type can disappear into their imagination, the analytical type has the self-discipline to remain objective and focused on the task in hand – qualities that the creative type would do well to incorporate. The creative type can learn from the analytical type how to be objective and how to critique their own behaviour. The creative type can also learn from the analytical type how to take themselves and life more seriously – in other words, rather than wasting time and resources on diversionary pastimes, the creative type can learn to take responsibility, choosing to face challenges and undertake unpleasant tasks because this will help to build a stable and strong existence.

Challenge: To the flamboyant creative type, the analytical type can seem nerdy, cautious and boring. The analytical type's parsimonious and sceptical attitude will feel stifling and full of criticism to the creative type, who likes to be playful and irresponsible, even wild. The analytical type's tendency to be cautious arises out of a fear that something might go wrong, and this will be deeply frustrating to the creative type who prefers to consider all the options and take risks in the hope that something new and different might emerge.

Relationship with the dedicated type

Connection: The creative type will be impressed by the dedicated type's ability to remain focused, enthusiastic and positive in the pursuit of a vision that reaches beyond mere self-interest. The creative type will also be inspired by the dedicated type's passion, sensitivity and loyalty to their core values and their desire to unlock potential in the search for a more meaningful way of life. The creative type will appreciate the dedicated type's ability to fight for what they hold dear, even if this means facing challenges or accusations that they are wasting their time.

Challenge: While aware with their intense feelings, the creative type will find the dedicated type to be overly serious and rigid in their thinking, such that the dedicated type can seem like a fanatic, unable to take time to smell the roses, out of which new and more interesting ideas can emerge. When these types meet, the intense and volatile temperament of the dedicated type will tend to create conflict and disturb the harmony that is dear to the creative type.

Relationship with the practical type

Connection: The creative type, with their love of beauty, will admire the adept way in which the practical type is able to focus, prioritise and organise ideas and resources in order to achieve concrete results. The creative type can learn from the practical type's self-discipline and skill in discerning whatever will be most useful for the realisation of their vision. In terms of manner and appearance, the creative type will admire the beauty, elegance and self-control of the practical type. The practical type can teach the creative type to express a more disciplined and organised energy that would help teo control the spontaneous impulses that cause the creative type to become sidetracked and loose connection with their purpose.

Challenge: The creative type thrives on the unpredictable and can even enjoy conflict and extreme emotions because all of this generates opportunities for new ideas and surprising outcomes. By contrast, the practical type's methodical approach will seem rigid, even controlling, which will leave the creative type feeling stifled and inhibited. The practical type's need to control even the smallest details will tend to block the creative type's creativity, which will be experienced as deeply frustrating. Similarly, the creative type will feel constrained by the practical type's predictability, focus on routine and need to achieve concrete results.

The Analytical Type

The Explorer and The Researcher

Likely partners: Dynamic, Mental, Analytical, Practical

Unlikely partners: Sensitive, Creative, Dedicated

Best friend: Mental

Relationship with the dynamic type

Connection: The analytical type will appreciate the direct, practical and logical style of the dynamic type. For the analytical type, who can get lost in detail and research, it is refreshing to see the disciplined and matter-of-fact way in which the dynamic type gets things done. The dynamic type's cool and impersonal style of leadership will be appreciated by the analytical type, as will the dynamic type's high energy and work capacity, which matches the work discipline of the analytical type. The dynamic type can teach the analytical type to think big and live courageously and adventurously. The analytical type could learn to be less self-critical by drawing on the dynamic type's authority, gravitas and self-confidence.

Challenge: The analytical type will feel hesitant around the dynamic type, whose tendency to ignore the detail and forge ahead with their own agenda is contrary to the analytical tendency to think things through. While the dynamic type is happy to dive into any situation that is going too slowly and assert their authority, the analytical type will tend to be overly-cautious and self-critical – an approach that could bring out a brutal response from the dynamic type.

Relationship with the sensitive type

Connection: The analytical type will admire the sensitive type's ability to handle people and situations with tact and respect. The sensitive type's warm and friendly qualities are what is needed to soften the analytical type's critical eye, which can be turned on both themselves and others. These two types are both interested in detail, albeit the analytical type has a focus on gathering objective information while the sensitive type is focused on the subjective world. The analytical type can learn from the sensitive type how to be more engaging and personal in relationships and how to be sensitive to their own needs. The analytical type can also learn from the sensitive type how to draw benefit from irrational impulses and how to take a more holistic look at life rather than getting stuck in the details.

Challenge: The objective analytical type will struggle with the sensitive type's tendency to mix feeling and fact, subjectivity and objectivity. The analytical type will become frustrated by the sensitive type's vulnerability to criticism and their corresponding difficulty in looking at others with a critical eye. The analytical type, who appreciates and values difference, will struggle with the sensitive type's resistance to recognising strong differences and contrasts.

Relationship with the mental type

Connection: The analytical type will admire, and perhaps envy, the mental type's comprehensive knowledge and ability to make connections and communicate with ease. The analytical type can also learn from the mental type's ability to multitask and to look at the big picture rather than losing themselves in the detail. The analytical type will appreciate the mental type's ability to communicate knowledge in a popular way so that it reaches a wide audience. The analytical type will want to learn from the mental type's skills in finance and trade because this will help the analytical type to generate a profit from their work.

Challenge: The analytical type is able to look deeply into their chosen subject and investigate whatever they find, even uncomfortable facts. As a consequence, the analytical type can experience the mental type's preference for breadth, rather than depth, as superficial and avoidant, even cowardly. The mental type's tendency to explain away or put a spin on uncomfortable facts will be highly frustrating to the analytical type, who likes to know the truth and the detail no matter how inconvenient or painful.

Relationship with the creative type

Connection: The analytical type, who tends to stick with tried and tested methods, will be impressed by the imaginative and intuitive way in which the creative type is able to come up with new ideas and fresh insights. The analytical type, who is most at home in the library or laboratory, can learn people skills from the warm and sociable creative type. The creative type's ability to understand and work with conflict to bring about a compromise will be appreciated by the analytical type who can get stuck in their own world and struggle to relate to others. And from the playful and humorous qualities of the creative type, the analytical type can learn to loosen up and relax.

Challenge: The analytical type, who enjoys working with facts and finds it easy to concentrate for long periods of time, will consider the playful nature of the creative type to be frivolous, and the creative type's reliance on imagination and intuition to be unscientific. The analytical type will become frustrated by the creative type's inability to concentrate when bored. Analytical types will also be frustrated by the creative type's tendency to exaggerate and embellish reality, thereby distorting facts.

Relationship with other analytical types

Connection: When analytical types get together they will appreciate each other's diligence, common sense and attention to detail. Whether at work or in a relationship, they will speak to each other in a manner that is fair and objective and, as a result, they will be able to tell each other the truth without the risk of causing offence – in this way they can help each other to clear away blind spots, leading to new discoveries. Together, they can pool their resources to reach deeper insights that lead to greater know-how.

Challenge: Analytical types have a tendency to become defensive and finds it difficult to receive personal criticism, so they can easily fall out with each other, either withdrawing or becoming passive-aggressive. This type's tendency to be critical for the sake of criticism, and to be cynical and negative about things they know little about, will create trouble. This type can be grumpy and anti-social which means it will be difficult for analytical types to establish a healthy professional relationships with each other.

Relationship with the dedicated type

Connection: The analytical type will admire the dedicated type's uncomplicated and honest nature and their capacity for hard work in the pursuit of goals. The analytical type can learn from the dedicated type's positivity, focus on values and refusal to give up. The analytical type appreciates, the dedicated type's desire to communicate their vision and knowledge in a passionate way in order to inspire a wide audience. The analytical type can learn from the dedicated type how to incorporate subjective values into their analysis in order to establish clarity around their values and beliefs. The pessimistic analytical type can also learn from the dedicated type how to have faith and how to dream dreams that may seem improbable but which may lead to new discoveries.

Challenge: The analytical type can be sceptical of the dedicated type's faith in their vision, which they see as based on subjective feelings rather than well-researched data. The dedicated type's emotional approach to life, which can veer towards fanaticism, will be experienced as alarming by the cautious analytical type. The activism and idealism of the dedicated type will strike the cautious analytical type as exaggerated and illogical.

Relationship with the practical type

Connection: The analytical type will be impressed by the practical type's ability to make use of specialist knowledge. The analytical type will appreciate the serious and down to earth attitude of the practical type and their capacity to take ideas and knowledge and translate them into useful and helpful activities, products and projects. The analytical type can learn from the practical type that outward appearance and performance are appealing and therefore important because they can be used to help to promote ideas. The analytical type would also benefit by learning from the practical type how to cooperate with experts from different areas so that knowledge can be shared, synthesised and expanded.

Challenge: The analytical type can feel invaded and offended when the practical type seeks to get involved with the details of a situation or process, which the analytical type will feel is part of their domain. The practical type has a focus on the end result, which means they can overlook individual contributions – and this can often leave the analytical type feeling ignored. The analytical type will feel frustrated if the practical type emphasises outward appearance and performance so much that facts and purpose disappear.

The Dedicated Type

The Visionary and The Activist

Likely partners: Sensitive, Creative, Dedicated

Unlikely partners: Dynamic, Mental, Practical

Best friend: Sensitive

Relationship with the dynamic type

Connection: The dedicated type is inspired by the dynamic type's power, authority and drive for excellence. The emotional dedicated type can learn from the dynamic type's self-control and capacity to take challenges and attacks in their stride without becoming emotional. Incorporating the pragmatic qualities of the dynamic type will help to moderate the dedicated type's idealism, which will make them more approachable and less prone to disappointment. The dedicated type can also learn from the dynamic type how to be a leader rather than a follower and how to think strategically before rushing into action.

Challenge: The dedicated type will disapprove of the dynamic type's ability to put ethical considerations aside in their pursuit of power. The dedicated type, who values loyalty and relationships, is averse to the dynamic type's ability to detach from people and act in ways that are cold, disloyal and even brutal.

Relationship with the sensitive type

Connection: The dedicated type appreciates the sensitive type's warmth, patience, and ability to accept all types of people. The sensitive type's psychological insight and ability to bring people together will impress the dedicated type whose goal is to inspire as many people as possible with their message – to this end, the sensitive type can teach the dedicated type how to be less reactive and better able to see different points of view. The dedicated type can acquire wisdom from the sensitive type and learn how to explore a range of possibilities before plunging into projects in a fanatical way.

Challenge: The dedicated type can perceive the sensitive type as being too passive and conflict-avoidant, which goes against the dedicated type's desire to shake people out of habitual ways of thinking and living. The dedicated type, who tends to feel sure about the rightness of their cause, can feel perplexed by the sensitive type's tendency to see all sides of an issue. The dedicated type will feel frustrated by the sensitive type's cautious nature when there is a need to be brave and try new things.

Relationship with the mental type

Connection: The temperamental dedicated type is impressed by the mental type's ability to connect easily with people and to remain calm even during a disagreement. The mental type is able to see life from many different angles, which is a quality that would benefit the dedicated type, whose focus is often locked on a single ideology. The dedicated type could also learn from the mental type's ability to strategise, work hard and get things done, as well as their gift for financial planning.

Challenge: The passionate dedicated type will become frustrated by the mental type's cautionary and neutral attitude and by their preference for considering all viewpoints rather than taking sides. The dedicated type might also question the ethics of the mental type, who might lack a sense of values and put profit ahead of ethics. The mental type's verbosity and sales tricks, which sometimes stretch the truth, will frustrate the dedicated type.

Relationship with the creative type

Connection: The dedicated type will appreciate the creative type's people skills and enthusiastic nature, albeit that the focus of the creative type is on new and aesthetic experiences, rather than a particular ideology. The dedicated type, whose single-minded pursuit of a vision can shut them off from new ideas, can learn from the creative type's ability to relax and enjoy company for its own sake. Indeed, learning from the creative type how to be playful, flexible and spontaneous would help the dedicated type to establish warmer relationships and to gain fresh insights, all of which could help with their cause.

Challenge: The mood swings of the creative type are likely to trigger the fiery temper of the dedicated type. The creative type, with their wandering imagination and changing opinions, will strike the idealistic and focused dedicated type as fickle and lacking in purpose. The dedicated type will see the creative type's sociability and playful nature as people-pleasing, and perhaps lacking in a sense of loyalty – but the dedicated type might also feel envious of the ease with which the creative type can establish relationships. The dedicated type might be jealous of the creative type's flirty style and ability to make intimate connections.

Relationship with the analytical type

Connection: The dedicated type will admire the analytical type's concern to work hard and focus, to discover the truth, and to share what they have learned in a clear and straight forward manner. The analytical type can teach the dedicated type how to critique their vision by considering the facts and by keeping a cool head when passion threatens to distort their perception. The dedicated type can learn from the analytical type how to be objective and hold their passion in check – to keep their feet on the ground even though their head is in the sky.

Challenge: The dedicated type will feel frustrated by the analytical type's critical and scientific attitude – this is the classic conflict between faith and reason. The cool and detached perspective of the analytical type will strike the dedicated type as negative and lacking in conviction, which will serve to deflate the enthusiasm of the dedicated type and even leave them feeling disillusioned.

Relationship with other dedicated types

Connection: When dedicated types get together, their enthusiasm is contagious: they will find in each other a loyal friend with whom to pursue their goals with renewed energy, perhaps setting their sights even higher. Dedicated types will support each other through difficult times, helping each other to see the potential in setbacks so they can renew their efforts. Dedicated types can help to curb each other's tendency to extremism and to see the dangers of adopting an overly intense and passionate approach.

Challenge: When dedicated types get together, they can get carried away by their enthusiasm which can lead to impulsive actions and naïve behaviour that they may regret. With their volatile temperament, dedicated types can argue fiercely, especially when core values are threatened. And if dedicated types fall out or betray one another, then the greatest of friends can become the greatest of enemies.

Relationship with the practical type

Connection: The dedicated type will admire the practical type's ability to get things done and achieve their goals. The dedicated type, who can hold on doggedly to unattainable ideals, will benefit from the practical type's pragmatism and ability to focus, organise and proceed in a clear and intelligent fashion. The practical type's reliability, competency and flexibility are all qualities that would help the dedicated type realise their vision, as will the practical type's ability to inspire people to contribute their skills and cooperate. Dedicated types, who have a tendency to do everything themselves or else to stick with their own kind, can learn from the practical type how to cooperate with a team of different types of people.

Challenge: The passionate dedicated type can experience the pragmatic approach of the practical type as cold and impersonal. Indeed, the practical type's sense of realism can deflate the dedicated type's enthusiasm and leave their dreams in tatters. The dedicated type, whose single-minded pursuit of a vision can result in asceticism, will consider the practical type's appreciation of physical beauty to be an irrelevance or an indulgence.

The Practical Type

The Creator and The Designer

Likely partners: Dynamic, Mental, Analytical, Practical

Unlikely partners: Sensitive, Creative, Dedicated

Best friend: Dynamic

Relationship with the dynamic type

Connection: The practical type will admire the strength and courage of the dynamic type to swim against the tide and press forward with new ideas in the face of challenges and conflict. The practical type can learn from the dynamic type's ability to make unpopular decisions and take responsibility. Adopting this approach would release the practical type from their adherence to systems and routines and give them the courage to explore new ideas and implement change, even if this means dropping their social façade, upsetting people, and temporarily creating chaos.

Challenge: The practical type, who likes to hold things together, can feel threatened by the dynamic type's tendency to break things down – even to destroy – before building something new. The practical type might also be alarmed by the tendency of the dynamic type to take power and play mind games in order to hold onto power. The practical type, who thrives on cooperation, will struggle to relate to the dynamic type's capacity to operate in isolation.

Relationship with the sensitive type

Connection: The practical type will admire the sensitive type's ability to establish warm relationships that recognise people's qualities and inspire them to cooperate. The practical type, whose focus is on planning, efficiency and end results, can learn from the sensitive type how to relax and how to relate in an empathic manner that seeks to enjoy people for who they are, rather than seeing people as tools to be used. The practical type will appreciate the sensitive type's ability to resolve conflict and heal relationships through their warmth, insight, psychological depth and understanding nature.

Challenge: The practical type, whose focus is on completing the job in hand, will consider the sensitive type's overly concern for people's well-being as an unnecessary distraction, even as something that could encourage dependency and a sense of victimhood. This tendency of the sensitive type to focus on feelings and intimacy will strike the practical type as a waste of time because there is work to be done – so these two types will have issues with each other.

Relationship with the mental type

Recognise: The practical type will admire the mental type's ability to think strategically and communicate how their ideas can be turned into reality, yet with a flexibility that can deal with any challenges that might arise. The practical type can learn from the mental type that it is ok to let go of tried and tested ideas and think outside of the box. The practical type will appreciate the mental type's knack for inspiring people to share a vision and work together to achieve a goal. The practical type will appreciate the mental type's skill ingenuity, innovation, drive, and ability to explain reality through attractive stories.

Challenge: The practical type will feel his plans are being frustrated by the mental type's hyperactivity and by their tendency to focus on intrigues rather than on what brings people together. The practical type, who simply wants to get on with the task in hand, will feel frustrated by the mental type's tendency to be manipulative and self-serving. The practical type will find the mental type to be unreliable because of their shifting opinions and opportunistic behaviour.

Relationship with the creative type

Connection: The practical type will relate to the creative type's aesthetic sense and be intrigued by their ability to improvise, and even break the rules, in their attempt to improve the cultural atmosphere. The practical type, who enjoys order and organisation, will appreciate the creative type's desire to establish positive and harmonious environments that value diversity and bring people together. The creative type can teach the practical type how to use play, humour and debate to release emotions and get the most out of people, which will in turn help with the realisation of goals.

Challenge: The disciplined practical type will feel frustrated by the unstructured and chaotic attitude of the creative type, whose mood swings and unwitting tendency to create conflict could interrupt the practical type's carefully made plans. The practical type will also feel frustrated by any attempt to engage the creative type in disciplined work, which will often result in the creative type becoming bored, passive or rebellious.

Relationship with the analytical type

Recognise: The practical type will appreciate the analytical type's discipline, technical skill, and ability to cut through superficial layers to get to the heart of an issue. The practical type will appreciate the analytical type's reliable knowledge and effective management of the tasks they undertake. From the analytical type, the practical type can learn the importance of paying attention to detail so that corrections can be made and plans adjusted in order to achieve the best possible results.

Challenge: The practical type, for whom speed and action are essential, will become frustrated by the analytical type's tendency to get lost in detail and to refuse to update tried and tested methods. The slow and painstaking approach of the analytical type will appear unnecessary and stubborn to the practical type. The practical type, who has a love for elegance and extravagance, will find the analytical type to be dour and nerdy in their love of precision and detail.

Relationship with the dedicated type

Connection: The practical type shares with the dedicated type an ability to focus and work hard in order to achieve a specific goal. The practical type can learn from the dedicated type that core values and ethics are important so that the end result can be beneficial and not merely an achievement for its own sake. The practical type would benefit from adopting the warmth and enthusiasm of the dedicated type, which would help the practical type to inspire people to give their best in support of a shared goal. The dedicated type could teach the practical type how to face challenges with unswerving commitment – this would help the practical type to ask openly for support for their vision, rather than locking themselves away and trying to do everything.

Challenge: The practical type can experience the dedicated type as naïve, impractical and even fanatical due to their belief in utopia. The practical type will be perplexed by the dedicated type's fiery temper and black or white thinking that often creates conflict and drama. Practical types favour rational and diplomatic behaviour, which will bring them into conflict with the activism and extreme sentiment of the dedicated type.

Relationship with other practical types

Connection: When practical types meet they can inspire each other to set their sights high and strive for new standards of excellence. Whether as friends, partners or colleagues, practical types will establish a spirit of fellowship and close cooperation that will work in an elegant, minimalistic and controlled fashion. The practical type's ability to organise, consider multiple perspectives and take responsibility means that their projects will run smoothly and efficiently and generate positive results.

Challenge: This practical type's wish to be in charge and make all the decisions, even to micro-manage, means that conflict and power struggles are almost inevitable when practical types get together. This can lead to a tendency to play the diplomatic, even to become manipulative, in an attempt to pull the strings from behind the scenes to try and make things happen.

Assagioli's egg-diagram and the seven energies

This article, which has been adapted from my book *Integral Meditation*, offers a brief exploration of how the seven energies or rays correspond to Assagioli's egg-diagram. The topic deserves in-depth study, but I hope this brief offering will stir your imagination and curiosity.

Let's start at the beginning: the Seven Rays constitute everything in existence, from the mineral world to the highest spiritual levels of being. From this perspective, there is no area of study where we cannot apply psychoenergetics.

Roberto Assagioli

The term "ray" should be understood to refer to the *quality* associated with it, and not the physical or psychological form in which it is expressed. For example, in the mineral world, metals are forms of energy that have a particular atomic pattern, with each metal having different qualities that emerge through the energy pattern – or "ray quality" – that created them. The same applies to human beings: the combination of rays that are most dominant in us will determine which psychological qualities define our character.

The energies of the rays are not outside us, but are within, making up the essence of who we are. We are energy! Sri Aurobindo poetically says that the rivers (another term for the rays) come from "a superior sea of light and power and joy" and that they reveal *Sat-Cit-Ananda*, which is "being, consciousness, bliss".[1] This deep insight is one of the concepts that makes psychoenergetics so fascinating: psychoenergetics provides a cosmic view of life, while also offering concrete practical advice for psychological application.

Psychoenergetics, as it is presented in the model of the Seven Types, is a spiritual typology comprised of levels of being, stages of development, states of being, seven types, and the quadrants of experience as described in Ken Wilber's Integral Psychology.

Wilber emphasises the concept of Spirit-in-Action, which he describes as the universal life force driving the evolution of consciousness. What Wilber calls Spirit-in-Action is the equivalent to the Universal Self in Assagioli's terminology – and this universal life force is the very fabric of life, the innermost power residing in all living beings. We all ride on the wave of this great evolutionary force: we *are* this wave – we *are* *Spirit-in-Action*.

An important teaching found in many religions concerns the transcendent unmanifest realm that exists outside of time and space. In Buddhism, this realm is called *Dharmakaya*; in Hinduism it is *Parabrahman*; in the Christian tradition it is God. Out of this ground of being emerges the will to manifest. The universe appears and continually actualises its potential: this gives us Spirit-in-Action and the Big Bang, which is how the physical realm was created. However, according to the processes of involution and evolution, the inner worlds appeared before the outer worlds. And these inner worlds constitute the manifest ground of reality; they are the source of what is known, in the perennial philosophy, as *the Great Chain of Being*; they are the "heavens" of an *interior* space (Sørensen, 2017b). The Seven Rays are

---

[1] Aurobindo, Sri, The Synthesis of Yoga, Complete Works, p. 423, 1999, Sri Aurobindo Publishing Department.

the seven streams of spiritual force produced by the Universal Self which shape and maintain creation.

But how do the Seven Rays manifest in us? The spiritual soul receives these energies from the Universal Self and channels them through the personality, and continues to do so throughout our life. The relationship between the three levels of Spirit, soul and personality and the Seven Rays is illustrated in Figure 1, which shows how the Seven Rays flow into the soul, which is depicted at the top of Assagioli's egg-diagram. From the soul, the rays flow through the superconscious into the conscious "I", or self, in the middle of the egg, and from here the rays move out into the personality through the agency of our psychological functions (will, feeling, thought, imagination, logic, passion and, eventually, physical action).

Figure1:
The seven rays and Assagioli's Egg-diagram – showing how the Seven Rays flow into the soul then down into the self and the personality via the seven psychological functions (only will, thought and feeling are listed).

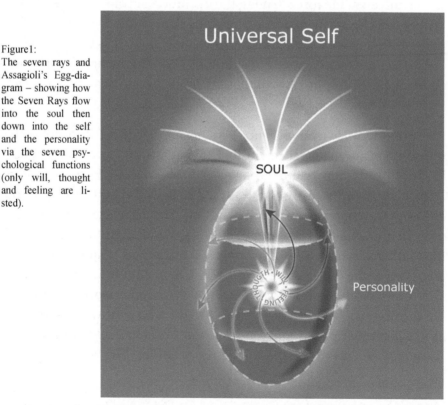

While we've seen that the rays and types are in some respect the same, it is still important to differentiate between the energies of the rays and the types, and the different ways that they both manifest.

The rays are ever-present in the great universal ocean; *they flow through every manifestation of the All*. A type, however, is a *particular vehicle for the soul*, an energy field, of which there are five different vehicles: the physical or etheric body, the emotional body, the mental body, the personality field, and the soul or causal body. These are the energy fields, or bodies, of which Assagioli (Undated: 6) stated: "The *Rays* which qualify his soul, his personality, and his mental, emotional and physical bodies."

Along with the physical body, we have subtle bodies (levels), or "sheaths" as they are called in yogic literature and in Ken Wilber's writing[2]. Each body has a particular type coloured by one of the seven rays.

Figure 2.
The Egg-diagram and the five bodies

[2] See note in chapter 9.

When we speak of the five dominant types, we are referring to how the seven rays, in a constant stream, are expressed in our lives *through the five bodies* (levels), *which act like coloured filters*. The seven rays, which are influencing us all the time, are filtered through the different types and bodies that express them. The different energy fields define how we seek meaning, our character, and how we think, feel and act.

To offer an example of how the seven rays might manifest in an individual life, Figure 2 shows the five levels (layers, bodies) of the inner house, which is made up of our soul and our personality (which contains the levels of body, feeling and thought). We are not aware of all the rooms or floors in our inner house – some have never been inhabited, and few of us know the layout of all the rooms. In the egg-diagram, we see the different holarchies (wholes within wholes) – i.e. each higher level incorporates all the levels beneath it. An exchange takes places through these levels, between the environment and the incoming energies of the different rays.

Moving down the levels, we can see from the symbols at each level that this diagram is depicting a person with a "7-2,521" combination of types: we can see the practical soul type (7), which comprises the red-brown soul body and which incorporates all the other layers in its totality; the blue field is the sensitive personality type (2), which includes the three lower levels, or bodies, of thought, feeling and body; the next layer is the analytical thinking type (5), which incorporates the levels of feeling and body; then we have the blue sensitive feeling type (2), which incorporates the level of body, and at the bottom we find the energy of the dynamic body type (1).

Assagioli and typology: Research notes

The following is a summary of some of the key findings I made while researching Assagioli's references to typology. Very often, Assagioli referred only in passing to the significance of typology, without elaborating on how to apply the theory of types. However, it is clear that, from early in his thinking, Assagioli held that typology was an essential element of psychosynthesis. The aim of my research was to draw out some of Assagioli's implicit

Assagioli meditating

thinking around typology so that a set of concrete principles regarding psychosynthesis typology could be established. For each of the following 24 principles I have referenced the source material so the reader can check out my interpretations in Assagioli's original writings.

Typology in Counselling

1. Typology help us to develop a true and profound self-knowledge (1933)
2. There is a specific psychosynthetic method for each of the types (1974: 249).
3. Meditation must be used with an understanding of how the types react to different forms of meditation (2007: 273; 1974: 223-224, 229).
4. The practice of psychosynthesis implies "the classification of his psycho-physical type" (1927).
5. Our understanding of how the psychological laws work must be adapted to the psychological type of the individual (1974: 54; Undated 12).
6. Typology offers awareness of the particular sensitivities and mentalities of individual clients, according to type (1983: 53-54).
7. Typology offers insight into how different types approach personal and spiritual psychosynthesis, thereby suggesting the most effective psychosynthetic task for each type (1983: 13-16).
8. The creative and analytic-scientific types have crises similar to those taking place before and after the "awakening" (1965: 48).
9. Having an understanding of the types will suggest the most effective methods or techniques for supporting clients, according to their psychological type (1965: 93, 94, 99, 109, 120, 141, 149, 162, 189-190, 222, 242, 247, 283; 1974: 77, 97, 100, 164-166; 1970; 1983c; 1933).
10. It is important to apply an understanding of typology when using the techniques of the Ideal Model and the Seven Ways (1965: 48-49; 201-202, https://kennethsorensen.dk/en/glossary/seven-ways).
11. The particular concept of ultimate reality will be biased or coloured by the different types of human beings who describe it (1974: 130).
12. Typology offers insight into the limitations, or "shadows" (Jung), that each type is prone to and how to work with each type most effectively to overcome these limitations (1970b: Year 3, https://meditationmount.org/study-courses/).

13. Typology offers insight into how clients will react to obstacles, challenges and awakening, according to type (1968b; 1975).

14. Typology offers insight into how clients react and approach a creative phase (2007: 52).

15. Typology offers insight into introvert-extrovert dynamics (1967b, 1931).

In working with couples and groups

16. Typology offers insight regarding the spiritual psychosynthesis of a couple or nation (Undated 4).

17. Typology offers understanding of the different nations (Undated 29; 1931; 1983: 22-23, 43; 1931b).

18. Typology offers insight for resolving conflict between different types (Undated 17).

19. Typology informs which approaches will be most effective for establishing balance between love and will in relationships (1974: 97).

20. Typology provides insight into how different types respond to falling in love (1974: 100).

In education

21. Typology provides insight for how to understand, teach and support children, especially super-gifted children (1968a; 1960).

22. Typology encourages an attitude of equality of opportunity through an acknowledgement of different types (1968a).

23. Typology informs how best to support future leaders and illuminators, according to type (1968a).

24. Typology informs how to promote language-learning, according to type (Undated 5).

An overview
of the Seven Types

Master Index: THE SEVEN TYPES

Type Function	Dynamic Will	Sensitive Feeling	Mental Thought	Creative Imagination	Analytical Logic	Dedicated Passion	Practical Action
Archetypal roles	Hero Manager Pioneer Leader Regent Warrior	Illuminator Guide Helper Healer Teacher Humanist	Genius Thinker Strategist Communicator Negotiator Innovator	Artist Aesthete Transformer Designer Psychologist Dramatist	Explorer Researcher Specialist Inventor Detective Fixer	Visionary Idealist Advocate Soldier Romantic Activist	Creator Orhestrator Organiser Systematiser Financier Entrepeneur
Highest goal	Victory	Love	Perspective	Beauty	Facts	Perfection	Manifestation
Basic technique	Grasping	Attracting	Choosing	Unifying	Separating	Responding	Coordinating
Symbols	Lightning Sword Diamond	Heart Sun The Pen	The Eye Spider (web)	Yin-Yang Scales	Key Magnifying glass Five-pointed star	Mountain top Flame Holy Grail	Rotating sun Seven-pointed star
Strengths	Strong Courageous Inspiring	Accepting Calm Insightful	Intelligent Strategic Sharp	Aesthetic Humorous Intuitive	Precise Persevering Discerning	Goal-orientated Loyal Sacrificial	Organising Effective Elegant
Weakness	Tyrannical Cold Power-hungry	Weak, Dependent Self-pitying	Manipulative Arrogant Unreliable	Chaotic Dishonest Anxious	Suspicious Critical Merciless	Naive Aggressive Dogmatic	Controlling Superficial Snobbish
Power strategies	Aggression that creates weakness	Sweetness that creates dependency	Speech that confuses and manipulates	Flattery that seduces	Criticism that points out mistakes and creates guilt	Moralising that creates shame	Correcting that creates fear
Must be developed	Inclusion	Centralisation	Silence	Endurance	Detachment	Stillness	Orientation toward purpose
Motivation	Power	Love	Intelligence	Harmony	Know-how	Faith	Results
Basic feelings	Courage Wrath	Love Hate	Curiosity Jealousy	Happiness Sadness	Neutrality Disgust	Devotion Shame	Control Guilt
Core fear	Humiliation or weakness	Separation or loss	Treachery or conspiracy	Unhappiness or boredom	Falsehood or lies	Disappointment or lack of meaning	Chaos or waste of resources
Greatest pain	Defeat	Loneliness	Stupidity	Depression	Dishonesty	Disillusionment	Incompetence
Meditations[1]	Dynamic and presence-based meditation	Insight and healing meditation	Reflective and receptive meditation	Creative and transformative meditation	Reflective and analytic meditation	Creative or mystic meditation	Integral and group meditation
Literature	Biographies Political debate Leadership philosophy Military strategy	Self-help literature	Academic literature History Philosophy	The classics Poetry	Detective stories Manuals Dictionaries Reference books	Romantic and religious literature	Business literature Science fiction
Teaching style	Challenging Discipline	Humanistic Appreciative	Topical Debating	Playful Experience-based	Academic Testing	Engaging Motivating	Group dynamic Project-orientated
Leadership style	Dynamic leader Inspire through ideas and examples	Sensitive leader Value-based leadership Focus on community	Innovative leader Strategic network	Creative leader Artistic Conflict resolution Experience-based	Academic leader Expertise Know-how	Advocating Value-based Motivating Visualising goals Branding	Project manager Organiser Administrator Implementer
Soldier style	The General Elite Soldier	Officer with the responsibility for education and welfare	Intelligence Officer Strategic planning	The tactical operational leader	Engineer and special forces. Mechanics	Commander that motivates and maintains focus in battle	Supply officer Logistics

THE SEVEN TYPES ON A GOOD DAY

Dynamic	Sensitive	Mental	Creative	Analytical	Dedicated	Practical
Independent,	Insightful,	Discerning	Creative	Independent	Idealistic	Powerful
Individualistic	Understanding	Intelligent	Poetic	Clear	Enthusiastic	Commanding
Detached	Illuminating	Smart	Imaginative	Analytical	Loyal	Disciplined
Sovereign	Wise	Alert	Aesthetic	Scientific	Self-sacrificial	Organised
Impersonal,	Self-aware	Acute	Intuitive	Keen	Ecstatic	Integrative
Governing	Intuitive	Reflective	Wise	Discriminating	Inspirational	Practical
Pioneering	Holistic	Thoughtful	Artistic	Lucid	Holy	Conscientious
Initiating	Enlightening	Strategic	Transformative	Factual	Blissful	Orderly
Decisive	Loving	Agile	Insightful	Sharp	One-pointed	Elegant
Dynamic	Empathetic	Abstract	Penetrating	Just	Intense	Excellent
Commanding	Compassionate	Excellent	Vibrant	Discerning	Aspirational	Graceful
Heroic	Accepting	Observant	Inspirational	Rational	Whole-hearted	Dignified
Organised	Inclusive	Clear	Graceful	Inventive	Courageous	Conservative
Majestic	Unifying	Sharp	Joyful	Experimental	Honest	Formal
Powerful	Sensitive	Curious	Witty	Technical	Earnest	Diplomatic
Influential	Receptive	Original	Entertaining	Enlightening	Sincere	Noble
Strong	Open	Foresighted	Amusing	Diagnostic	Humble	Group conscious
Victorious	Warm	Concentrated	Charming	Revealing	Pure	Dignified
Energetic	Kind	Broad-minded	Improvisational	Honest	Supportive	Rhythmic
Inspirational	Benevolent	Analytical	Process-orientate	Accurate	Faithful	Balanced
Liberating	Nurturing	Ingenious	Playful	Objective	Loyal	Transformative
Firm	Altruistic	Innovative	Musical	Detached	Devoted	Masterful
Resolute	Cooperative	Skilful	Communicative	Neutral	Romantic	Systematic
Concentrated	Egalitarian	Vocal	Connective	Fair	Generous	Creative
Disciplined	Accommodating	Accurate	Outgoing	Truthful	Caring	Productive
Confident	Appreciative	Persuasive	Literate	Impartial	Serious	Industrious
Self-controlled	Caring	Communicative	Spontaneous	Focused	Motivating	Methodical
Principled	Forgiving	Accommodating	Present	Observant	Uplifting	Skilful
Synthetic	Trustworthy	Flexible	Quick	Precise	Persistent	Balanced
Large-minded	Tolerant	Impersonal	Candid	Meticulous	Enduring	Ritualistic
Honest	Patient	Neutral	Vocal	Practical	Persuasive	Philanthropic
Courageous	Faithful	Adaptable	Compromising	Patient	Engaging	Economic
Daring	tactful	Quick	Harmonious	Tenacious	Optimistic	
Fearless	Gentle	Conversational	Peaceful	Persevering	Passionate	
Vigilant	Humble	Objective	Unifying		Energetic	
Truthful	Magnetic	Economical	Generous		Adventurous	
Victorious	Attractive	Practical	Sensitive			
Enforcing	Serene	Active				
Guarding	Calm	Effective				
Defending	Healing	Efficient				
Just	Sensual	Philanthropic				
Purposeful						

THE SEVEN TYPES ON A BAD DAY

Dynamic	Sensitive	Mental	Creative	Analytical	Dedicated	Practical
Oppressive	Deluded	Proud	Self-absorbed	Hyper-critical	Fanatical	Ritualistic
Domineering	Seductive	Cold	Narcissistic	Irreverent	Extreme	Formal
Aggressive	Popularity-seeking	Cunning	Self-centred	Rigid	Manipulative	Pompous
Brutal	Vague	Critical	Appeasing	Prejudiced	Manic	Excessive
Destructive	People-pleasing	Complicated	Ingratiating	Judgmental	Militant	Fixated
Ruthless	Manipulative	Careless	Seductive	Narrow-minded	Repressive	Controlling
Hard	Fearful	Manipulative	Flattering	Arrogant	Domineering	Conceited
Cruel	Hyper-sensitive	Secretive	Melodramatic	Dogmatic	Dogmatic	Power-hungry
Despotic	Avoidant	Suspicious	Moody	Suspicious	Blind	Greedy
Dictating	Anxious	Devious	Over-dramatic	Fixated	Self-abasing	Intrigant
Pompous	Sentimental	Opportunistic	Suspicious	Judgemental	Naïve	Dogmatic
Militant	Weak	Amoral	Anxious	Awkward	Conflicted	Compulsive
Power-hungry	Despondent	Deceitful	Impractical	Insensitive	Impatient	Bigoted
Grandiose	Whining	Cynical	Manipulative	Merciless	Dramatic	Biased
Controlling	Symbiotic	Calculating	Agitated	Unforgiving	Jealous	Superficial
Greedy	Over-protective	Dishonest	Unstable	Boring	Possessive	Obsessive
Reckless	Clingy	Deceptive	Unpredictable	Miserly	Masochistic	Neurotic
Impatient	Passive	Conspirational	Unreliable	Predictable	Superstitious	Materialistic
Irritable	Powerless	Untruthful	Indolent	Obsessive,	Aggressive	Indulgent
Violent	Non-assertive	Hyperactive	Lazy	Short-sighted	Brutal	Wasteful
Egotistical	Over-inclusive	Restless	Conflict-avoidant	Sense-bound	Harsh	Pedantic
Arrogant	Self-pitying	Vague	Extreme		Hard	Earth-bounded
Proud	Inferior	Absent-minded	Combative		Polarising	Over-perfectionistic
Stubborn	Depressive	Busy	Inert		Impractical	
Obstinate	Over-indulgent	Disorderly	Ambivalent		Fierce	
Stiff	Hoarding	Chaotic			Impulsive	
Static		Disorganised				
Isolating		Superficial				
Disruptive		Indecisive				
Insensitive		Perplexed				
Solitary		Confused				
Lonely						
Loveless						

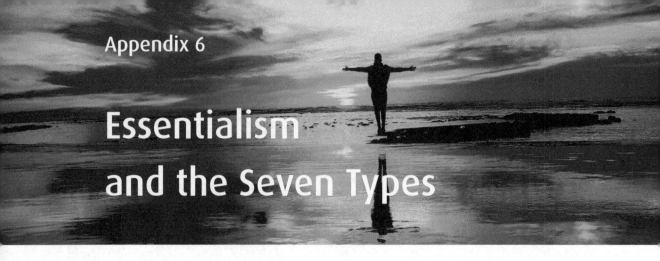

Appendix 6

Essentialism and the Seven Types

Both psychosynthesis and the theory of the Seven Types are based on the philosophy of essentialism. This becomes clear when we investigate the grand narrative that underpins Assagioli's conception of psychosynthesis.

In my article *Psychosynthesis and Evolutionary Panentheism* (2017c; see also Sørensen, 2008 and 2017b), I demonstrate how Assagioli drew upon the concepts of the Great Chain of Being, involution and evolution, thus aligning himself with the perennial philosophy and the essentialist position. Let me offer the following quote as sufficient to illustrate this point (Assagioli, 2007: 241):

> In order to fully understand the nature and power of beauty we need to remember the spiritual concept which states that everything that exists externally, in concrete form and individually is the manifestation, effect and reflection of a higher, transcendent, spiritual Reality. It is the great principle of involution or emanation. From a basic, original absolute reality, a series of levels of life, intellect, feeling and material life has developed, through gradual differentiation, to the point of inorganic matter. Thus every quality or attribute of the eternal world, of matter itself, and of the countless different creatures is but a pale, obscure reflection of a quality or attribute of the spiritual Reality, the Divine Being. This is particularly true when it comes to Beauty.

This quote demonstrates that Assagioli was influenced by Plato's ladder of love and beauty and the neo-Platonic idea of emanation. Accordingly, there is an assumption underlying psychosynthesis and the Seven Types that each individual has an essential spiritual core that is predisposed to grow, like a seed, via an evolutionary journey from the pre-personal to the personal, and then to the transpersonal. In psychosynthesis, this developmental concept is expressed in the idea of the soul's calling, which implies that each individual has a soul path that must be followed if the soul's purpose is to be fulfilled. In the Seven Types, the essentialist philosophy is found in the theory of the Seven Ways and the idea that we each have *essential energies* that we are here to manifest.

Assagioli was well aware of the postmodern critique that ancient wisdom and the ancient narratives are socially constructed and culturally biased. In response, Assagioli, drawing upon the thinking of William James, argued that the spiritual experience described in ancient wisdom is real, but how this experience is described may be inaccurate due to our limited understanding and vocabulary. Assagioli (2007: 18) explained:

> Furthermore, each person has recounted his or her own experience in words which imply serious discrepancies; the experience produces different emotional reactions within each individual which they interpret in differing, and at times contradictory, ways. To use James's own well-chosen words, each individual adds to the original experience a series of imprecise personal structures, to which they are often firmly attached both mentally and emotionally. This diversity has caused confusion, misperceptions and doubts that surround the subject under discussion.

It therefore follows that, when attempting to interpret our soul's calling and our essential qualities, we need to navigate carefully between factual experience and the theory we use to describe that experience.

I take the position that there is a spiritual essence (the soul) guiding my path, but how I choose to manifest my soul's qualities is a creative collaboration involving my limited personal self and whatever illumination I have gained about my soul's calling.

From this perspective, I see the five dominant types – i.e. the dominant energies at the levels of body, feeling, thought, personality and soul – as our *soul seeds* (referred to elsewhere as our psychological DNA. This DNA is *what we are here to give* and contain our potential for how we can develop and manifest in the world. Of course, we are not left to undergo this process alone: we live in a social context – among family and friends, in groups and in our nation – which means we are also here to *receive* qualities from our social environment. And it is through this interaction with our environment that our essential qualities can emerge so we can begin to realise our soul's calling.

Does essentialism equal determinism? Yes and No!

To borrow an analogy, an acorn has the potential to become an oak tree – the acorn is *determined* to grow in this way because of its inherent *oakness*. How the acorn unfolds its potential and develops its particular qualities as an oak will be influenced by the particular DNA and the quality of the soil and weather conditions, but the life inherent in the acorn will always strive towards manifesting its oakness. The same applies to the human being, except that we can consciously participate in the growth process towards becoming a fully functioning human being. So, from this perspective, every person is *determined* to evolve because there is in life an inherent evolutionary drive towards synthesis and towards becoming all that we can be. Assagioli explains this evolutionary drive in the following way (1965: 31):

From a still wider and more comprehensive point of view, universal life itself appears to us as a struggle between multiplicity and unity – a labour and an aspiration towards union. We seem to sense that – whether we conceive it as a divine Being or as cosmic energy – the Spirit working upon and within all creation is shaping it into order, harmony, and beauty, uniting all beings (some willing but the majority as yet blind and rebellious) with each other through links of love, achieving – slowly and silently, but powerfully and irresistibly – *the Supreme Synthesis.*

In life itself there is an organic drive towards unity that we are determined to follow, with some following willingly, while others follow blindly and rebelliously, according to the perennialist paradigm as expressed by Assagioli.

Because we now have an understanding of the process of psychosynthesis, human beings can choose to cooperate with life and choose how our particular journey will unfold – and in this lies our freedom. This process does not lead to the development of sameness, rather our uniqueness and particularity will unfold in what Assagioli calls a *unity in diversity*, meaning a balance between universality and individuality.

As soon as we wake up to the universal process of psychosynthesis, we can start to exercise our free will and decide which qualities we want to bring forth, even though, at the same time, the voice of conscience from the Higher Self, or soul (our self in a deeper state of being), will be guiding our path to wholeness by bringing to fruition a particular set of qualities. The qualities we are able to manifest are fixed or determined: an oak tree will not develop into a pine tree; similarly, if we are a dynamic soul type we are determined to bring to fruition dynamic qualities, however we are free inasmuch as we can participate in shaping how our particular soul qualities unfold.

References

Much of this material is hard to find. Information has been provided where known (albeit incomplete). Many of the Assagioli articles were found and archived after his death and have never been published. A large number of the articles can be retrieved at www.kennethsorensen.dk/en/sitemap/

Assagioli, R. (1927). *A New Method of Healing.* Archive Assagioli, Florence. Lecture delivered at the English Speaking Union in Rome, on 1 May 1927. Read at www.kennethsorensen.dk/en/sitemap/

Assagioli, R. (1930). *Individual Psychology and Spiritual Development: Introductory Survey of Individual Psychology.* The Beacon, Vol. IX (Oct.) p. 147.

Assagioli, R. (1930b). *Individual Psychology and Spiritual Development, Personality and Individuality.* The Beacon, Vol IX (Nov.) p. 178.

Assagioli, R. (1930c). *Individual Psychology and Spiritual Development: The Four Fundamental Types.* The Beacon, Vol IX (Dec.) p. 214.

Assagioli, R. (1931). *Individual Psychology and Spiritual Development, Extraverts and Introverts.* The Beacon, Vol IX (Jan.) p. 250.

Assagioli, R. (1931b). *Individual Psychology and Spiritual Development, Psychological Types According to the Personal and Egoic Rays.* The Beacon, Vol IX (Feb.) p. 289.

Assagioli, R. (1931c). *Astro-Psychology – Emotional Control.* The Beacon, Vol X (Dec. p.) p. 272.

Assagioli, R. (1932). *Spiritual Development and Nervous Diseases.* The Beacon, Vol. XI (Dec.) p. 246. (This article is the transcript of a lecture delivered by Dr Assagioli at the Third Summer Session of the International Centre of Spiritual Research at Ascona, Switzerland, in August 1932. It was later revised and included in his book *Psychosynthesis* (1965), in chapter 2: *Self-Realisation and Psychological Disturbances.*)

Assagioli, R. (1933). *Practical Contributions to a Modern Yoga, part I.* The Beacon. Vol. XII (Oct.) p. 182.

Assagioli, R. (1934). *Practical Contributions to a Modern Yoga, part II.* The Beacon. Vol. XII (Mar.) p. 346.

Assagioli, R. (1934b). *Practical Contributions to a Modern Yoga, part III.* The Beacon. Vol. XIII (Apr.) p. 18.

Assagioli, R. (1934c). *Loving Understanding, Wisdom and Love in Action.* The Beacon (July). Read at www.kennethsorensen.dk/en/sitemap/

Assagioli, R. (1935). *Psychoanalysis and Psychosynthesis.* The Beacon, Vol XIV. p. 34. Read at www.kennethsorensen.dk/en/sitemap/

Assagioli, R. (1942). *Spiritual Joy,* The Beacon. Read at www.kennethsorensen.dk/en/sitemap/

Assagioli, R. (1960). *The Education of Gifted and Super-Gifted Children.* Psychosynthesis Research Foundation, Issue No. 8. Read at www.kennethsorensen.dk/en/sitemap/

Assagioli, R. (1961). *Self Realization and Psychological Disturbances.* Psychosynthesis Research Foundation, Issue No. 10. Read at www.kennethsorensen.dk/en/sitemap/

Assagioli, R. (1963). *Creative Expression in Education: It's Purpose, Process, Techniques and Results.* Psychosynthesis Research Foundation. Read at www.kennethsorensen.dk/en/sitemap/

Assagioli, R. (1965). *Psychosynthesis.* Hobbs, Dorman & Company: New York.

Assagioli, R. (1965b). *Psychosynthesis: Individual and Social: Some Suggested Lines of Research.* Psychosynthesis Research Foundation, Issue No. 16. Read at www.kennethsorensen.dk/en/sitemap/

Assagioli, R. (1966). *Dialogue with Roberto Assagioli (with Martha Crampton and Dr. Graham C. Taylor).* Psychosynthesis Trust (unpublished). Read at www.kennethsorensen.dk/en/sitemap/

Assagioli, R. (1967a). *Psychosomatic Medicine and Bio-Psychosynthesis.* Psychosynthesis Research Foundation, Issue No. 21. Read at www. kennethsorensen.dk/en/sitemap/

Assagioli, Roberto (1967b). *Jung and Psychosynthesis.* Psychosynthesis Research Foundation, Issue No. 19. Read at www.kennethsorensen. dk/en/sitemap/

Assagioli, R. (1968a). *Notes on Education.* Psychosynthesis Research Foundation. Read at www.kennethsorensen.dk/en/sitemap/

Assagioli, R. (1968b). *The Science and Service of Blessing.* Sundial House. Read at www.kennethsorensen.dk/en/sitemap/

Assagioli, R. (1968c). *The Scientific Way.* Archive Assagioli, Florence.

Assagioli, Roberto, (1969), *Symbols of Transpersonal Experiences.*

Psychosynthesis Research Foundation, Reprint No. 11. Read at www. kennethsorensen.dk/en/sitemap/

Assagioli, R. (1970). *The Technique of Evocative Words.* Psychosynthesis Research Foundation, Issue No. 25. Read at www.kennethsorensen. dk/en/sitemap/

Assagioli, R. and MGNA. (1970b). *The Meditation Group for the New Age.* Read at https://meditationmount.org/study-courses/

Assagioli, R. (1972). *The Balancing and Synthesis of Opposites.* Psychosynthesis Research Foundation, Issue No. 29. Read at www. kennethsorensen.dk/en/sitemap/

Assagioli, R. (1973). *The Conflict Between the Generations and the Psychosynthesis of the Human Ages.* Psychosynthesis Research Foundation, Issue No. 31.

Assagioli, R. (1974). *The Act of Will.* Penguin Books.

Assagioli, R. (1974. *Training: A Statement.* Istituto di Psicosintesi, Florence. Read at www.kennethsorensen.dk/en/sitemap/

Assagioli, R. (1975). *The Resolution of Conflicts and Spiritual Conflicts and Crises.* Psychosynthesis Research Foundation, Issue No. 34. Read at www.kennethsorensen.dk/en/sitemap/

Assagioli, R. (1976). *Transpersonal Inspiration, and Psychological Mountain-Climbing.* Psychosynthesis Research Foundation, Issue No. 36. Read at www.kennethsorensen.dk/en/sitemap/

Assagioli, R. (1983). *Psychosynthesis Typology.* Institute of Psychosynthesis.

Assagioli, R. (1983b). *Cheerfulness (A Psychosynthetic Technique).* Pasadena California: Psychosynthesis Training Center. (First print 1973, P.R.F., Issue 33.) Read at www.kennethsorensen.dk/en/sitemap/

Assagioli, R. (1983c). *Life as a Game and Stage Performance* (Role Playing). Pasadena California: Psychosynthesis Training Center. (First print 1973, P.R.F., Issue 33.) Read at www.kennethsorensen.dk/en/sitemap/

Assagioli, R. (2007). *Transpersonal Development.* Inner Way Productions.

Assagioli, R. (Undated 1). *Psychosynthesis in Education.* Psychosynthesis Research Foundation, Issue No. 2. Read at www.kennethsorensen.dk/en/sitemap/

Assagioli, R. (Undated 2). *Talks on the Self.* Hand out. The Psychosynthesis and Education Trust, London. Read at www.kennethsorensen.dk/en/sitemap/

Assagioli, R. (Undated 3). *The Superconscious and the Self.* The Psychosynthesis and Education Trust, London. Hand out. Read at www.kennethsorensen.dk/en/sitemap/

Assagioli, R. (Undated 4). *From the Couple to the Community.* Unknown source. Read at www.kennethsorensen.dk/en/sitemap/

Assagioli, R. (Undated 5). *A Psychological Method for Learning Languages.* Psychosynthesis Research Foundation, Issue No. 3. Read at www.kennethsorensen.dk/en/sitemap/

Assagioli, R. (Undated 6). *Discrimination in Service.* The Institute of

Psychosynthesis, London. Read at www.kennethsorensen.dk/en/sitemap/

Assagioli, R. (Undated 7). *Music as a Cause of Disease and as a Healing Agent.* Psychosynthesis Research Foundation, Issue No. 5. Read at www.kennethsorensen.dk/en/sitemap/

Assagioli, R. (Undated 8). *Smiling Wisdom.* Psychosynthesis Research Foundation, Issue No. 4. Read at www.kennethsorensen.dk/en/sitemap/

Assagioli, R. (Undated 9). *Synthesis in Psychotherapy.* Psychosynthesis Research Foundation, Issue No.15. Read at www.kennethsorensen.dk/en/sitemap/

Assagioli, R. (Undated 10). *The Psychology of Woman and Her Psychosynthesis.* Psychosynthesis Research Foundation, Issue No. 24. Read at www.kennethsorensen.dk/en/sitemap/

Assagioli, R. (Undated 11). *The Self a Unifying Center.* Hand out. The Psychosynthesis and Education Trust, London. Read at www.kennethsorensen.dk/en/sitemap/

Assagioli, R. (Undated 12). *Training of the Will.* Psychosynthesis Research Foundation, Issue No. 17. Read at www.kennethsorensen.dk/en/sitemap/

Assagioli, R. (Undated 13). *Transpersonal Inspiration and Psychological Mountain Climbing.* Psychosynthesis Research Foundation, Issue No. 36. Read at www.kennethsorensen.dk/en/sitemap/

Assagioli, R. (Undated 14). *Transmutation and Sublimation of Sexual*

Energies. Psychosynthesis Research Foundation, Issue No. 13.

Assagioli, R. (Undated 15). *What Is Synthesis?* Hand out. The Psychosynthesis and Education Trust, London. Read at www. kennethsorensen.dk/en/sitemap/

Assagioli, R. (Undated 16). *The Cognitive (Scientific-Philosophic) Way.* Archive Assagioli, Florence, in folder *Height Psychology.*

Assagioli, R. (Undated 17). *Unity in Diversity (translated by Gordon Symons).* Archive Assagioli, Florence.

Assagioli, R. (Undated 18). *The New Dimensions of Psychology: The Third, Fourth and Fifth Forces.* (First published in AAP Online Journal, Sep. 2016.) Read the article at www.kennethsorensen.dk/en/sitemap/

Assagioli, R. (Undated 19). *The Heroic Approach.* Archive Assagioli, Florence.

Assagioli, R. (Undated 20). *The Seven Ways.* Hand out. The Psychosynthesis and Education Trust. Read at www.kennethsorensen.dk/en/sitemap/

Assagioli, R. (Undated 21). *Meditation.* The Norwegian Institute of Psychosynthesis, Oslo. Handed out. Read at www.kennethsorensen.dk/en/sitemap/

Assagioli, R. (Undated 22). *The Illuminative Intuitive Approach.* Archive Assagioli, Florence.

Assagioli, R. (Undated 23). *The Way of Active Service.* Archive Assagioli, Florence.

Assagioli, R. (Undated 24). *The Aesthetic Way.* Assagioli's Archives, Florence, originally in *Italian Magazine of Psychosynthesis* (April 2013). Read at www.kennethsorensen.dk/en/sitemap/

Assagioli, R. (Undated 25). *The Cognitive (Scientific-Philosophic) Way.* Archive Assagioli, Florence.

Assagioli, R. (Undated 26). *The Path of Regeneration through Ethics.* Archive Assagioli, Florence, originally in *Italian Magazine of Psychosynthesis* (April 2013). Read at www.kennethsorensen.dk/en/sitemap/

Assagioli, R. (Undated 27). *The Mystical Approach.* Archive Assagioli, Florence.

Assagioli, R. (Undated 28). *The Ritualistic and Ceremonial Way.* Archive Assagioli, Florence.

Assagioli, R. (Undated 29). *The Psychosynthesis of the National Entity.* Archive Assagioli, Florence.

Bailey, A. (1962). *Esoteric Psychology, volume 1.* Lucis Trust.

Besmer, By. (1973-74). *Height Psychology: Discovering the self and the Self.* Interpersonal Development, Vol. 4, pp. 215-225. Read at www.kennethsorensen.dk/en/sitemap/

Crampton, M. (1966). *Dialogue with Roberto Assagioli.* Hand out. The Norwegian Institute of Psychosynthesis. Read at www.kennethsorensen.dk/en/sitemap/

Cullen, J. (1987). *Applications of Esoteric Ray Theory to Manager and*

Organizational Development. The Journal of Esoteric Psychology, Vol. 3, No. 1.

Cullen, J. (1988). *The Manager of the Future.* International Association for Managerial and Organizational Psychosynthesis.

Eastcott M. (1980). The Seven Rays of Energy, Sundial House

Ferrucci, P. (1982). *What We May Be.* Tarcher/Putnam.

Ferrucci, P. (1990). *Inevitable Grace.* Tarcher/Putnam.

Freund, D. (1983). *Conversations with Roberto.* Psychosynthesis Digest (Spring). Read at www.kennethsorensen.dk/en/sitemap/

Miller, S. (1972). *The Will of Roberto Assagioli.* Intellectual Digest (October). Read at www.kennethsorensen.dk/en/sitemap/

Miller, S. (1973). *The Rebirth of the Soul.* Intellectual Digest (August). Read at www.kennethsorensen.dk/en/sitemap/

Keen, S. (1974). *The Golden Mean of Roberto Assagioli (interview).* Psychology Today. Read at www.kennethsorensen.dk/en/sitemap/

Nardi, D. (2011). *Neuroscience of Personality.* Radiance House.

Rosenthal, V. and Rosenthal, Pat. (1973). *The Gentle Synthesizer.* (Interview with Roberto Assagioli.) Voices: The Art and Science of Psychotherapy, Vol. 9, No. 3, Issue 33.

Robbins, M. (1988). *The Tapestry of the Gods, volumes 1 & 2.* The Seven Ray Publishing House.
Robbins, M. (Undated). *Combinations of Soul Rays and Personality Rays.*

Read at www.sevenray.org/robbins.html

Sørensen, K. (2008). *Integral Psychosynthesis*. MA-Dissertation. Read at www.kennethsorensen.dk/en/sitemap/

Sørensen, K. (2015). *The Soul of Psychosynthesis*. Kentaur Publishing.

Sørensen, K. (2017). *Integral Meditation*. Kentaur Publishing.

Sørensen, K. (2017b) *Why Assagioli Put a Star in the Sky*. Read at www.kennethsorensen.dk/en/sitemap/

Sørensen, K. (2017c). *Psychosynthesis and Evolutionary Panentheism.* Read at www.kennethsorensen.dk/en/sitemap/

Sørensen, K. (2018). *Psychosynthesis and Psychoenergetics*. Read at www.kennethsorensen.dk/en/sitemap/

Sørensen, K. (2018b). *Psychoenergetics and The Seven Rivers of Life*. Read at www.kennethsorensen.dk/en/sitemap/

Sørensen, K. (2018c). *The Seven Types and Seven Ways: Your Psychological and Spiritual DNA*. Read at www.kennethsorensen.dk/en/sitemap/

Vargiu, J. (1977). *Creativity*. The Synthesis Journal, Vol. 3-4. Synthesis Press. Read at www.kennethsorensen.dk/en/sitemap/

Vargiu, J. and Firman, J. (1977). *The Dimensions of Growth*. The Synthesis Journal, Vol. 3-4. Read at www.kennethsorensen.dk/en/sitemap/

Wilber, K. (2006). *Excerpt G: Toward A Comprehensive Theory of Subtle*

Energies. Retrieved from http://wilber.shambhala.com/html/books kosmos/excerptG/part1.cfm/

Wilber, K. (2000c). *Integral Psychology.* Shambhala.

Wilber, K. (2006). *Integral Spirituality.* Shambhala.

Wilber, K. (2007). *Sidebar G: States and Stages. Retrieved from* www.kenwilber.com/Writings/PDF/G-states%20and%20stages.pdf

Wilber, K. (1999a). *The Collected Works of Ken Wilber.* Vol. 2, Shambhala.

Wilber, K. (1999b). *The Collected Works of Ken Wilber.* Vol. 3, Shambhala.

Wilber, K. (2000a). *The Collected Works of Ken Wilber.* Vol. 7, Shambhala.

Wilber, K. (2000b). *The Collected Works of Ken Wilber.* Vol. 8, Shambhala.

Wilber, K. (2017). *The Religion of Tomorrow.* Shambhala.

Other books by Kenneth Sørensen

The Soul of Psychosynthesis

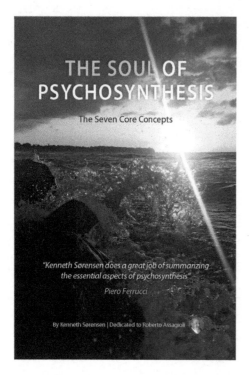

Shortly before his death at 85, in 1974, Dr Roberto Assagioli, one of the founding fathers of transpersonal psychology, described what he regarded as the essence of psychosynthesis. It was, for him, a psychology which placed the soul as a spiritual Being at its centre. It is no surprise that psychosynthesis has since been seen as a "Psychology with a Soul".

The Soul of Psychosynthesis aims to understand what this means. It presents the essence of psychosynthesis through the Seven Core Concepts that Assagioli defined as the foundation of his work, and which some today see as his "Last Will", his final statement about his ideas and their practical application.

The Soul of Psychosynthesis will enable the reader to discover the wisdom in the Seven Core Concepts and realise that:

Disidentification – is a way to Freedom
The self – is a way to Presence
The will – is a way to Power
The ideal model – is a way to Focus
Synthesis – is a way to Flow
The Superconscious – is a way to Abundance
The Transpersonal Self – is a way to Love

The Soul of Psychosynthesis is a concise introduction and practical guide to the fundamental ideas of one of the most important therapeutic approaches in the modern world.

The Soul of Psychosynthesis

Kenneth Sørensen, 190 pages, Kentaur Publishing, 2016.

———————————

"Assagioli's psychosynthesis spreads far and wide. It is ambitious in scope and subject matter. For this reason it may be hard at times to understand its essence – with the risk of being lost in the details. Kenneth Sørensen does a great job of summarising in a short and well-researched book the essential aspects of psychosynthesis, offering an overview that will allow the reader to grasp its main themes in theory and practice, as well as its historical development."

Piero Ferrucci, is an international bestselling author, a psychotherapist and philosopher

Integral Meditation

– The Seven Ways to Self-realisation

In *Integral Meditation*, Sørensen offers a lively and comprehensive introduction to the esoteric philosophy of the Seven Rays (also known as the Seven Rivers of Life), which teaches how we can achieve self-realisation by integrating and embodying the seven essential energies that underpin the universe.

Sørensen explains how each of the Seven Rays can be navigated using a particular type of meditation that must be modified according to the meditator's personal blueprint of spiritual energy. The result is a unique path to the soul for every seeker.

While reflecting with unflinching honesty upon his own spiritual journey, Sørensen shows how the application of tried and tested techniques of meditation can bring inspiration, transformation and spiritual breakthrough. The formula is as simple as it is challenging: the integration of a variety of meditation techniques can result in the manifestation of universal energies that will profoundly change our relationship to ourselves, to those around us and to the universe as a whole.

Drawing heavily on the teachings of psychosynthesis, energy psychology and ancient wisdom, *Integral Meditation* presents an approach to the psycho-spiritual journey that can be summed up in the invitation: *"Meditate, love and choose freedom every day."*

Integral Meditation, Kenneth Sørensen, 260 pages, Kentaur Publishing 2017

––––––––––––––

"Integral meditation is an illuminating and wise presentation of the science of meditation. It is a candid spiritual autobiography – a magnificent synthesis of the author's life to date and what he has discovered by consciously treading the path of the Soul."

Michael Lindfield, Board President of Meditation Mount

CPSIA information can be obtained
at www.ICGtesting.com
Printed in the USA
BVHW050512040222
627987BV00001B/1

9 788792 252395